LASAGNA GARDENING
for Small Spaces

LASAGNA GARDENING
for Small Spaces

A Layering System for Big Results
in Small Gardens and Containers

Patricia Lanza

RODALE

RODALE

WE **INSPIRE** AND **ENABLE** PEOPLE TO IMPROVE
THEIR LIVES AND THE WORLD AROUND THEM

Editor: Fern Marshall Bradley
Cover and Interior Book Designer: Chris Neyen
Contributing Designer: Dale Mack
Interior Illustrators: John Gist and Leigh Wells
Cover Illustrator: Leigh Wells
Layout Designer: Jennifer H. Giandomenico
Researchers: Diana Erney, Sarah Heffner,
    and Pamela R. Ruch
Copy Editor: Erana Bumbardatore
Product Specialist: Jodi Schaffer
Indexer: Nan N. Badgett
Editorial Assistance: Kerrie A. Cadden
    and Dolly Donchez

Rodale Organic Living Books

Editorial Director: Christopher Hirsheimer
Executive Creative Director: Christin Gangi
Executive Editor: Kathleen Fish
Art Director: Patricia Field
Production Manager: Robert V. Anderson Jr.
Studio Manager: Leslie M. Keefe
Copy Manager: Nancy N. Bailey
Projects Coordinator: Kerrie A. Cadden

Designer of gardens on pages 70, 73, and 93:
    Pamela R. Ruch

**Library of Congress Cataloging-
    in-Publication Data**

Lanza, Patricia.
    Lasagna gardening for small spaces : a layering system for big results in small gardens and containers / Patricia Lanza.
        p.   cm.
    Includes bibliographical references (p.   ) and index.
    ISBN 0–87596–859–7   (hardcover : alk. paper)—
ISBN 0–87596–886–4   (pbk. : alk. paper)
    1. Organic gardening.   I. Title.
SB453.5 .L36   2002
635'.04844—dc21   2001005501

Distributed in the book trade by St. Martin's Press

2 4 6 8 10 9 7 5 3 1   hardcover
2 4 6 8 10 9 7 5 3 1   paperback

To my family: Debbie and Steve Donothan; Alex and Mike Orr; Mickey Lanza; Judy, Rich, and Melissa Bakunas; Mike, Pam, Brian, and Jackie Lanza; Rich, Juliet, Anthony, Sean, and Dominick Lanza; Melissa Lanza; Kaitlin Butler; Elizabeth, Harry, Malorie, Matthew, and Tyler Copeland; Tom and Cheryl Neal; and Ruth Neal.

RODALE
ORGANIC GARDENING STARTS HERE!

Here at Rodale, we've been gardening organically for more than 60 years—ever since my grandfather J. I. Rodale learned about composting and decided that healthy living starts with healthy soil. In 1940, J. I. started the Rodale Organic Farm to test his theories, and today the nonprofit Rodale Institute Experimental Farm is still at the forefront of organic gardening and farming research. In 1942, J. I. founded *Organic Gardening* magazine to share his discoveries with gardeners everywhere. His son, my father, Robert Rodale, headed *Organic Gardening* until 1990, and today a third generation of Rodales is growing up with the new *OG* magazine. Over the years we've shown millions of readers how to grow bountiful crops and beautiful flowers using nature's own techniques.

In this book, you'll find the latest organic methods and the best gardening advice. We know—because all our authors and editors are passionate about gardening! We feel strongly that our gardens should be safe for our children, pets, and the birds and butterflies that add beauty and delight to our lives and landscapes. Our gardens should provide us with fresh, flavorful vegetables, delightful herbs, and gorgeous flowers. And they should be a pleasure to work in as well as to view.

Sharing the secrets of safe, successful gardening is why we publish books. So come visit us at www.organicgardening.com, where you can tour the world of organic gardening all day, every day. And use this book to create your best garden ever.

Happy gardening!

Maria Rodale

Maria Rodale
Rodale Organic Gardening Books

CONTENTS

DISCOVERING THE JOYS
OF SMALL-SPACE GARDENING

While researching and writing my first book, *Lasagna Gardening*, I realized that I needed to downsize my gardens. In a way, I was a victim of my own success. My lasagna gardening method made installing gardens so easy that I had created more gardens than I'd ever had in my life. Also, it was such a pleasure to motivate other gardeners by sharing my method that I was writing gardening columns and magazine articles, plus traveling all over the country to present lasagna gardening lectures. On top of that, divorced and with all my children grown, I was living by myself in a large, old, two-story house that needed lots of maintenance.

For awhile, the feeling of empowerment was heady, knowing I could accomplish so much alone. But when my obsession led to the installation of lights for night gardening, when I dug an 80-foot-long path through 4 feet of snow so I could get to my greenhouse, and when I turned down an all-expenses-paid vacation because I couldn't trust anyone else to water my seedlings, I finally admitted I was a garden-aholic who needed help.

I put together my own 12-step program for recovery, and step one was a biggie: downsizing. I decided to sell my mountain farm and move to smaller living and gardening spaces. Sounds simple, but it was painful. I had to say good-bye to my 30 display and production gardens, that wonderful old house, and my collection of eclectic furnishings. Selling the farm also meant giving up frequent contact with old friends and neighbors. It meant abandoning long-term plans and dreams grown way too large, and starting over.

The property sold quickly. One day a couple came to buy a pot of herbs and fell in love with my house and gardens. Two days later they returned, and within a few minutes we agreed on price and terms. I wasn't prepared for such rapid change, and my heart hurt for weeks as I packed and prepared to leave my beloved Shandelee Mountain.

Preparing for the move, I took small cuttings, divisions, and a few seeds of favorite plants. I edged and mulched all the old free-form gardens, letting the black, rich soil slide through my fingers for the last time. I removed my most treasured garden statuary and gave it to family members to safeguard. I layered a new lasagna garden for a special friend and planted my cuttings and divisions there.

On the day of the closing, only my determination to stick to my program, plus the check I carried in my pocket, gave me the strength to say good-bye. Tears blurred my vision as I walked down the farm's path and through the gate. I took several deep breaths, wiped my eyes, and turned for a last look. As I surveyed the property, I noted all the projects still left to tackle—new garage doors, a roof and railing for the deck, another layer of mulch on 30 gardens, four composters to be emptied, grape vines to prune, and more. My pain lessened, my heart felt lighter, and I was ready to move on.

What came next? My daughter Mickey and I had bought an old church in the small village of Wurtsboro for a new gift shop, garden center, and café business. The property was only half an acre, and it became abundantly clear that I would have to become very inventive to display all the plants I needed to show. And so began a 3-year experiment in getting the most results from every small space.

We called our new business The Potager. At The Potager, there was a small, square front lawn, a tiny side lawn with a huge maple tree, and another side lawn with three old maple trees. What had been the back lawn quickly became just a memory as the regulatory agencies insisted on lots of off-street parking and the septic system from hell. All that was left of the yard were several long, narrow strips inside the fence. For a recovering gardenaholic, it was just perfect.

We spent the first year layering all the beds, moving perennial plants into place, and mulching. I filled gaps in the new gardens with flashy annuals and planted entire gardens in containers. I grew vine crops on every section of fence, up bamboo poles, and over all sorts of discarded tools and building materials from farm auctions and tag sales. It was close to instant gardening. I had drastically downsized and my recovery program was working.

Gardening in small spaces certainly taught me to "grow up," and I've become a master of devising interesting yet simple trellises and plant supports. By combining the unique beauty of old wrought iron, wood, and bamboo with today's innovative products and the ease of my layering method for creating easy, bountiful gardens, you can have the garden of your dreams, no matter how small your space. All it takes is creativity, understanding plants and how they grow, learning how to use vertical supports, and developing your own flair for combining plants in interesting containers.

CHAPTER 1

GETTING STARTED
WITH LASAGNA GARDENING

Starting a garden, even a very small one, is a favorite project of mine. It's creative and new, and that's what makes life fun. I'm lucky, too, because I've developed an easy layering system for making garden beds—large or small—without digging or tilling. It's called lasagna gardening, and it will work as well for you as it does for me.

From Large to Small

Once upon a time, I was a country innkeeper in the Catskill region of New York State. The inn was surrounded by 7 acres of lawn and landscape. I loved to garden, and I needed bushel baskets full of vegetables, fruits, and herbs to serve guests at the inn's 250-seat restaurant, so I built *lots* of big gardens. This was when I developed the method of garden making that I call lasagna gardening. It's a no-dig, no-till method that proved so successful and attracted so much interest that I wrote a book about it called *Lasagna Gardening.* I also began giving talks to garden clubs and at garden shows. Now I travel all over the country to tell people about my system!

Since I wrote *Lasagna Gardening*, I've moved from my inn to a farm, and more recently, to an apartment where I garden in small terraced beds, mostly in the shade. I'm no longer an innkeeper; now I'm the proprietor of The Potager, a 115-year-old former church on half an acre that I've turned into a garden center, gift shop, and small café.

As my life changed, my gardening style changed, too—from large-scale gardens to small, intimate gardens. I've discovered that small-space gardening is twice as creative because it makes me rise above the limited dimensions of a small bed to create a diverse and beautiful garden. Quite literally, the gardens rise up, too! Many of the plants grow up on decorative trellises and other supports that become as much a part of the garden as the plants themselves. Choosing plants that will fit the space available is an art I've enjoyed mastering.

JOIN THE SMALL-GARDEN CROWD!

Small-space gardening appeals to many types of people, not just those with limited outdoor space. Maybe you'll identify yourself in this list:

- Parents who want to introduce their small children to the wonders of growing plants, but who don't have time for a big garden.
- Working people with busy lives who enjoy gardening for stress relief and thus don't want a big garden that might stress them out!
- Apartment- and condo-dwellers who are limited to gardening on an outside patio or balcony.
- Beginners who want to experiment without investing too much time or money.
- People who own a vacation home and want to enjoy a *little* gardening when they're on their summer getaway.
- Mature gardeners (like me) who need to take care not to overdo it in the garden.

I was having so much fun with my small-space gardens that I realized it was time to write another book—and here it is. I've packed these pages with all the tricks, techniques, plant combinations, and design ideas that I've developed since I switched from big-time to small-space gardening. I've also refined my lasagna gardening method over time, and I've included all my updates here, too. Of course, I'll still tell you about the basics of lasagna gardening and growing flowers, vegetables, herbs, and fruits. So whether you're a neophyte lasagna gardener or an expert at building lasagna layers, read on and enjoy!

Lasagna Gardening: From the Ground Up

Lasagna gardening is a layering system for bountiful gardens that requires no digging, no tilling, and no weeding. It's an organic process that is neat and efficient, using materials found around your yard or neighborhood to create wonderful soil.

All you need to build a lasagna bed is some newspaper and a variety of natural ingredients such as compost, grass clippings, chopped leaves, and peat moss. To start, you'll spread thick sections of wet newspaper over the ground. On top of the paper, you'll add alternating layers of the organic materials you've collected. It's that simple!

Once you've gathered all your materials, building a small-space lasagna bed like this one takes less than an hour.

There's no magic formula for a lasagna bed. I use whatever materials I can get my hands on easily. Sometimes that includes composted manure or composted barn litter, because I live in a rural area. You'll soon discover what materials you can scrounge for free in your area, and of course, you can always buy bagged organic materials at a garden center.

The bottom layer of a lasagna garden is always newspaper. By covering the sod with wet newspaper, you eliminate the need to dig or till. That's because you've created the perfect environment (one that's dark and moist) for earthworms. Earthworms are natural tilling marvels. They tunnel through the soil, consuming and digesting organic materials as they go. Their work creates channels that allow air and water to move through the soil. Their excrement, called castings, is a high-quality source of nutrients in a form that plant roots can absorb. Essentially, earthworms convert the raw materials you've layered in a lasagna bed into rich garden soil. (Microorganisms and other soil-dwelling critters play a role in this process, too.) There's no need to mix up the layers—Mother Nature will take care of that. Gardening just got a whole lot easier!

Mother Nature Wrote the Recipe

I didn't invent the layering process I call lasagna gardening—Mother Nature did! She's been doing it for eons. A forest is a perfect example of nature's version of lasagna layering. Trees are always shedding dead leaves, twigs, and branches. After this debris drops to the forest floor, it decomposes and eventually becomes a rich, dark, organic material called humus. More debris drops each year, so the forest floor is carpeted with fallen leaves covering a soft cushion of humus that every nature lover enjoys walking on.

Mother Nature isn't very tidy, and her helter-skelter method of layering wouldn't pass the "neat gardener test" in suburbia. Also, in nature, decomposition can be a very slow process. Sometimes it takes years to transform organic materials into a single inch of rich, black soil. I've refined Mother Nature's method so it's faster, neater, and more manageable on a small scale.

Lasagna gardening mimics Mother Nature's recipe for converting organic waste into food for plants. It's easy and fast, but more than anything, it's a wonderful way to reuse what we have rather than consigning it to a landfill. Lasagna gardening is smart recycling! I can't help but wince every time I see a trash-hauling crew picking up bags of leaves and throwing them into a garbage truck. I think about all the food and flowers that could have grown in those leaves if they'd been used for lasagna gardening, instead. So I do my share by putting as much waste to good use as I can and by sharing my recipe for gardening success with everyone I know.

My Lasagna Gardening Story

Before I developed my lasagna gardening method, I was frustrated with my gardens. I was busy at the inn from early morning until night. I would find time to plant a vegetable garden each spring, but it always suffered from neglect as the season wore on. My flower gardens never looked as pretty and colorful as I wanted them to. It seemed my little herb garden at the bottom of the kitchen steps was the only thing I could do right!

Composting Complications

My composting efforts were out of control, too. I had enormous composting resources: vegetable peelings from the inn's kitchen, 7 acres of grass clippings, and more than 200 bags of leaves each year. But transporting all this material to the composting area and turning the huge compost piles was way too much work. Poor me!

One fall day, I ran away to the woods in back of the inn. I needed to escape and take time to be alone. I came to a place where loggers had cleared hardwoods a few years before, and I was amazed by the change. The last time I'd been there, the scene was felled trees and raw earth scarred by heavy machinery. Now the area was sprouting a new miniature forest. Nature was hard at work, and without any help from humans, in fact *in spite of* their destructive efforts, a steady growth of trees, shrubs, and wildflowers was reestablishing itself.

I stooped to brush fallen leaves aside and scooped up handfuls of rich brown earth. Earthworms wiggled to the surface where I had

Beneath the forest floor (*below left*), natural layered composting takes place: Leaves and other debris build up in layers that gradually decompose to make rich soil. When you make a lasagna bed (*below right*), you're imitating this natural process.

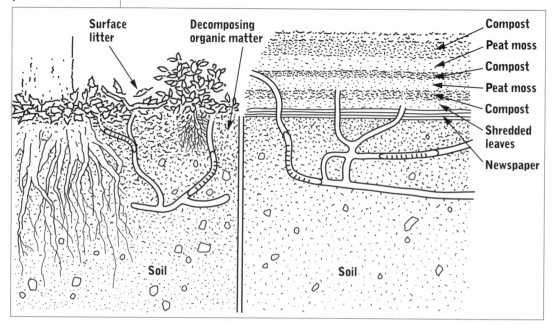

swept aside their cover. It occurred to me then that I was approaching my composting system all wrong. Here was proof that I could create gardens that would grow anything just by applying layers of organic materials to the earth and letting nature take its course. Instead of struggling with my oversize compost pile, what if I just put it all right on the garden in layers?

Layering the Lasagna Way

That fall, I layered the vegetable garden for the first time by covering the soil with fresh horse manure. It was convenient and free, and I had all winter to let it mature. I covered the manure with leaves and grass clippings.

In spring, the results weren't as successful as I had hoped. My soil was easier to work, but I had a bumper crop of weeds. No wonder— they'd grown up through the layers and were deliriously happy in the rich composted manure, grass, and leaves. It was clear I needed something to block the weeds.

One day, while I was bundling up the week's newspapers, inspiration struck. I thought about times when I had put the papers out for pickup and it had rained. The recycling crew wouldn't take wet paper, so the bundle had sat on the grassy area next to the curb for a week. When I'd moved the bundle, the grass underneath was yellowed and dying, and I could see earthworms right on the surface. This was the answer to my weed woes: newspaper under the organic layers to block the weeds.

Back in the garden, inspired, I stomped the weeds down and covered the entire area with thick pads of newspaper before I began to layer. With the newspapers as a base, I realized I could then pile up my organic materials without fighting weeds along the way. I've made many lasagna gardens since then, large and small—and in containers, too. (I'll show you the ropes of lasagna gardening in containers in Chapter 2.) I've found that no matter what size or shape the garden, my lasagna system works to produce beautiful soil without back-breaking work.

Lasagna Gardening Basics

I hope my story has convinced you that lasagna gardening is a better way to garden because it saves you time and effort while giving you great results. You simply layer organic materials and let Mother Nature do the rest!

No Digging!

Lasagna gardening saves you from hours of digging. By covering the sod with newspaper and organic materials, you create the perfect environment—dark, warm, and moist—for earthworms to do their stuff. They churn the soil, so you don't have to! Plus, the thick base layer of newspaper will choke out the plants on the site, so you don't need to dig out weeds or grass before you start, either.

Pick a Garden Spot

The first step in building a lasagna bed is to mark your site (or for a container garden, to choose your container). I like to use stakes and string to lay out a square or rectangular garden. For a garden with a curved outline, such as a small bed for a mix of annuals and perennials, you can use a garden hose or rope to lay out the design. When you're satisfied with the shape, gather a bucket of sand, a cup, and a funnel. Use the cup to pour sand into the funnel and follow along the hose or rope with the funnel. Then you can remove the hose or rope, and the sand will remain as your guideline.

Start Layering

Now comes the no-dig part: Leave the ground surface of the bed as it is—whether it's grass, weeds, or open soil—and blanket it with wet newspapers. I wet the newspapers thoroughly, so that even in windy conditions I can work without them blowing around.

Use entire sections of wet newspaper. One or two sheets aren't enough—you need layers thick enough to block light to the grass and weeds underneath. It will take months for thick layers of paper to decompose, and during that time, the plants underneath the paper will die. If you use too little paper or dig through the paper, you are defeating its purpose. Overlap the edges of each section so that weeds and grass can't sneak through in between.

Cover the newspaper with a layer of straw, spoiled hay, peat moss, or compost. Next, spread a layer of a different organic material, such as chopped leaves, composted manure, or composted kitchen waste. Keep on alternating materials until you have a bed of the desired height.

When I first started lasagna gardening, I layered on 3 or 4 inches of materials at a time, building beds 18 to 24 inches tall. But over the years I've discovered that sometimes that's overkill. Now I match the bed height to the type of plants I'm using. Six-packs of bedding plants

SMALL SECRETS FOR BIG SUCCESS

Recycling Redux

Working with wet newspaper when you build a lasagna bed is a good idea because the paper stays in place much better than dry newspaper does. I stick newspapers in a large plastic container with handles (I bought it at my supermarket for about $7), and I use the hose to add water to the container. It's easy to drag the container around as I lay out the newspaper. (I also use containers like these for garden cleanup in fall.)

After a couple of seasons in the garden, the bottom on this great container split. But I'm a die-hard recycler, so I wasn't about to throw it away. Instead, I filled the container with lasagna layers and planted a garden in it! The split bottom made for good drainage.

will slip into a bed just 3 to 6 inches high. Planting flowers growing in 4-inch pots? A 6-inch bed will do. For gallon-size perennials, build up layers 8 to 10 inches high. For shrubs or berry bushes in 2-gallon pots, don't stop layering until your bed is at least 1 foot high.

Remember, you can use any combination of organic materials you have handy, but if you're building a shallow bed, stick with fine materials like compost, peat, and chopped leaves. Coarse materials like straw, kitchen wastes, or spoiled hay will lose a lot of bulk as they settle, which could leave you with a skimpy bed.

Control the Heat

One caution when building a bed that you plan to plant the same day or week: Don't use too many materials that are highly rich in nitrogen (such as alfalfa hay, alfalfa meal, bloodmeal, or fresh grass clippings). If you build a pile that provides too much nitrogen, microorganisms will swing into high gear. All that biological activity will drive up the

(continued on page 20)

HELPFUL HINTS FOR GATHERING INGREDIENTS

Here's a rundown of some common and not-so-common organic materials that you can layer in your lasagna garden, add to your compost pile, or use as mulch around your garden plants. You'll find some of these materials in your own yard, and you may be able to glean some from neighbors who aren't as resourceful as you are. You can create wonderful garden soil from what some people would throw away! Think about what unique materials might be available from farms or businesses in your local area, too.

MATERIAL	WHERE TO FIND IT	HOW TO USE IT
Newspaper	On your doorstep every morning and around your neighborhood on recycling day.	Discard glossy, colored pages. Wet it thoroughly and use it as the growth-smothering base layer of every lasagna bed you make.
Compost	Your backyard compost pile, local recycling center, or bagged at garden centers.	Simply the best material for layering in your garden. Also good for creating seed beds and for boosting fertility in planting holes.
Peat moss	Garden centers and hardware stores.	Good for lasagna layers, but not as a top mulch because it tends to wick water away from the soil beneath.
Grass clippings	In your lawn-mower bag; try asking your neighbors for theirs.	In thin layers in a garden bed or as a top mulch.
Leaves	Your backyard, your neighbors' yards, and bagged at curbside around your neighborhood.	Great to use as a generous lasagna layer or top mulch. Use a shredder or your lawn mower to chip leaves.
Bagged, composted cow manure	Garden centers and hardware stores.	Good for lasagna layers because it's odorless and rich in nutrients.
Garden wastes	Home gardens—your own or your neighbors'.	Run spent plants through a shredder and use as a lower layer in a lasagna bed, or throw them in your compost pile.
Spoiled hay	Farms, racetracks, and riding stables.	Use as a bottom lasagna layer just above newspaper. Breaks down slowly.
Straw	Garden centers and farms.	Use as a mulch under strawberries and leafy food crops. Also good as a thin lower layer of a lasagna bed.
Shredded office paper	Local businesses; check the curbs in front of office buildings on trash day.	Use as a top mulch or as a lower layer in a lasagna bed. A caution: Office paper may contain more dioxin residues than newspaper because it is heavily bleached during manufacturing.
Leaf mold	Old leaf piles.	Excellent for lasagna layers and as a top mulch.

MATERIAL	WHERE TO FIND IT	HOW TO USE IT
Seaweed	Seashore.	Makes a great nutrient-rich lasagna layer.
Mushroom compost	Mushroom farms.	Perfect as either a layer in a lasagna bed or as a top mulch.
Composted animal manure	Farms, racetracks, and riding stables.	Use as a bottom layer in spring and as an upper layer in fall. It's best to obtain manure from organic farms, because manure from conventional farms may contain antibiotic residues. Never use raw manure because of the risk that it may carry lethal strains of bacteria. If the manure has an off odor, it's a sign that it hasn't been composted fully.
Salt marsh hay	Farms near the sea.	Works well as a lasagna garden layer.
Cornstalks	Your vegetable garden or farms that grow feed for cattle.	Chop them up and use them as a bottom layer in a lasagna garden or as a rough top mulch. Not for use in an ornamental garden.
Well-aged sawdust	Lumber yards, sawmills, and woodworking shops.	Use well-aged sawdust as a mulch or lasagna layer. Always ensure that the sawdust isn't from treated wood.
Spent hops and hulls	Breweries and microbreweries.	Use as a bottom layer of a lasagna bed (they're too smelly for a top layer). These materials break down quickly, and worms love them.
Fruit pulp	Fruit processing plants, wineries, and cider mills.	Use as a lasagna layer when you make beds in fall. This material needs to sit for a season or over winter before you plant the bed.
Pine needles	Your yard, your neighbors' yards, and in bales at garden centers.	If you collect needles from your yard or your neighbors', use your lawn mower to chip them before layering them in a lasagna bed. Or, use them as a top mulch. If you buy pine needles, ask your supplier about the source. Don't buy pine needles collected from public lands, as this collection can harm the ecosystem.
Sand	Garden centers and stone yards.	Use as a fast-draining medium in a rock garden or trough. Sprinkle on top of a lasagna garden to mark rows for planting seeds.
Wood ashes	Woodstoves and fireplaces.	Sift before using to remove cinders. Wood ashes can raise soil pH, so use in small quantities only when you first build a lasagna bed and not at all in a bed where you'll plant acid-loving plants. Don't apply more than 2 pounds per 100 square feet.
Shredded bark	Bagged at garden centers, or ask local landscapers or tree trimmers.	Use in a thin layer as a top mulch for gardens with long-term plantings.
Buckwheat hulls	Garden centers and flour mills.	Use as a decorative top mulch (my favorite for the display gardens at The Potager).

temperature inside the pile, especially if rain wets the materials. Temperatures may shoot up above 120°F, cooking the roots of tender young plants.

On the other hand, if you have lots of materials available and you don't need to plant right away, you may want to assemble a bed that will heat up and break down fast. To do so, pile the materials high, and use lots of nitrogen-rich materials. You can add a compost activator if you want, though it isn't necessary. (A compost activator is a packaged mix that contains the beneficial bacteria that drive the decomposition process. You can buy it at some garden centers or from mail-order suppliers; see "Resources for Lasagna Gardeners" on page 271.) Adding a little rich soil or compost to the layers should have the same effect as adding a compost activator.

After you build the bed, cover it with black plastic and place bricks or stones around the edges to keep the plastic in place. (This is one of the few times I will ever tell you to use black plastic.) If outside temperatures are warm, a few weeks under the plastic should do the job. When you remove the plastic, most of the pile will be decomposed and ready for you to plant anything, even small seeds or seedlings.

Some Thoughts about Peat Moss

You can use any organic materials you have on hand to cover the newspapers when you're preparing a lasagna garden. At The Potager, I've covered every inch of what used to be lawns with lasagna beds and paths. Because of that, I don't have any grass clippings. The only time I have leaves to work with is in fall. I do have lots of compost, made from kitchen waste from The Potager café. So these days, I rely primarily on alternating layers of compost and peat moss when I build a lasagna bed.

I use peat moss for several reasons. Peat moss is inexpensive and lightweight. It's not a nutrient-rich type of organic matter, but it's an extender for nutrient-rich materials like compost. Peat also holds lots of moisture. Mainly, I use peat moss because it's convenient for me and easy to handle.

My friends from *OG* magazine tell me that compost is king when they build lasagna beds, and because they have materials like grass and leaves to use for alternating layers, they don't find any need to use peat moss. Those Rodale folks like using compost because it contains lots of the beneficial microorganisms that drive the decomposition process.

So a lasagna bed made with lots of compost will probably mature faster than one made with peat moss, because peat moss is a sterile medium. Also, Rodale gardeners like compost for the top layer of a lasagna bed because when you plant into compost, your plants' roots are immediately surrounded by rich nutrients.

The challenge with compost can be making enough of it to go around. If you only tend a few small-space beds and containers, though, it's not too hard. You can make compost almost anywhere, even if you don't have much yard space. (See "Brewing Compost" on page 24.)

Ready, Set, Plant

Once you've layered materials to the proper depth, you're ready to plant. Mind yourself—no digging! Just pull the layers aside, set a plant in place, push material around the stem, and water. In a shallow bed, you may be setting the bottom of the rootball directly on the newspaper, but never disturb or cut into the base layer of newspaper.

Take time to prepare your plants before you set them in place. It helps to tease apart the roots of bedding plants and potted perennials, especially if the roots are dense or circling. Fan the roots out in all directions as you set the plant into the bed. You want the roots to grow laterally through those wonderful lasagna layers. Eventually, as the paper disintegrates, the roots will also reach down into the soil beneath.

A lasagna garden offers plants nearly ideal growing conditions. It's nutrient rich, because there's so much organic matter. All that organic matter retains moisture, too, so plants won't suffer water stress. They're unlikely to become waterlogged, either, because the beds are raised above ground level and excess water will tend to drain away quickly. The soil medium is loose and airy because it has never been compacted by people walking on or driving machinery over it, which means roots can get plenty of air and extend through the layers easily. Because conditions are so wonderful, you can set plants closer than standard spacing recommendations. For example, the garden encyclopedia I use says to plant annuals 10 to 12 inches apart. But I tuck in annual bedding plants just 4 to 6 inches away from their neighbors. That way my beds look full and colorful right from the start, and the plants quickly spread to fill every inch of space with foliage and flowers. This is terrific news for small-space gardeners, because it means you can fit in more plants than you might expect.

Adding Mulch

It's important to keep adding organic materials to your lasagna garden. Topping the bed with mulch will help suppress germination of any weed seeds that find their way into the bed and will conserve moisture in the original surface layers, where root growth is heaviest. In summer, mulch with grass clippings: Apply them in a 2- to 3-inch layer. When leaves fall in autumn, run over them with your lawn mower to shred them, then put them on the garden in a 4- to 6-inch layer as a winter mulch.

Gardening lasagna-style produces such rich soil that you can plant intensively, increasing yield by as much as 100 percent!

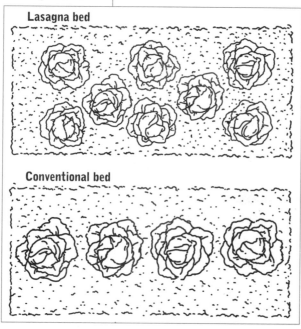

Lasagna bed

Conventional bed

Adding organic mulches also renews the bed's fertility by providing more nutrients. The most nutrient-rich mulch is compost. In most cases, adding ¼ to ½ inch of compost as a yearly mulch is enough to renew soil fertility. If you have sandy soil or live in the deep South (where heat causes organic matter to break down faster), apply ½ to 1 inch yearly.

Mulching is certainly practical, but you can also use a decorative mulch to add a special accent to a garden bed. Pine bark, buckwheat hulls, and crushed stone can all work well as decorative mulches. For a shrub in a large container, I'll even use a living mulch of a low-growing flower or herb, such as violets (see page 189 for a description of this technique). Because I set plants so close together, it's usually not necessary to mulch them once they're established. Foliage covers every inch of the surface of the beds. However, I do use lots of grass clippings and leaves to renew the soil at the end of the season and protect it over the winter. The secret to keeping lasagna beds productive is to keep the soil growing as well as the plants!

No Tilling!

There's never a need to plow, rototill, or otherwise move earth around when you use the lasagna gardening method. Remember, you're following the model of Mother Nature, and she lets earthworms work the soil for her. Even if earthworms seem to be absent from the soil

UNDERLYING ISSUES

Even though you'll build and plant a lasagna bed above ground level, the native soil underneath the bed can affect how your plants grow. As the bed matures, roots will penetrate the base layer of crumbly newspaper and delve into the soil beneath. If your soil has a pH problem, your plants might end up showing nutrient deficiency symptoms. The pH is a measure of the acidity or alkalinity of soil; it's expressed as a number from 1 to 14. On this scale, 1 is most acid, 14 is most alkaline, and 7 is neutral. Most plants grow best in soil that's neutral or close to neutral. At a high or low pH, plant roots sometimes can't absorb nutrients properly.

Organic matter tends to buffer soil, bringing it closer to neutral. But if your soil is strongly acid or alkaline, the organic matter you supply with your lasagna layers may not be enough. To correct the pH, you may need to add lime to your lasagna bed to correct acid soil beneath, or sulfur to correct alkaline soil. You can buy a simple test kit from a garden center to check pH.

Another problem, especially in urban areas, is soil contamination by heavy metals like lead. If you live in a city or town, especially near businesses or factories, it's wise to have your soil tested for contaminants. Think about it: Even though your lasagna layers are full of only good things, once those roots hit the soil beneath, they can absorb toxins. Those toxins will end up in your harvest. For information on having soil tested for contaminants, check with your local cooperative extension office, or see "Resources for Lasagna Gardeners" on page 271 for some listings of soil-testing laboratories.

around your yard, don't worry. Your soil may be low in organic matter and it may not have much life to it. Feed the soil with layers of organic material, and earthworms will come.

No Weeding!

Lasagna layers create a dense barrier to light, and without light, weeds won't grow. It's important to remember that when you plant your lasagna garden, you shouldn't cut through the base layer of newspaper. Plant your seeds or seedlings only in the layers of soil amendments that are on top of the paper. If you cut through the paper layer, light can get to the levels below and weeds will grow up through your lasagna layers.

Now I'm not promising you a garden with no work at all. But I am promising that if you follow my directions and continue layering around your plants as they grow, you will not have to weed. In addition, watering isn't as important as it would be if your soil were bare. After a few seasons of applying layers of mulch to your gardens, a few weed seeds may get in, but dealing with them is easy. The soil will be so loose that seedlings will uproot easily with a gentle tug.

AWAY WITH WEEDS

Every winter, the road crews drive their trucks right by the curbside gardens at **The Potager**, applying sand to the street to keep it free of ice. The sand is pushed up on the gardens whenever the snowplows go by to remove snow. The sand is full of weed seeds, and they get a tiny hold in my gardens. Each spring, without fail, the weed seeds sprout and seedlings cover the bed. But because the soil of my lasagna beds is so loose and light, I can pluck the seedlings out easily. One short session in spring, and the problem is solved.

Brewing Compost

Guess what? Lasagna gardening is a way of making compost in place in the garden. You layer organic materials to create raised beds, and then you let them break down, either before or after you plant the bed. It's the beauty of the lasagna gardening method—composting is an easy and natural part of the process.

On occasion, I do build a classic compost pile at The Potager during seasonal peaks in the supply of garden wastes, and I sometimes make a small-scale compost pile in a plastic sweater box (see page 249 for more about this method). I use the compost from compost piles as layers in lasagna beds, as an organic fertilizer, and as a primary ingredient for potting mix (for planting small pots and growing plants from seed).

You may want a supply of homemade compost for bed-making, fertilizing, and planting containers, too. If so, you'll want to set up a dedicated compost pile. The best place for a compost pile is a level, well-drained site in full sun. If you can, also pick a site that's sheltered from wind and screened from your neighbors.

Get It in Shape

A classic compost pile should be 3 to 4 feet high and wide to promote decomposition. Smaller piles will still break down, but they will take longer. You can make a freestanding pile, or you can buy or build an enclosure. Enclosures can be made from anything you have handy, such as lumber, chicken wire, fence wire, hardware cloth, bricks, cinder blocks, hay bales, or wooden pallets.

Composting bacteria and fungi need oxygen to do their work. It's a good idea to lay some heavy brush or scrap wood directly on the ground before you start building layers; that will allow some air to reach the lower layers of the pile. If you build an enclosure for your pile, make sure air can circulate through the sides, too.

Feed Your Pile

Food for a compost pile includes just about any plant material, plus certain animal-based products. To create your pile, start with a layer of brown, dry materials such as leaves, straw, and hay. Then add a layer of green, moist materials, such as grass clippings, kitchen waste, and composted manure. If you don't have enough green, high-nitrogen material, you can substitute a thin layer of bloodmeal (available from garden centers). Continue alternating layers of brown materials with layers of green materials until the pile is 3 to 4 feet high. (It does sound like lasagna gardening, doesn't it, only taller!)

If you're enthusiastic about composting and want to speed up the composting process, chop the ingredients before you add them to your pile. (Small pieces break down more quickly than large chunks do.)

THE KRICKET KRAP KING

Talk about using what you have! I have long admired the ingenuity of retired Army Colonel Bill Bricker of Augusta, Georgia. Kricket Krap, a terrific organic fertilizer product, is one of Bill's most creative business ventures.

Bill, an environmentalist of long standing, was appalled by the amount of raw materials that some of the large manufacturers were dumping in landfills. He set himself on a course that would eventually put him in a position to change his city.

First, Bill took the city's collected leaves and limbs and ground them into mulch. Then he added the peelings (potato, carrot, and onion) from a canning factory. He mixed the two together, using a front-end loader to turn the pile. As the mixture decomposed he added other yummy ingredients.

He obtained the contents of cow's stomachs, called paunch, from a slaughterhouse. This undigested vegetable matter is full of nitrogen, which makes his compost piles heat up. I was at the Bricker Organic Farm when an enormous dump truck pulled in and unloaded paunch onto a prepared draining bed. We had moved quickly to an upwind area to watch, but even that wasn't enough to dilute the smell!

Over a period of time, the materials compost and evolve into a rich, black mixture that, when added to Georgia red clay, produces incredible garden soil. I have never seen such vegetables and flowers as those at Bricker's.

This isn't how Bill's business got its interesting name, though. During his quest to find materials to compost, Bill discovered Ghan's Cricket Farm. The farm raises crickets for use as bait and pet food. Cricket waste is second only to bat guano in nitrogen content. Bill took cricket droppings from the farm by the truckload. He then composted it into a product that stimulates plants to grow so fast that they seem to jump out of the ground. His wife, Lou Ellen, dubbed it Kricket Krap.

I use Bill's fertilizer sparingly on my small lasagna beds to help speed decomposition (sometimes a small bed is slower to break down than a large one). Kricket Krap is an absolutely perfect fertilizer for containers, and this is how I most often use it.

Kricket Krap and a related product, Pansy Mate, are now available from some mail-order suppliers and garden centers, or directly from Bricko Farms. (See "Resources for Lasagna Gardeners" on page 271 for contact information.)

You can chop kitchen scraps in a blender or food processor and crush eggshells with your hands. Run newspapers, leaves, stalks, twigs, and branches through a chipper/shredder. A lawn mower also works well for chopping up leaves.

What doesn't belong in your compost pile? Avoid adding fats, meat, bones, and oils. These are slow to decompose, they'll make your pile smell bad, and they'll attract animals to your pile. Also, don't add droppings from dogs or cats; these materials can carry diseases.

A compost pile also needs air and water to encourage decomposition. That's why you've heard that you should turn your compost pile. (I *never* bother turning my compost—it's too much work.) A compost pile will break down even if you never turn it; it will just take more time: a few months instead of several weeks. When you want compost fast, turn the pile about once a week (using a pitchfork) to let in air. It also helps if you keep your compost pile about as moist as a damp sponge. Do this by sprinkling the layers with a garden hose as you build the pile. When you turn the pile, you'll be able to see if it's still moist or if it's drying out. If it's dry, add more water when you turn it. If it's sopping wet, add an absorbent material like shredded dry leaves.

Compost in a Can

Even in a very small yard, you can still compost—in a trash can! Make a simple compost bin by cutting out the bottom of a metal trash can. Drill a few holes in the sides and the lid to let in air, then layer the organic ingredients as you would in a regular, larger pile. Shred your materials as finely as you can to speed up the decomposition. Don't fill the can completely, or you won't be able to turn the compost.

Since a pitchfork won't fit into a trash can, use a stick to turn the compost. Turn it every few days and check the moisture content. It's best to keep garbage-can compost a bit on the dry side.

You can set up your compost can in a garage or shed, too. Don't cut out the bottom of the can for this setup, but add a catch tray underneath the can to contain any excess liquid that drips from the air holes and to catch any materials that fall out when you turn the pile.

More Compost Choices

If you can't make enough compost for your needs, here are two other options. One is to buy bagged compost—it's available at any garden or

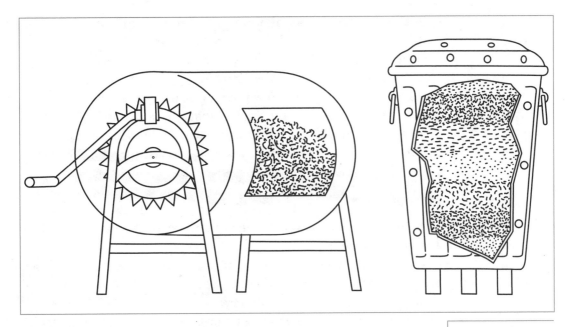

home center. *OG* magazine has tested bagged compost, though, and they find that the quality varies dramatically. It probably will cost more than peat moss, too. If you do buy bagged compost, look for a product that is dark brown or black and has a loose texture. If you can see lots of wood or bark, it's a sign that the material hasn't composted thoroughly. The compost should be moist—not too wet and not too dry. Avoid composts that smell bad (like ammonia, for example); they may not be properly composted either.

Check the label on the bag to see whether the nitrogen content is listed. If you're using compost as mulch, keep in mind that supplying ⅓ pound of nitrogen per 100 square feet of bed surface is plenty to maintain fertility.

Another option is to check the local recycling center run by your city, township, borough, or village. Many centers allow residents to drop off yard waste, which the recycling center staff then uses to make yard waste compost. This compost is usually available free in any quantity you feeling like hauling away.

A compost tumbler (*above left*) will disguise your compost, but it's a costly cover-up! Another option for camouflaging your compost is to make compost in a garbage can set in a corner of your yard or inside your garage (*above right*).

Questions, Questions

As I travel and teach my lasagna gardening techniques to gardeners across the country, people ask me some interesting and practical questions about my methods. Here are the ones I'm most often asked.

Q. Should I add layers of paper in the middle of lasagna beds as I build them?

A. Once you spread the base layer of wet paper on the ground, you don't need to spread any more layers of paper, just layers of organic material. However, after a few growing seasons, weed seeds may invade a lasagna bed, especially a bed that's been planted with annual vegetables or flowers each year. Don't spend your time painstakingly pulling out the weed seedlings. Instead, in spring, top the bed with a layer of newspaper (two or three sheets are sufficient to repress seedlings) and a layer of compost 2 to 3 inches thick. You're ready to plant, and no weed seedlings will trouble your plants.

Q. Can I use cardboard as the bottom layer of a lasagna bed instead of newspaper?

A. I used to recommend cardboard as a substitute for newspaper, but I've come to think that it doesn't work as well. If you want to build a garden with soft, friable soil, newspaper is preferable because it's softer. Worms are more likely to munch on paper than on cardboard, and plant roots can push through decomposing newspaper easier than through cardboard. Newspaper also decomposes faster than cardboard.

Cardboard is a good material to use as the base layer of a path or for a garden bed that you're not planning to plant for at least a full year. I also use cardboard as the base for an "instant patio" (see "Patio on Demand" on page 263 to learn how I do this). Also, if you have an area of really nasty perennial weeds or plants that you want to kill—like bamboo—try covering the area with stiff cardboard weighted down with rocks. Leave it in place for several months, or even a year. Then you can remove the cardboard and build a typical lasagna bed. Some aggressive plants like bamboo might be able to push through newspaper and take over a lasagna bed, so using cardboard to smother it first is the safest course of action.

Q. My perennial garden is a weedy mess. How do I get the weeds under control?

A. To fight weeds in an established perennial bed, cover all the weedy areas between the plants with wet paper. You'll have to fold the paper to fit and tuck it under and around the plants. Top the paper with an attractive mulch such as chopped leaves or buckwheat hulls, keeping the mulch away from the bases of the perennials. If there are desirable plants in the bed that perpetuate themselves by self-sowing, you'll lose them. You can't save every little plant or you'll never reclaim the garden. Watch for weeds that sneak through the foliage of your perennials and pull them out frequently.

Q. Do I have to build a frame around a lasagna garden?

A. No, it's not necessary to box your garden in unless it's on a slope. Even then, laying a low fieldstone wall on the downhill side will be enough to keep the layers in place, as shown in the illustration on this page. To do this, add extra newspaper or cardboard along the low end of the bed, and stack the fieldstone on top of it. In each layer, alternate the seams between the rocks to keep the wall stable. You may have seen complicated directions for building stone walls, but my philosophy is to keep it simple. As long as you're sticking with a fieldstone wall that's two or three layers (6 to 8 inches) high, you probably don't need to fuss with digging a base. Some little walls I built at my inn have remained standing for 25 years. If frost heaving is a big problem in your area, though, it may be safer to dig down several inches to ensure that you have a stable base for the stone.

A low edging of rough fieldstone will help keep a lasagna bed from washing out if it's on a slope.

Q. What keeps grass or weeds from invading a lasagna bed from the side?

A. Cutting an edging gives lasagna beds a nice, clean appearance and helps prevent roots of surrounding plants from growing into the lasagna layers. I like to edge my beds with a sharp-pointed shovel. When you cut a strip of sod from around the edge of a new garden, turn the sod upside down on top of the garden to decompose.

Q. Can I plant a lawn using the lasagna garden method?

A. Absolutely! The best time to plant grass seed is spring or early fall. Follow the same procedure you would to create a new garden bed, starting with the wet newspaper. Alternate layers of fine organic materials such as peat moss, finely chipped leaves, or screened compost to make a bed just 3 to 4 inches high. Lightly rake the top of the bed to make sure it's smooth and level, then scatter the grass seed. Rake the area again to lightly cover the seed, and gently tamp the bed surface with the back of your rake so the seed makes contact with the materials in the bed. Mulch lightly with straw or hay, and keep the area well watered. Don't rush to cut the grass when it appears! Remember, the grass is growing in just a few inches of surface material, and it needs time to anchor itself through the paper and into the soil beneath. Mow too soon, and you'll ruin your efforts. Let the grass grow to 8 inches or more before cutting. When you're ready to mow, set your mower at the highest possible setting so you remove only a few inches of growth.

Q. I love wildflowers. Can I plant a bed of wildflowers using the lasagna garden method?

A. Yes! You have two choices: seed or growing mats. Starting a bed from seed is certainly less expensive, but using growing mats is the easiest method.

If you're starting from seed, follow the instructions above for preparing a bed and planting grass seed. For best results, buy wildflower seed appropriate for your zone and regional conditions from a reputable nursery or mail-order supplier.

After sowing the seed, keep the bed watered the first year. There will be some weeds mixed in with the wildflowers, but unless you consult a wildflower guide, you may not be able to tell which seedlings are weeds and which are wildflowers. In fall, after the plants set seed, cut them back. You may also want to spread additional seed in fall to help regenerate the garden for the following year.

If you develop a passion for wildflowers, you'll discover that there's plenty to learn about them. Some are annuals, while others are biennials or perennials. Some of the plants we call wildflowers truly are flowers that grew wild in North America from the time that European explorers first arrived. Other plants we call wildflowers are plants introduced by settlers from their homes in Europe and Asia that now grow wild along roadsides and in wetlands and wooded areas. If you become interested in native wildflowers, you may want to grow a garden of natives only, in which case you'll want to order specific seeds or plants from a wildflower nursery. You'll also need to spend some time learning to identify plants and weeding out nonnative invaders that show up in the bed.

Q. I've read that manure can be contaminated with bacteria that can make people very sick or even kill them. Is it safe to use manure in my lasagna beds?

A. News stories about deadly strains of *E. coli* in animal manure are frightening, and this is an important question. I've used manure in my lasagna beds for years, and I've recommended it to others. But because of these reports of diseases spread in manure, I asked my friends at *OG* magazine what they're telling gardeners about using manure. They told me that until there are studies that reveal more about the risks of using animal manures, the magazine is recommending that people never use *raw* manure in home gardens. Composted manure should be safe to use. To be truly confident that the manure is fully composted, add it to your own compost pile and compost it a second time. Or, use it for lasagna layers in a bed that you plan to let sit for a season or over the winter before planting. It's also best to seek out organic farms for manure because manure from conventional farms may contain antibiotic residues.

CHAPTER 2

SMALL-GARDEN POSSIBILITIES

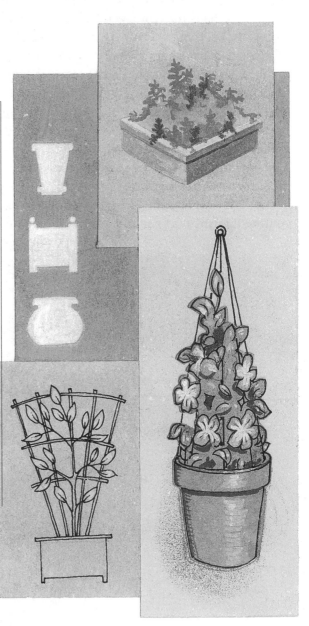

A small garden is a real garden, not just a poor substitute for a large garden. No matter how small your property is, you can still have the garden of your dreams. You may find that you become more discriminating, carefully choosing distinctive plants instead of settling for the ordinary. Creativity is the key! Designing your own plant supports and container gardens also adds to the fun of small-space gardening. So enjoy dreaming and designing your small-space gardens and containers. After all, you have the time because small-space lasagna gardens are so easy to install and maintain.

Make the Most of Small Spaces

Many of my visitors at The Potager are amazed by how many gardens and containers I've crammed into my half acre. Sometimes people ask me why I've worked so hard on my gardens. First of all, I tell them, it's not hard! Because all my gardens are lasagna gardens, they were easy to make and require very little maintenance. I also tell them that for me, gardening is sheer pleasure. I love the challenge of finding places for small gardens. Plus, I depend on my gardens to produce many of the vegetables, fruits, and herbs used for the meals that we serve in The Potager café.

Most people don't grow food as a business anymore, or even to feed themselves. They garden for enjoyment and therefore don't need a big garden. First-time homeowners may have a small home or townhouse on a small lot. Busy working families may have a big yard, but limited time for gardening. Retirees are giving up their big houses and yards for something smaller. I made the same change when I began a new life as a single person and needed less space to live in—of course, I also ended up with less space to make a garden in. My new home had so little land that at first I thought it would be impossible to create a garden. After taking a better look, though, I saw possibilities for creating an outdoor garden retreat with plenty of plants and lots of style.

My Garden Wonderland

My garden at my home in the woods is a wonderful example of how ideas for small-space gardening can evolve. I don't have one-tenth of the area that I had at my beautiful farmhouse. But even though my home garden is limited to a courtyard area that's only about 20 × 20 feet, I've created a small garden wonderland that I truly love.

The courtyard is mostly shaded because it's situated between my house and my daughter's house. When I moved in, the only things planted in the courtyard were four large boxwoods, English ivy against the wall of my daughter's house, and an old planting of hostas and bleeding hearts along the base of the stone wall at the rear of the courtyard. A curving fieldstone pathway divided the courtyard area in two.

GARDEN DREAMING

In winter, when there's time for some serious garden planning and dreaming, the postman brings me garden catalogs from around the world. Stacks of them pile up on my nightstand and cover my kitchen table. Out of this chaos comes my garden plan. I start with my dream garden, listing every flower and vegetable I could possibly want. Of course, my small garden can't hold all those plants, so I've learned to use a pencil with a good eraser! You, too, should plan and dream about your garden, no matter what its size. With my lasagna method, you can turn even the tiniest speck of land into a thriving garden.

With careful planning, I found I could turn that courtyard into an outdoor room that would give me a secluded place to sit, a mini nature retreat to enjoy, and space to display some of the containers I love to decorate with. My courtyard even includes a small water feature.

The main sitting area is on the right-hand side of the courtyard. The two chairs and table are made of an aluminum alloy that looks like heavy wrought iron. They're a gift from my son Michael and his wife, Pam. Each time I go in or out of my house, I see the seating area and am reminded of Michael and Pam. Personal connections like this are very important to me, and I've filled my small garden spaces with plants and objects that bring to mind special people and memories. Adding this type of romantic touch to a garden, especially a small garden, is one of my favorite pastimes. (See "Set a Garden Personality" on page 264 for a basketful of sentimental ideas for giving your garden a romantic flavor.)

The foundation beds along my daughter Mickey's house are just 2 feet wide. They're still a project in progress, but I plan to plant them

My courtyard garden proves that you can have it all in a small space: plenty of beautiful plants, special features for style and to attract wildlife, and places to sit and enjoy the beauty around you.

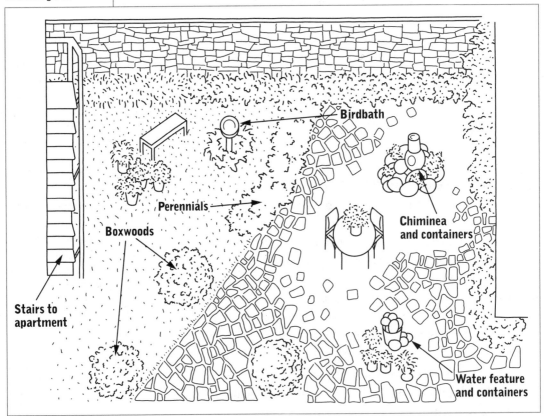

Birdbath

Perennials

Boxwoods

Chiminea and containers

Stairs to apartment

Water feature and containers

with shade-loving perennials, and I'll preserve the clematis with deep purple blooms that climbs the front corner of her house.

Near the seating area, I made a pile of stones for a small rock garden, and on top of it I put a Chiminea stove as a conversation piece. Among the stones, I planted a lovely collection of red, magenta, white, and bicolor cheddar pinks. It looks like a bright quilt when they're all in bloom. This side of the courtyard also includes the water feature—an old ice cream mixer with a recirculating pump hidden inside under pretty stones, surrounded by container plantings.

On the left side of the path, I've made a lasagna garden that includes 'Rheinland' astilbes, 'Rotblum' bergenia, and columbines, with lady's mantle edging the path. I set up a birdbath among the hostas and placed a very low wooden bench and containers of shade-loving annuals beside the birdbath. I enjoy the different viewpoint of the garden that unfolds when I sit on the bench. I can see the details of the hosta leaves and the impatiens blossoms in the containers. I can spy on the insect residents of my courtyard—ants, beetles, and spiders that scurry between the plants and stones. It's a child's-eye view of the garden, and I am always particularly pleased when a visiting child spots the bench and spends time there discovering the small wonders of nature.

Analyzing Your Site

How can you go about creating your own dream garden? Even if you only have a small yard or patio area to work with, I recommend that you begin by drawing a map of your property. It's easy—you don't need to be a professional artist. Your map is a tool that will help you discover possible spaces to plant, because looking at a map gives you a new perspective on your surroundings.

You can use plain white paper for your site map, or use graph paper if you want to draw things to scale. First, sketch the outline of your property. Then draw the outline of your house and any outbuildings. Draw circles to indicate trees and shrubs. Be sure to sketch in your driveway (if you have one) and any existing pathways. That's all there is to it.

I also encourage you to take photos of your property from all sides and angles. Snapshots from a disposable camera will do the job. The camera sees more than the human eye, and you may be surprised by things you've never noticed before that suddenly seem obvious in a photo of your deck or front entry area.

Places to Sneak in a Small Garden

Spend some time looking at your map and photos, and also walking outside looking at your yard. You're sleuthing for garden sites, and you should look low and high. When your space is limited, you'll find valuable gardening opportunities by picturing where trellises, arbors, and arches would fit into the scene. Once you start growing some plants vertically, you free up valuable ground space to grow even more plants. Here are some ideas to kick-start the process:

Under the roof overhang. We tend to write off the space immediately next to a house or outbuilding if it's a narrow strip of soil bordered by a path or the edge of the property. Also, if it's under an overhang, the soil may be very dry because rainwater doesn't reach it, and it may not get much sun. But why let that stop you? With the right choice of plants, you can create a super garden in a long, narrow space, whether it's sunny or shady. And dry soil is no problem—just run a soaker hose or drip irrigation hose through the bed, and you can water on a regular basis with very little effort.

Along pathways. Pathways don't have to be bordered by grass. I create little borders of flowers and herbs along all walkways, putting ground-hugging herbs right at the edge.

On the steps. Are there steps leading to your front or back door? Set a potted plant or two on each step to create a multilayer garden. Unless your steps are extremely narrow, you can surely find containers that will fit without blocking traffic.

Let a garden of containers cascade down the steps to your front door or your deck. Choose a variety of containers, and set some of them on overturned pots for a tiered effect.

In your front lawn. We take our front lawns for granted, but have you ever wondered why you need a front lawn? You probably don't use it for playing or entertaining; you do that out back. Why not turn that front lawn into a garden with a grass path running through it? It's so easy with lasagna gardening.

From the rafters. If you have a front or back porch or a covered patio, you can create an entire garden above the ground using hanging baskets. Annuals, foliage plants, herbs, and even some vegetables will grow well in hanging baskets. You can also set up containers on the porch or patio and guide twining vines like morning glories or peas to grow up strings attached to the roof.

On your deck or patio. Surely your patio furniture and grill don't take up every inch of your deck or patio surface. Fill the unused areas with groups

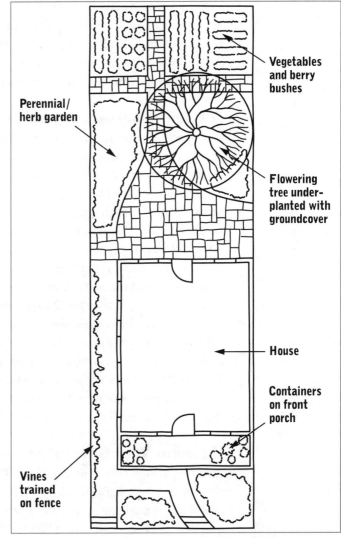

Perennial/herb garden

Vegetables and berry bushes

Flowering tree underplanted with groundcover

House

Containers on front porch

Vines trained on fence

of lushly planted containers. It will transform the atmosphere of your deck or patio, and you'll feel like you're sitting in the middle of a garden.

Up a fence. If there's a fence between your property and your neighbor's, dress it up with climbing plants. All you need is a 6-inch-wide strip of soil at the base of the fence. In that small space, you can plant tomatoes, clematis, or even fruit trees, and train them to a trellis or directly on the fence. *No* soil at the base of the fence? Mount planters right on the fence at about eye level, and fill them with smaller plants or cascading plants, such as trailing nasturtiums or petunias.

Whether you live in a city row home or a suburban townhouse, you can find plenty of spaces that invite a garden, either in small beds or in containers.

Over your head. Install an arbor over a pathway and grow flowering vines. Have an exposed patio? Instead of covering it with an awning or roof, build an overhead sunshade and train grapevines or scarlet runner beans to grow up and overhead. (Suspend hanging baskets from the rafters of the sunshade, too.)

A Dream Garden Takes Shape

Once you've brainstormed some ideas, make another drawing that shows your new gardens in place. Don't hold back—at this stage, it's your dream garden and it's only on paper! Garden dreaming like this is such a pleasure that you may surprise yourself with the ideas you come up with. Dream gardens can be a great place to start, and somewhere between the dream and the reality, an actual garden will evolve.

Your lifestyle will affect the look of your small garden, too. Will it be a place for rest and reflection? Will children or animals share the space? Will you be cooking and eating meals in the garden? Will you need protection from the sun or rain? Don't overlook any features that a larger garden would have. Small gardens are limited only by your imagination.

While you're dreaming about gardens, think about other features that you'd like to include, such as paths and a seating area. Have some fun, too, like I did with my Chiminea stove and ice-cream-mixer fountain. The rewards will far outweigh the cost and labor, which, because they are on a small scale, may be considerably less than you think.

Keeping Your Garden Fresh

This may be the first time you have taken an overall view of your property with the goal of finding space for a new garden, but don't let it be the last. I repeat my map-making exercise once a year, both at home and at The Potager, because the landscape changes. Trees cast more shade as they grow, and paths become overgrown. Each year, I choose something new to work on, and I also check in on how the things I've planted in past years are faring. This kind of yearly check-in also allows you to work in new ideas from photos you've seen in magazines, gardens you've visited, or programs you've seen on television.

Design Tricks for Small Gardens

Basic garden design principles apply to gardens large and small. I take my design inspiration from many sources, and I don't always play by classic garden design rules. It's up to you how much you want

SMALL SECRETS FOR BIG SUCCESS

Tips from Abroad

I've taken inspiration for my small gardens from British gardeners, who are experts at creating wonderful gardens in very little space. Here are a few of the gardening tricks I've learned from my friends across the Atlantic:

- Use rows of short plants as living borders between crops and at the edges of beds. Some of my favorite plants for edging a bed are alpine strawberries, curly parsley, and a closely trimmed hedge of hyssop.

- Keep plants in reserve to fill garden holes. There's a little area behind my garden shed where I grow flowers in pots. Whenever I harvest a vegetable crop like beans, I pull up the veggie plants and set a container of flowers in its place.

- Set plants close together, so you can fit more of them in a bed. This also results in fewer problems with weeds, because the plants grow leaf-to-leaf and shade weeds out.

- Extend your garden with containers. Line containers along pathways, decks, and patios, and up the steps to your door.

to consult gardening books, magazines, or fellow gardeners for garden design advice. I think the first rule with small gardens is this: Choose plants that you like! That said, here are some of my best ideas for creating interest and appeal in small gardens.

Garden in 3-D

To maximize space in a small garden, think in 3-D. Of course, gardens are always three-dimensional, but if you choose only small plants for a small garden, it may end up looking flat. A garden is more interesting when the plants in it vary in height, width, and depth. You can fit a wide variety of plant sizes and shapes in a narrow bed by building a graduated garden. Start with the tallest plants in the back, tuck in medium-height plants around and under the tallest, and plant the ground-huggers at the front. A garden designed this way is pleasing to the eye and makes maximum use of a small space.

I've used old-fashioned hollyhocks, which grow up to 8 feet tall, as the background of one of my 2-foot beds, and I've planted impressive 'Morning Light' miscanthus in another. Remember, your garden space may be small, but that's no reason not to grow a few large plants!

As you plan your dimensional plantings, try to set a rhythm that carries the eye from the front to the back by repeating certain plants or colors. I use plants with gray foliage, such as artemisias, repeatedly in my small garden to create rhythm and highlights.

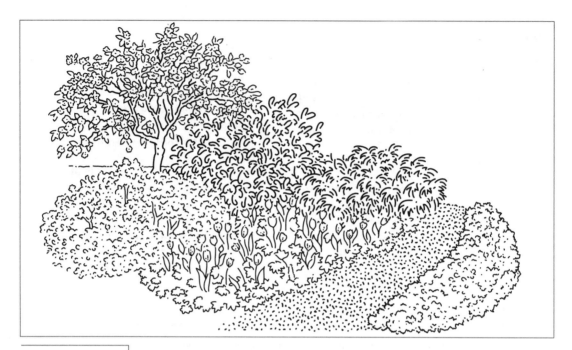

Springtime in this small garden includes lots of 3-D effects, with azaleas blooming in the shade of a small tree and tulips poking through a bed of perennials.

Put Yourself in the Garden

When you have a large property to landscape, it's important to think about the vista from your house windows or from the street. But if you're gardening in a small city backyard or just around your patio, your garden may never be exposed to public view. All the more reason to be sure that *you* enjoy the view of your garden. The best way to do that is to include a seating area in your garden: a table and chairs, a bench, a lounge chair, or whatever suits your taste.

Design for the Front Door

Another important place to include plants is by your front door. The entrance to your home is your first impression on visitors. You can change the look of your front entryway with the seasons by planning a small, in-ground garden (if possible), then adding a variety of plants in interesting containers. Even if your entryway has no other space than what immediately surrounds your front door, it can still be home to a charming garden. You may want to plan plantings that match the color of your front door or choose containers that echo the materials of your house or the front path.

My brother and sister-in-law, Tom and Cheryl Neal, of Springfield, Illinois, use black iron urns flanking each side of their front door as planters for dwarf Alberta spruce. The black iron picks up the black of their window shutters and contrasts nicely with their house's brick exterior. With each change of season, Cheryl adds potted plants and other touches for color and interest. Spring brings tulips, daffodils, and a darling cement rabbit. In summer, the urns hold pots of zonal geraniums, petunias, and nasturtiums. Fall is my favorite time, when Cheryl displays potted mums, small bales of hay, pumpkins, and gourds.

Create a Focal Point

Insert an attention-getting plant as a focal point (use plants that stand taller or have more striking foliage than others) when you want to draw attention to a certain part of the garden. Color can make this trick work, too. A light-color plant highlights and attracts attention to a background planting. Daffodils and light-flowered tulips can serve this role in a spring garden, and a white-flowering shrub such as 'Abbotswood' shrubby cinquefoil (*Potentilla fruticosa* 'Abbotswood') will draw your gaze when planted behind flowering perennials or annuals. An ornamental arbor or trellis that supports a

Lush hanging baskets and containers perk up standard entry gardens without requiring lots of space.

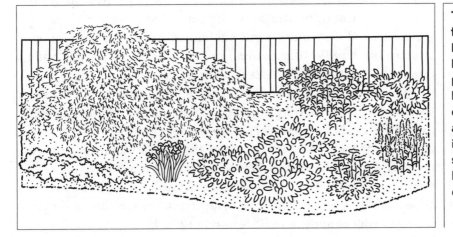

The spreading foliage of the cut-leaf maple tree at left is the focal point of this lasagna bed, changing it from an ordinary bed into something special by adding height, color, and contrast.

Tall delphiniums and hollyhocks command attention in this small garden, luring visitors to stroll to the bench where they can admire the flowers at close range.

tall background plant also serves as a focal point. I used a black wrought iron trellis this way in a small foundation garden that I reworked for a friend of mine. It bridges the gap between some evergreens and a lilac bush, and it is covered with an old-fashioned climbing rose and a clematis vine.

A tree or large shrub could also be a strong focal point. If you have space for only one tree or shrub, try to find one that has interest in all four seasons. For example, paperbark maple (*Acer griseum*) has bluish green leaves in spring and summer; good fall color; and ornamental bark for winter interest. There are plenty of plants to choose from if you do a little research. Ask a knowledgeable local nursery owner for advice. You may need to prune the tree or shrub occasionally to keep it inbounds.

Space-Saving Structures

If you want to garden successfully in small spaces, you have to "grow up"! That means growing plants vertically on fences, trellises, arches, arbors, and other ingenious plant supports of your own devising. Arbors, trellises, and other plant supports are some of your most important design tools in a small garden because they allow you to vary the height of your garden in a small space; they introduce interesting shapes and textures; and they free up valuable ground space for other plants. My daughter Debbie, who gardens in Atlanta, has used trellises to dress up the view of her garage. It's a large, two-car garage, and it's the first thing you see when you drive up to her house. The garage looked very stark until she added an Italian jasmine vine (*Jasminum humile* 'Revolutum'), which has large, butter yellow flowers that cover the trellises from spring to fall.

I love coming up with ideas for plant supports. Whenever I travel for speaking engagements or to attend gardening conferences, my favorite part of the trip is touring local private gardens. I always discover wonderful new ideas, and I find some of the most unique space-saving structures in small gardens. Walled or fenced properties in cities may offer only a few inches of soil between the wall or fence and the walk or patio, but I've seen flowering dwarf fruit trees, bulbs, and perennials growing happily in as little as 6 to 12 inches.

Gardening vertically isn't difficult. The basics are to match plants to supports of the right size and strength, to learn how to train plants to climb the supports, and to anchor the supports when needed.

Encouraging Plants to Climb

Some plants will climb almost any support without any encouragement. Ivy is the most common example—it has sticky rootlets that adhere to surfaces. That sticky adhesive can also remove paint from your house or damage mortar, though, so be careful!

Other plants have stems that naturally coil around vertical uprights. Pole beans and morning glories climb this way. Clematis, cucumbers, and peas have tendrils that grasp hold of supports. Some plants, like tomatoes and climbing roses, need to be tied to supports. Twist-ties, string, or pieces of old panty hose work well to fasten vines to supports. Be sure to leave some slack so you don't strangle the stems when you tie them.

Regardless of the type of support you lend your plants, placement of the trellis is important. Most freestanding supports will create a shadow, cutting off light to another area and inadvertently creating a shade garden. Watch how the sun travels over your area and place the arbor so it is not a problem. On the flip side, if you garden in the South or Southwest, you may want to take advantage of shade cast by a trellis to protect plants that can't take the blazing summer sun.

Working with Walls

It's a cinch to turn the walls of your house into plant supports. For a lightweight vine like sweet peas, all you need to do is attach plastic netting to the wall. If your house has wooden or aluminum siding, you can hammer galvanized nails into the siding (add a little caulk around the base of each nail) and attach wires to the nails for training plants. Some plants, like Virginia creeper, will climb a wall without any support.

Fences are great plant supports, too, either with nails and plastic netting or all by themselves. Just be sure to check the fence posts or other supports to make sure they're not rotting or damaged. The weight of a heavy vine can pull down a rickety fence.

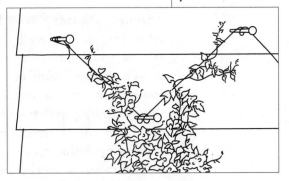

Wires on a house wall for training plants should be very taut so they won't sag under the weight of the plants.

Clematis climbing on a wooden tower is a classy focal point for a small garden.

Trellis Tips

Simple wooden and plastic trellises are available for sale at any garden or home center. You can set these trellises against a wall and secure them in place in a few spots. You can also set up a freestanding trellis in a garden bed.

There's no limit to the materials and styles of homemade trellises. Here's a sampling of the possibilities:

- One standard trellis is stakes and strings. There are seemingly endless variations on this type of trellis: the stakes can be made of bamboo, wood, plastic pipe, or copper tubing.
- For a heavy-duty trellis to support a mix of crops, use rebar or metal posts driven about 1 foot into the ground to support strong wire-mesh fencing.
- An old wooden stepladder is an instant trellis that you can train almost any vine to climb, from honeysuckle to pumpkins. Or, put potted plants on the rungs and hook hanging baskets onto the side supports for an instant multilayer garden.
- Old tools and metal wagon or tractor wheels are some of my favorite trellises. An iron wheel, for instance, can lean against a fence for sweet peas to climb.
- With some 2 × 4s and pieces of lattice, you can erect a trellis to shade a deck or patio on one side, or create a four-sided column for a vine to climb.
- Tepee-style trellises of bamboo or wood are popular for beans, morning glories, and other annual vines.

Keeping Trellises in Place

When you attach a trellis to a wall, use spacers between the trellis and the wall so air can circulate freely around the vines and so the vines can wrap completely around the trellis supports. Choose good-quality, rustproof screws.

Freestanding trellises often need anchoring so they won't topple over in the wind or from the weight of the growing vines. For a stake-and-string trellis, all you need to do is push the stakes 6 inches or more into the soil. For more elaborate trellises, you may need to

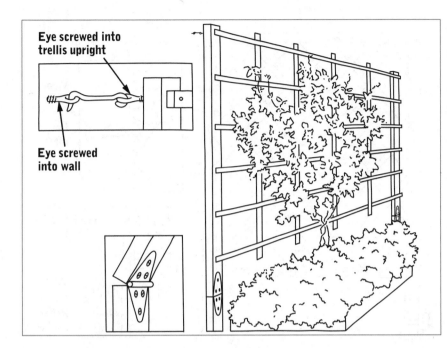

Eye screwed into
trellis upright

Eye screwed
into wall

Include hinges
and a hook-and-
eye setup when
you install a
trellis against the
wall of your
house or shed.
That way you
can easily move
the trellis out of
the way when
you want to
paint the wall.

fasten the trellis to a length of rebar or iron pipe sunk into the ground, as shown in the illustration on page 46.

If you want to go beyond a flat trellis, you can try using an arch or arbor for supporting plants, too. These are especially effective over a pathway or seating area. Plants with scented flowers, such as moonflower and roses, are wonderful choices for an arbor near a seating area. (For more details about using arches and arbors in your garden designs, see "Supporting and Training Vines" on page 95 and "Arches and Arbors" on page 256.)

Invite visitors
to enter your
garden through
a classic vine-
covered arch.

Finding Trellis Materials

Most of my gardening friends love to scrounge materials for making their own trellises and plant supports. One discovery of mine is the small saplings that the local road maintenance workers cut down while clearing roadsides to keep vegetation from blocking the view of drivers. After they fell trees and shrubs, they pile the trunks in place for chipping. I watch for these piles and raid them before they're turned into wood chips. These small saplings are perfect for making beautiful trellises and tepees to place around the garden.

Use wood screws to fasten diagonal crosspieces to the rectangular frame of a rustic wooden trellis like this one. Anchor the trellis to a length of rebar or an iron fence post, and it will be ready to support vines or climbing roses.

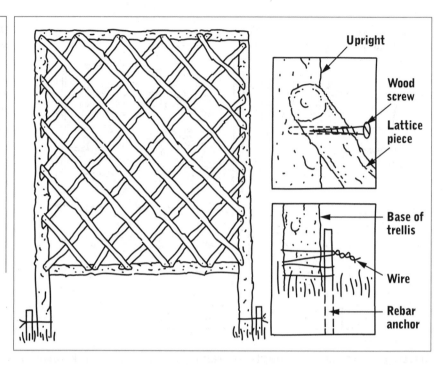

When I'm ready to build a new support, I select some saplings from my supply of rescued trees. I use a measuring tape and bow saw to measure and cut the saplings to the lengths I need. With the help of my power screwdriver, I then fasten the saplings together with wood screws to make a rustic trellis or arch. These supports are usually heavy enough to stand alone, but to stabilize a plant support in a windy area, you can wire the base to rebar or an iron fence post that has been driven into the ground at least 1 foot deep, as shown above. (See page 249 for more information about using rebar.)

Cages and Other Supports

Some plants don't need a full-fledged trellis but will do best with some type of plant support that prevents them from sprawling. Tomatoes are the most obvious example, but the same is true for many tall perennials, such as peonies, lupines, and tall asters. You can buy plant supports, such as tomato cages or peony rings, and you can also fashion your own sturdy cages for tomatoes. With perennials, you'll probably want to choose more discreet homemade supports. You can push bamboo poles into the soil near the base of

HILDA'S 2-TOWER GARDEN

At age 90, my neighbor Hilda Spraque was still an attractive woman, tall, slim, and crowned with healthy white hair pulled back in a bun. She was independent and just a little sassy. I always enjoyed talking with Hilda—I think she had forgotten more than I will ever know!

Hilda had a small backyard with one garden area—a plot about 12 × 14 feet. I helped Hilda make two layered lasagna beds with a path down the middle. For the centerpiece of each plot, we set up a bean tower. A bean tower is an amazingly efficient plant support made of galvanized metal that can support up to 12 pole bean plants in less than 5 square feet of garden space. (Bean towers are available from many mail-order garden supply and seed companies; they cost about $25.) We planted Hilda's whole garden around these towers. We left space for a narrow path, just wide enough for one person, around each tower, so that Hilda could reach them

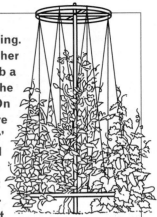

easily for harvesting. Hilda planted all her crops to either climb a tower or huddle at the bottom of one. On one tower, there were 'Kentucky Wonder' pole beans, small cucumbers, old-fashioned sweet peas, and tomatoes. At their feet, her favorite herbs and flowers grew: sage, parsley, thyme, and bold-colored zinnias. The other tower supported scarlet runner beans, which she grew not for the beans but for the red flowers that would lure bees and butterflies. After a couple of seasons I also noticed the early spring bloom of 'Yellow Queen' clematis on the tower. Around the base a riot of annuals bloomed all summer.

I miss that lovely old lady, but I will always remember her as a great gardener.

a plant and weave twine among the poles as a framework to support the growing stems. Twiggy brush poked in among plant stems is another unobtrusive support. As with trellises, it's important to put these plant supports in place at the beginning of the season, so that the plants can grow up and through them.

Watch for castoffs that will work as plant supports. In my garden, an abandoned bar stool without a seat is the perfect plant support for gladiolus. I added a terra-cotta saucer to the top, and it doubles as a birdbath. For more hints on finding treasures from trash for your garden, see "Trash or Treasure?" on page 266.

Get Creative with Containers

Growing plants in containers is one of the best parts of small-space gardening. Once a garden is in the ground, it isn't easy to get creative with new arrangements—not without digging, anyway. But when you plant in containers, flexibility and change are the norm. Containers also add color and interest to a small garden. If the planting arrangement doesn't look right, pick up your containers and try again.

Container gardening allows you to "plant" on deck steps, at front entrances, on patios, in window boxes—anywhere there's room for a container or two—which means that even the most land-deprived gardener can grow flowers, herbs, and even vegetables in the smallest amount of space.

Give Me a Pot and I'll Grow You a Garden

I've grown some of my favorite foods in containers on my deck. It's so easy to pick tiny alpine strawberries when they are growing in a window box hanging from the railing just outside the kitchen door. Cucumbers are practically at arm's length in a self-watering pot that stands near an outdoor table, with a twig trellis supporting the vines. Lettuce in a wooden box sitting atop the railing is but a step away from becoming a salad. Fast-growing radishes and slow-growing carrots grow in another railing box. (The radishes will all be eaten long before the carrots need the extra room to grow.)

Matching the plant to the space available is the key to success with container gardens. Read plant tags and catalog descriptions and watch for plants described as compact, dwarf, or good for containers. It helps to know the minimum size container for the plant. For example, most annuals, perennials, and herbs will grow well in containers that hold from 2 to 4 gallons of planting mix. Vegetables vary in their needs—check "Mix-and-Match Containers" on

Mixed herbs, tomatoes with a lettuce border, and gorgeous combinations of perennials and annuals will thrive in large containers filled with rich lasagna-style layers of organic ingredients.

page 106 for specific guidelines. If you don't know the volume of a container, ask a salesperson for information. For containers you already have, eyeball an approximation by imagining how many gallon jugs would fit in the container.

You'll want to plant containers fairly densely—nothing looks more forlorn than a big container with gaps between scrawny plants. But keep in mind how much the plants will expand during the growing season. Deciding what plants will share container space well takes a little practice. Container gardens are everywhere these days, so keep your eyes open for combinations you like, and try recreating them. Think about sun and shade needs—you wouldn't want to plant a shade-lover like coleus in the same container with sun-loving salvias and petunias. It's also a good idea to mix plants of different heights and textures to create interest. Choosing a color theme may help you plan your container plantings, and in Chapter 3 you'll find plenty of great ideas and plant suggestions for color-theme combinations.

Choosing and Using Containers

Containers come in many wonderful shapes, sizes, and materials. Some are easier to maintain than others, and some are more beautiful than others. New, lightweight, self-watering containers seem to have it all. So why do I keep using old stuff that I can't bear to throw away? I think it's because I've been able to use my well-worn containers to maximize the gardening potential of my small space. I couldn't have a garden at all if I didn't own a collection of pots. My collection includes containers that will hold any size plant. Here's how I put them to good use:

- Terra-cotta strawberry pots are filled with herbs.
- A mesa or Mayan planter (which is usually made of terra-cotta and has 11 separate openings) holds several different kinds of lettuce, salad herbs, and edible flowers, as well as a patio tomato in the large, main opening.
- Four terra-cotta pots of graduated sizes are stacked high, one inside the other, all planted with strawberries that spill over the sides.
- An old watering can holds thyme, rosemary, and baby basil.
- Plastic planting bags are a new type of container that can hang from a wall or fence and are easy to use.

Window boxes aren't just for flowers. Combine vegetables and herbs with flowers for a unique window-sill garden that you can harvest right through the window.

- Window boxes are pretty and productive because I use them for flowers, culinary herbs, and even carrots.
- An old metal trash can may not be glamorous, but it's an excellent size for growing hearty tomato plants. You could also let vining plants spill over the sides to disguise it.

Basic Considerations

My favorite container is a deep plastic planter, about 24 inches in diameter, that's a light shade of terra-cotta. I love the color, and plastic doesn't dry out as quickly as clay. It's wide enough to hold plenty of soil for several plants and deep enough to sink tall bamboo poles into as plant supports.

As you work with containers, you'll decide for yourself which materials you like best. All types of containers have their pros and cons, and I've outlined some of them in "Know Your Containers" on the opposite page.

Whatever type of container you select, make sure it has drainage holes in the bottom. If it doesn't, make some. (For most materials, you can use an electric drill to open drainage holes in the bottom of the container.) Good drainage is the difference between success and failure in a potted garden.

Planting Containers

Most potted plants that you buy at a garden center are planted in a "soilless mix" made from peat moss, perlite or vermiculite, and perhaps a little organic matter. Some have chemical fertilizers added right to the mix. Plus, these plants have likely been fed with liquid chemical fertilizer.

KNOW YOUR CONTAINERS

You may be a bit overwhelmed when you see the variety of containers available for sale at your local garden center. To help you make choices, here are some pros and cons of the most popular types of containers.

TYPE OF CONTAINER	GOOD POINTS	DRAWBACKS
Cast iron	Beautiful and weather-resistant; retains moisture well.	Heavy! Prone to rusting.
Growing bags	Reusable; these hang from fences or walls so they don't take up any ground space.	Need frequent watering.
Plastic, fiberglass	Lightweight, inexpensive, and weather resistant.	May blow over on windy days.
Pottery	Beautiful and distinctive.	Fragile; not weather-resistant.
Terra-cotta	Beautiful; provides bottom weight to counterbalance tall plants.	Dries out quickly in hot weather; cracks if it freezes; heavy.
Wire	Attractive; plants can be set between wires for lush effects.	Needs liner and frequent watering.
Wood	Versatile; insulates roots in hot weather.	May rot.

We want our container gardens to be all organic, just like our in-ground gardens are, so we need to create a root environment that will supply nutrients naturally. But using garden soil in containers isn't the answer, because natural soil tends to pack down in containers. Once the soil becomes compacted, it's difficult to water the plants because the water runs off the top of the container or down the sides instead of being absorbed. The roots struggle to absorb air and water in the compacted soil and your plants may grow poorly.

The solution is to make lasagna layers in your containers! You won't use rough organic materials like straw or kitchen wastes, because the decomposition process won't happen readily in containers. Instead, the layers should be fine-textured materials, with a heavy emphasis on compost. It's fine to use a commercial potting mix as one ingredient, but shop around for one made with all-organic ingredients, or at least one without added chemical fertilizers. If you're not sure where to look for one locally, try ordering it from a garden supplier who specializes in organic products.

SUPERCHARGE A CONTAINER

Heavy feeders such as tomatoes and peppers need a rich source of food to produce a good crop. So do fruit trees and bushes, because you'll harvest from them over several years. In the garden, their roots can spread to find food, and the soil's fertility is renewed as earthworms and microorganisms digest the mulch layers that you add each season. The system doesn't work quite that way in containers, so you may want to add some extra nutrients as you fill the containers. To make a special nutrient booster, mix 1 part bloodmeal with 1 part rock or colloidal phosphate and 1 part greensand. (You can buy these soil amendments at garden centers.) When you're filling containers with layers, sprinkle this mixture lightly on each layer. Use about 1 cup total for every 5 gallons of container volume.

Compost not only supplies nutrients to your plants, it also adds disease-preventing microorganisms to the root environment. It's also okay to add a small amount of garden soil to a container, equal to about 10 percent of the container's volume. This can help increase the weight of a container for a tall tree or shrub, counterbalancing the top so the container won't tip over in windy conditions.

With small pots, you don't need to bother making layers. Just put a coffee filter or paper towel in the bottom of the pot to cover the drainage holes, add some compost and some potting mix, and use a small stick or an old kitchen fork to gently stir them together. Set the plant in place, top the container with a little more mix if needed, and that's it.

When you're planting a large container, there's a bit more to think about. Here's a step-by-step rundown for hassle-free planting.

1. Move the container to the spot where you want it to be—it's much easier to move a large container when it's empty than after you fill it! I also like to set containers up on bricks to help ensure good drainage.

2. Place 1 or 2 sheets of wet newspaper in the bottom of the container to prevent materials from leaking out through the drainage holes.

3. Decide whether you need to fill the entire container with soil. If the container is very deep, chances are the plant roots won't penetrate all the way to the bottom. Save on materials by putting a base layer of lightweight filler in the

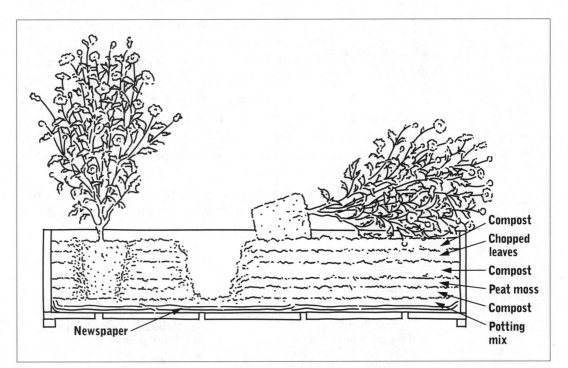

Compost
Chopped leaves
Compost
Peat moss
Compost
Potting mix
Newspaper

bottom of the container. You can use empty cans turned up-side down, or even foam peanuts. Put another layer of newspaper on top of the filler material.

4. Begin layering peat moss, potting mix, and compost in 1 to 2 inch layers in the container. You can also mix in some sand for plants that like very good drainage. I occasionally use thin layers of chopped leaves and grass clippings in my containers, too, and my plants seem to like it.

5. When the container is nearly full, pull back the layers and set the plants in place, as you would in a lasagna garden. Top with potting mix or compost if needed.

6. Water the container thoroughly and mulch the surface with grass clippings, chopped leaves, or shredded bark to help retain moisture and keep the roots cool.

I used to empty my large container gardens each fall and roll them to a new location in the spring—I thought the change was important. Those days are gone, and now I look at large containers as permanent garden sites. Each year I add additional layers, but I don't remove the layers from the previous year.

Avoid the fuss and mess of mixing ingredients for a container planting mix. Instead, spread layers of potting mix, compost, and other organic materials and amendments lasagna-style.

A Strawberry Jar Garden

These distinctively shaped containers aren't just for growing strawberries. You can design an ornamental strawberry jar garden of colorful annuals mixed with sedums or ivy, or an edible garden of cut-and-come-again lettuce, a dwarf tomato, parsley, cilantro, chives, and edible flowers.

Planting a strawberry jar is a bit different from planting other containers. There are openings at the sides that need to be planted before you fill the container completely.

I like to install a watering reservoir in a strawberry jar to channel water throughout the tall container. The reservoir is simply a piece of perforated plastic pipe filled with gravel.

Materials

Newspaper or a large coffee filter	**Compost**
Strawberry jar	**Pea gravel or pebbles**
Piece of 2-inch-diameter perforated plastic pipe, approximately the same height as the strawberry jar	**Small bedding plants, herbs, or foliage plants**
	Potting mix
	Peat moss

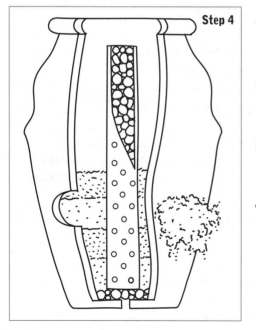

Step 4

1. Line the bottom of the jar with newspaper or a large coffee filter, and then stand the plastic pipe in the empty jar.

2. Add your first lasagna layer to the container. I recommend a layer of rich compost, up to the level of the first side pocket.

3. At this point, the pipe should be steady enough that you can fill it with pebbles or pea gravel.

4. Select the plants you want to position in the lowest side pockets. (Choose the plants that will tolerate wet conditions best, because the lower layers of the container may not dry out as quickly as the top.) Push the rootball of the plant from the outside of the container through the side pocket and into

the jar. Make sure the leaves remain on the outside of the container, with the plant stem resting on the pocket.

5. Add another lasagna layer or two, until you reach the next level of pockets.

6. Set more plants in place in the side pockets as before.

7. Continue layering and planting until the soil level is 2 inches below the lip of the jar.

8. Set your plant choices for the top of the pot in place between the lip of the jar and the top of the pipe. Fill in carefully around the roots with potting mix. Cover any exposed soil around the plants with a single sheet of wet newspaper and top that with finely chipped leaves or another decorative mulch.

9. Gently water from the top, and also slowly fill the watering channel.

Set your strawberry jar in a sunny location. If it mainly receives sun from one side, remember to rotate the pot every few days so that all the plants growing out of the side pockets get enough light. To keep your plants growing strong, fill the watering reservoir with a dilute solution of fish emulsion or other liquid organic fertilizer once every 2 weeks. Use garden shears or scissors to trim away faded leaves and to clip sprigs of fresh herbs as needed for cooking or garnishes.

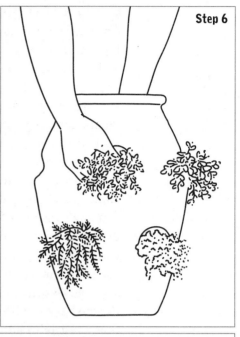

Step 6

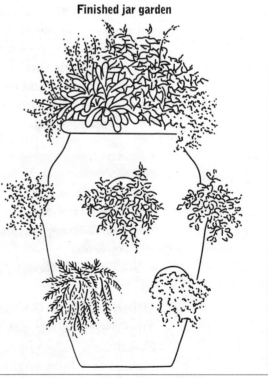

Finished jar garden

Grow a Hanging Garden

Once you get the hang of planting hanging baskets, I guarantee you'll include them in your gardening plans every year. Like pictures on the walls of indoor rooms, hanging baskets are the finishing touch for any outdoor area.

There are two basic types of hanging baskets: plastic and wire. Plastic hanging baskets are convenient to plant, and many feature a special self-watering system. But I love the elegant look of a wire hanging basket.

One drawback to wire hanging baskets is that they are relatively shallow and they dry out quickly. Also, because they are shallow, you can't build lasagna layers in them. I try to counteract the tendency toward drying out by using an inner plastic liner to retain water. I first line each basket with an attractive lining, such as cocoa hull matting. I cover that with a thin sheet of plastic (such as a grocery-store bag) and cut several slits in it for drainage. Then I fill the basket with potting soil mixed with some extra compost. All that's left is to add the plants and water them. I fill in around the plants with mulch to help retain water, but even with all these precautions, I still sometimes must water my wire hanging baskets daily, depending on the weather.

There's no rule that says hanging baskets are only for flowers. I've also grown herbs and even cherry tomatoes in hanging baskets with great success. Here are some of my favorite plants and combinations for hanging baskets:

- Alpine strawberries
- Petunias
- Prostrate rosemary
- Dahlberg daisies
- 'Sweet Million' cherry tomato with a fine-leaved basil such as 'Spicy Globe'
- 'Sun Gold' tomatoes (which have grape-size fruit) and curly parsley

Window Box Gardens

Almost every window at The Potager showcases a window box, and I attach them to deck railings, too. Most commercial window boxes are plastic and lightweight, but you can also buy or build wooden window boxes. If your windowsill isn't deep enough to support a window box, take a trip to your local garden center for sill extenders. Once you install them, you're ready to plant.

Window boxes are the ultimate in narrow gardening—they're usually just 6 to 8 inches wide. You can create a big effect in that small space when you pack it with bright colors. For example, try a window box full of bedding dahlias in hot colors—it's a showstopper. You can plant window boxes in layers, too. Use the outside edge for plants that will cascade over the side, such as lutea, prostrate rosemary, or trailing nasturtiums. That leaves the bulk of the box for other annual flowers and herbs. With the addition of a small trellis, you can grow tomatoes, basil, and parsley. I also like to interplant petunias, pinks, and variegated ivy in window boxes.

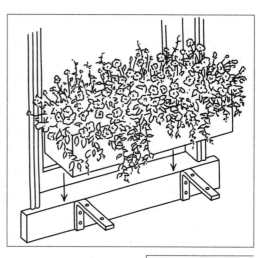

L-shaped sill extenders are easy to install, and they allow you to add a cheery window box to almost any window.

Window boxes will do fine in shady sites, too; in fact, they'll be less prone to drying out. If you have a shady window, try growing impatiens, begonias, and pansies together.

Caring for Potted Gardens

Potted plants and container gardens need the same care as regular gardens do: mulching, watering, deadheading, and harvesting—plus a little extra attention. Your container gardens will need to be watered more often than in-ground gardens. Watering containers can be a very pleasant ritual—it gives you time to admire each container and see how it's changing. You'll notice what's in bloom and what's ready to harvest. If you have a large number of containers, you can set up a drip irrigation system among the pots. A watering reservoir can also help in large containers (see page 149 for an illustration of a homemade reservoir).

Plants in containers may need supplemental fertilizing, too, depending on what you filled your containers with. I use a liquid seaweed fertilizer that is diluted in water, and I feed nutrient-demanding crops such as tomatoes every 2 weeks. (Foliage plants and perennials don't need nearly as much fertilizer.) Keep track of feedings so you will not overfeed. Your goal isn't to have the biggest tomato—it's to have a plant that will give you the *most* tomatoes.

Container plants may suffer from insect and disease problems, just as plants in garden beds do. In general, I find that plants growing in healthy, nutrient-rich lasagna beds and containers have few problems. If you have plants that are suffering, check Chapter 8 for advice on how to deal with the problems.

At the end of the growing season, take inventory of your containers and decide what to do with them over winter. Here are some options:

- Dump the contents of small containers of annuals and harvested vegetables on the compost pile, and scrub and store the pots.
- Group potted perennial flowers and herbs in a sheltered spot and surround them with bags of leaves to provide some insulation for the roots. Or, wrap individual containers with bubble wrap or some other insulating material, and then with burlap.
- If you have a greenhouse, move containers indoors for the winter.
- Bring containers into your house, if you have room. Some plants will adjust better to indoor conditions than others. Don't be too disappointed if some of the plants languish indoors. As you gain experience, you'll discover which plants you can overwinter indoors successfully.
- Dig nonhardy plants out of large planters that are permanently in place. Compost the plant wastes, and cover the surface of the planter with a thick layer of mulch for the winter.

Small Gardens Galore

As you gain experience with vertical gardening and gardening in containers, you may be surprised how many and varied your small garden spaces become. At The Potager, I've turned every inch of what used to be lawn into gardens, and I have more than 75 containers planted. There's something interesting in those containers in every season, too.

Containers of annual flowers and vegetables will look great in spring and summer, but what to do with the containers for the rest of the year? I use my containers for seasonal decorations after the plants pass their prime. I clean out the spent plants and then arrange corn-

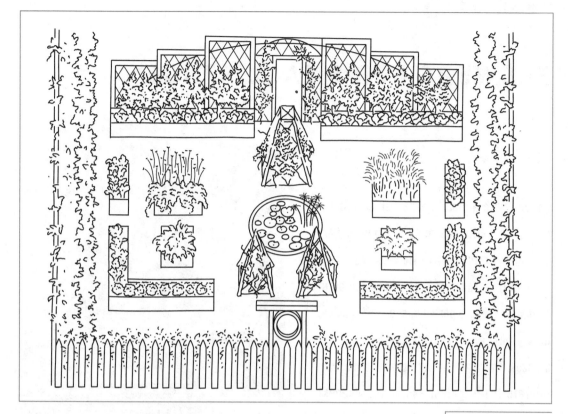

husks, colored corn ears, and pumpkins for late fall. Over the winter, I use fresh-cut greens, twigs, and berries. There's plenty to keep you interested and happy dabbling in your small-space gardens year-round. Throughout this book, I'll share with you many of the special tricks and secrets I've learned for growing all types of plants in small spaces and containers: flowers, vegetables, herbs, and fruits. I'll tell you about my small-space rock and trough gardens, and last but not least, I'll tell you some great stories about special romantic touches that make a small garden extra special.

This view of some of my gardens at The Potager proves my point that you can bring all your garden dreams to reality in small-space beds.

CHAPTER 3

FLOWERS FOR SMALL SPACES

Anyone with a small garden or a balcony, porch, or patio can have wonderful gardening adventures with flowers. You have an exciting range of choices—colorful annuals, exquisite perennials, cheerful bulbs, lush vines, and even elegant ornamental grasses. There are flowering plants that can tolerate the brightest sun or the deepest shade, and they look just as beautiful in a small bed or container as they do in a grand flower border.

The Joy of Flowers

As the years go by, I appreciate flowers more and more. I no longer have the tireless energy of my youth, and I find it harder to rebound from overwork, stress, or worries about a problem one of my children is having. Flowers, with their beauty and grace, comfort and inspire me when I'm feeling worn down. I give flowers the place of honor in my small gardens, and they reward me many times over. Flowers bring as much joy as a perfect sunset, are as satisfying as Mom's Sunday dinner, and give me a reason to look forward to another growing season.

Even if you're a city dweller without a backyard, you can grow flowers on your terrace or balcony, or perhaps up on your rooftop. If nothing else, you can have window boxes on your windowsills! The urge to garden is so strong that the folks with the least space often end up with the most creative and colorful flower gardens.

Deciding What to Grow

Now in the third quarter of my life, I have only touched the tip of my floral education. When I was a child, I could count on one hand the flowers I knew by name. Now I can't begin to count the names of all the species and varieties I know, but what I've learned is still only a drop in the bucket of knowledge. Some flowers I know by their Latin botanical names, others only by their common names. The more I learn, the more I want to know, and I think you'll find the same is true for you.

On the broad scale, your flower garden will be a combination of flowering annuals, bulbs, perennials, and vines. (You may even opt to try a few ornamental grasses—they don't have showy flowers, but their beautiful foliage and seedheads make them great garden accent plants.) So many flowers are beautiful and easy to grow. With some six-packs of annuals and a sampling of potted perennials from your local garden center, you can truly have an instant garden planted lasagna-style in just an hour or two.

Just as there may not be enough space in your small garden to grow *every* flower you'd like to try, there's not enough room in this book for me to describe all the wonderful flowering plants that I enjoy growing. But

PLANT BIG IN SMALL SPACES

Gardeners put too many limits on themselves when they think about planting flowers in pots, and often they won't venture beyond petunias or zonal geraniums. But here's my advice: **Don't plant small plants exclusively, or you'll end up with a too-cute doll's garden.**

Instead, think big and put some punch in your design. After all, people grow shrubs and trees in containers, so why not try some big flowers, such as sunflowers and delphiniums, in containers? Try something unexpected, as well. For instance, Japanese blood grass or another moderately sized ornamental grass can be a knockout focal point for a small garden.

throughout this chapter you'll find charts and special features that highlight some of my favorite annuals, perennials, bulbs, vines, and ornamental grasses that perform beautifully in small gardens and container gardens.

Annuals

Annuals are the precocious members of the flower family. Annuals such as marigolds and petunias go from seed to seed in one growing season: You plant a seed, and it grows into a plant that flowers within a few months. The flowers fade, leaving behind seedheads. This signals to the plant that its job is done and it can die. If you pinch off the faded flowers, seeds won't form, and the plant will continue blooming until cold weather kills it.

Annuals are commonly called bedding plants because they fill garden beds with carpets of color. They're easy to grow and inexpensive—for the price of a packet of seed, you can have a garden of bloom for an entire season. Rely on annuals for garden color while new, slower-growing perennials take hold and fill in. Plant annuals among bulbs—the annuals will mask the bulb foliage as it ripens and dies back. Annuals are also great long-blooming edging plants for the front of a garden.

A BIT ABOUT BIENNIALS

A few familiar garden flowers are biennials, or plants that go from seed to seed in two growing seasons. You plant a seed in spring, and it germinates and grows as a leafy plant. Over winter, the plant lies dormant in the garden. The following spring, the plant resprouts and blooms. After the flowers fade and the seed sets, the plants die. Foxgloves and sweet William are biennials. Sow biennial seeds for 2 consecutive years to ensure that you'll have some plants in bloom every year.

Perennials

Long-lived perennials are worth their weight in gold. They're not as flashy as annuals, and most of them only bloom for part of the growing season, but perennials are the hardest working and most reliable sources of flower pleasure in the garden. A perennial is a plant that lives for more than 2 years, but many perennials live much longer than that. Botanically speaking, shrubs and trees are perennials, as are most ornamental grasses. But for our purposes, we'll talk mainly about herbaceous flowering and foliage perennials such as hostas, peonies, and daylilies. Most of these plants die back to the ground each winter and resprout the following year.

Perennials vary in hardiness (ability to withstand winter cold). We rate the hardiness of perennials according to hardiness zones developed by the USDA.

Forget-me-nots (*Myosotis scorpioides*) and tulips is one of my favorite combinations for spring.

Each zone number corresponds to areas that have a particular average minimum winter temperature. To see what zone you live in, check the USDA Plant Hardiness Zone Map on page 288.

The world of perennials is one where the range of choices can be overwhelming, even if you limit yourself to what's available at your local garden center. Unlike annuals, most of which grow well in full sun and well-drained soil, perennials vary widely in their growing-site preferences. There are perennials for sun, for shade, and for wet or dry soil. And then there's the bloom-time factor to consider and co-ordinate. With proper planning, if you match the right plant to the right place and grow some in containers, your perennials will come in and out of bloom just like clockwork.

I think the best way to learn how to grow perennials is just to do it! I assure you that once you make some choices and fit them to the right locations, you'll find that perennials are easy to grow and very rewarding, as they come back year after year.

Bulbs

Flowering bulbs are perennials that sprout from an underground root or stem. These wonderful self-contained flower packages can bring the earliest bloom to your garden and are remarkably self-sufficient. The emergence of snowdrop flowers in February or March is what keeps my spirits up during the long, dark days of winter. Once snowdrops poke their heads up, I know spring can't be far behind.

It's remarkably easy to plant bulbs when you garden lasagna-style, so be sure to include some in your gardening plans. Bulbs vary in hardiness, and in some regions, gardeners treat tender bulbs like they would annuals, planting new ones each year. Or they dig up the tender bulbs in fall, store them in a protected spot over winter, and replant them the following spring. Gladiolus are an example of tender bulbs; north of Zone 7, they need to be "lifted" or replaced each year.

Vines

Flowering vines can be tender annuals or hardy perennials. What they have in common is how they grow: Vines produce very long stems, some as long as 20 feet in one year! Morning glory is a beloved annual vine that needs to be replanted each year; clematis is one of the most popular perennial vines.

I pay special attention to flowering vines, because these vines and climbers can expand a small garden space to new heights. The roots of these wonder plants may be grounded, but given support, they can make your garden take flight. I like working with vines in small-space gardens because I enjoy brainstorming interesting and unique trellises, arches, arbors, fences, and other plant supports that vines require. Given the right support, any vines will adapt to container growing, too.

Creating Great Flower Combinations

Whole books are written about garden design, but I don't fuss much about design rules. In my opinion, one word describes how your garden should look to you: pleasing. If your garden pleases you, then

TAGS DON'T TELL THE WHOLE STORY

I like to read the information on the plastic tags stuck in pots at the garden center. These tags confirm that I'm really getting the plant I want to buy, and they remind me about the conditions where the plant will grow best, including the hardiness zone, in wet or dry soil, and in sun or shade.

I advise you to read plant tags, too, but don't rely on them as your sole source of information about a plant. Buying plants can be a considerable investment, and in a small garden, you want to be sure you've chosen plants that will fit the space and conditions to a tee. Before you buy a plant,

especially a perennial or other long-lived plant, do a little research in plant encyclopedias, magazines, or on-line.

This extra research is necessary because there's no room on a plant tag to tell you about a plant's special eccentricities. Is the plant generally short-lived? Does it spread rapidly, consuming all other plants in its path? And if the tag told you these things, would you still buy the plant? Probably not! It is up to you to learn as much as you can about individual plants. You'll also discover the almost infinite variety of plants that will thrive in your zone and conditions. It pays to be an informed buyer.

you must be doing something right! With small-space gardens, the shape or form of the garden is usually dictated by the space available. I don't see that as a limitation—it's one less decision to trouble me. There are small ways to adapt a site if desired. You can soften a square-edged bed by simply cutting curves into the surrounding grass. Or you can add some attractive stones or ornamental accents to make a small garden more interesting.

In a small-space garden, your most important decision is likely to be which plants to group together as partners. Again, don't get hung up trying to follow too many rules when creating plant combinations. Think of these partnerships as experiments that you can learn from. Most plants, even perennials, are easy to transplant, especially in the loose soil of a lasagna bed.

One rule you should always follow is to match plants to site. If your garden bed is in the sun, choose sun-loving plants. If your only in-ground beds are stuck in the shade, plant woodland wildflowers there, and grow your sun-loving annuals in containers on a sunny deck or beside your driveway.

With lasagna-style beds, soil usually isn't a limitation. The raised beds are naturally well drained, and they're certainly fertile. If plants need to be constantly moist, keep them well mulched and water them frequently. You can even grow plants that like wet conditions in the same bed with plants that prefer things on the dry side. Snake a soaker hose through the bed so that it's tucked close to the moisture-loving plants and gives a wide berth to those that need less moisture, as shown in the illustration on page 83.

Aim for All-the-Time Bloom

Even in my small gardens, I aim to keep something in bloom all the time. That means choosing plants for a sequence of bloom and including some long-bloomers in each bed or grouping of containers to sustain interest during lulls in seasonal blooming.

For example, tulips and daffodils are dependable sources of bloom in my spring gardens, but I've learned not to plant them alone. I pair early-blooming tulips of any color—red, pink, or white—with an underplanting of blue grape hyacinths. Dainty fern-leaf pink bleeding heart is a great partner for late-blooming pink tulips. The bleeding heart foliage provides a lovely green backdrop for the bold tulip blossoms.

Later in the growing season, combinations of perennials, or perennials mixed with annuals, are the ticket for stunning effects. Colorful or variegated foliage can be as exciting as flowers! For example, try miniature hostas with 'Burgundy Glow' ajuga and alpine lady's mantle in a partly shaded bed. Showy herbs work well in flower gardens. Try 'Snow Bank' sweet alyssum with 'Tricolor' sage.

Garden mums tend to dominate fall gardens, but there are other great fall combinations, too. For a combination of the familiar with the unusual, try 'Autumn Joy' sedum with ornamental pink ribbon grass (*Phalaris arundinacea* 'Feesey') and dwarf purple asters.

Play a Color Theme

If you have several small gardens, whether they're in-ground beds, groups of pots, or window boxes, it can be fun and satisfying to develop a color theme to tie them together. Choose your favorite color and go for it! This can increase the overall impact of the garden spaces, just as using a color theme can unify the spaces inside your house. Of course, a single-color garden is almost always a two-color garden, because you're working with a base palette of green foliage.

I've created one all-pink garden (shown on the opposite page) and used many pink plants in other beds, too. You can find pink flowers for every season, starting with tulips and daffodils in spring. For May and June bloom, look to peonies underplanted with pink-flowered cranesbills or 'Burgundy Glow' ajuga. I've recently added 'Pink Pewter' lamium to my pink garden, and everyone who's seen its beautiful pink flowers and bright silvery leaves has wanted it. (Lamium can be a fairly aggressive spreader, so if you decide to plant it, make sure you choose a site with equally strong companions, or use it as a groundcover in a place where it won't have close neighbors.)

The list of choices for pink summer bloomers is a long one, including bee balm, campanulas, clematis, coreopsis, hollyhocks, irises, lupines, phlox, pincushion flower, pinks, poppies, and sedums. In fall, mums and fall asters top the list of pink flowers.

What Goes Where?

As you choose plant partners and decide how to arrange them in a bed, keep two basic ideas in mind: repetition and contrast. These are simple concepts to understand, and thinking about them as you make combinations will set you on the road to success.

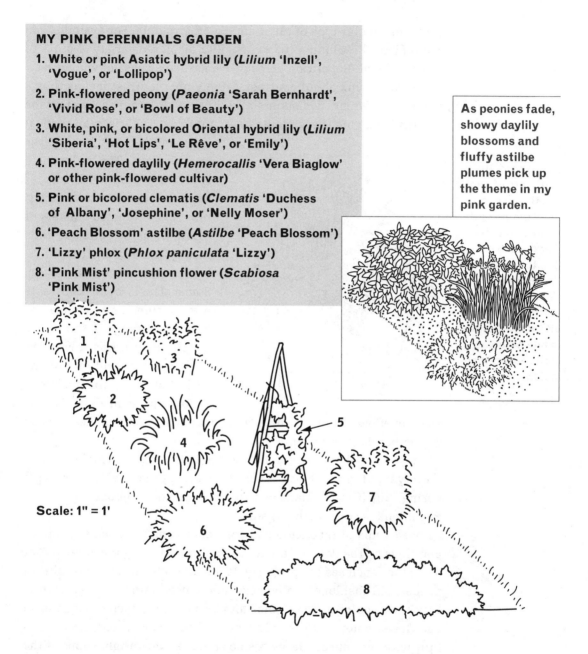

MY PINK PERENNIALS GARDEN

1. White or pink Asiatic hybrid lily (*Lilium* 'Inzell', 'Vogue', or 'Lollipop')

2. Pink-flowered peony (*Paeonia* 'Sarah Bernhardt', 'Vivid Rose', or 'Bowl of Beauty')

3. White, pink, or bicolored Oriental hybrid lily (*Lilium* 'Siberia', 'Hot Lips', 'Le Rêve', or 'Emily')

4. Pink-flowered daylily (*Hemerocallis* 'Vera Biaglow' or other pink-flowered cultivar)

5. Pink or bicolored clematis (*Clematis* 'Duchess of Albany', 'Josephine', or 'Nelly Moser')

6. 'Peach Blossom' astilbe (*Astilbe* 'Peach Blossom')

7. 'Lizzy' phlox (*Phlox paniculata* 'Lizzy')

8. 'Pink Mist' pincushion flower (*Scabiosa* 'Pink Mist')

As peonies fade, showy daylily blossoms and fluffy astilbe plumes pick up the theme in my pink garden.

Scale: 1" = 1'

Let's start with the idea of repetition. If you choose three different perennials with the same general shape, perhaps a rounded mound, and use them together in a bed, that's repetition. The color-theme garden shown above is a perfect example of repetition; it includes several different plants of the same basic color: pink. You can also repeat a particular type of plant among other plants. For example, you could plant three clumps of a particular bicolored variety of pinks in one small bed. Repetition helps give a garden a sense of wholeness.

Now let's think about contrast. Simply put, contrast means things that look different. Two perennials with very different shapes provide contrast. Imagine irises planted next to phlox. The iris is all vertical lines and has big, bold leaves and flowers. The phlox is a rounded clump with lots of small leaves that blend nicely, plus fluffy rounded clusters of small flowers. Contrast adds some pizzazz to a garden.

I love containers with lots of contrast, so I combine plants with contrasting foliage, such as hostas and Siberian iris. Sweet alyssum softens the edge of this container, while petunias add season-long color.

Colors can contrast, too. Some classic color contrasts are purple and yellow or blue and orange. I think that purple and yellow always work well together, and one of the easiest plantings for summer is yellow and gold daisylike orange coneflowers with the upright bright purple flower spikes of spike gayfeather (*Liatris spicata*).

In a small bed, you want a little bit of both repetition and contrast. If every plant in a bed looked similar to every other plant, it could get boring. But if every plant contrasted with its neighbors, your bed might look hectic and disorganized.

I used a mix of repetition and contrast in one of the most admired plantings at The Potager, a 2-foot-wide garden along the green picket fence that encloses the property. It includes cleome, cosmos, Shasta daisies, old-fashioned hollyhocks, and a porcelain vine (*Ampelopsis brevipedunculata*). The cleome and cosmos echo each other in form and flower color, but the bold leaves of the cleome contrast beautifully with the delicate, ferny cosmos foliage. The upright stems of the hollyhocks provide a strong vertical accent, and the porcelain vine creates a lush backdrop and gives fall interest with its blue berries. (I must caution you, though, that porcelain vine is considered invasive in many areas, so please check with your local extension service before planting to see whether it's a problem in your area.)

CEMETERY GARDENS

OUR BELOVED SISTER

A chance meeting with two elderly sisters at The Potager one spring led me to discover a unique opportunity for creating a small-scale lasagna garden. For many years, the sisters had been traveling from Florida to New York on Memorial Day weekend to decorate their deceased sister's gravesite. Because of their age, this would be the last Memorial Day that the two women could manage the trip. Touched by their devotion, I offered to continue the tradition on their behalf. They bought some potted annuals that day and took my business card. When the holiday season came, they called and my daughter Mickey made the trip to the gravesite.

It's 4 years and many trips to the cemetery later. It was on one of those trips that I began to think about permanent plantings at grave-sites. I had seen some beautiful graveside plantings of evergreens and ivy while on a garden tour in Boston. It seemed to me that even in the small space around a headstone, I could build one of my lasagna gardens.

For permanent plantings, use a dwarf shrub, a few small bulbs, and a pint-size perennial. After all chance of frost is past, add a few annuals and the gravesite will look special year-round. The very nature of lasagna gardening is conducive to gardens you don't visit frequently. Remember to bring a gallon jug of water with you when you visit the cemetery and a small bag of shredded leaves each spring and fall to renew the mulch. We do this now for many of our deceased relatives, and I draw great comfort from seeing how the plantings cradle and soften the headstones.

Contrast is effective in container plantings, too. One of my favorite window box combinations is pinks with petunias and ivy. I like the way the spiky points of the ivy leaves set off the round petunia flowers and the feathery foliage of the pinks. Containers are great places to try out new combinations because it's so easy to deal with experiments that don't turn out right. If you decide you don't like the effect or combination of colors, you can set the container in a less-noticeable spot. Or, you can pull the plants out and start all over again!

Planting and Caring for Flowers

You've chosen your plants and worked out combinations, so it's time to get down to the planting. No matter what kind of flowers you want to grow, you start out the same, by covering your site with wet newspapers and layering organic materials on top. What you do from there varies a little depending on what kind of flowers you're planting.

Growing Annuals

Planting annuals in large gardens year after year can add up to a lot of work, but on a small scale, planting annuals is a cinch. Some annuals, such as marigolds and zinnias, grow quickly and easily from seed right in the garden. Others, including petunias and pansies, need some coaxing. I've started my share of seeds indoors, and I still do, when I want to grow a special variety. But for the most part, I don't bother starting annuals indoors because it's so much easier to buy bedding plants. (Check "Pat's Favorite Annuals for Small Spaces" on page 74 to see whether an annual is easy to start from seed outdoors.)

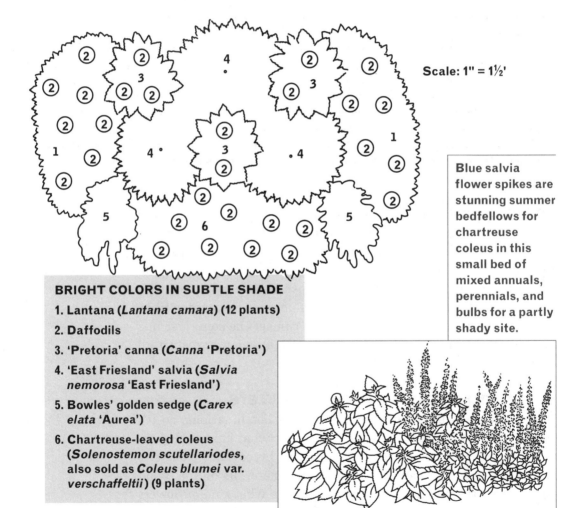

Scale: 1" = 1½'

Blue salvia flower spikes are stunning summer bedfellows for chartreuse coleus in this small bed of mixed annuals, perennials, and bulbs for a partly shady site.

BRIGHT COLORS IN SUBTLE SHADE

1. Lantana (*Lantana camara*) (12 plants)

2. Daffodils

3. 'Pretoria' canna (*Canna* 'Pretoria')

4. 'East Friesland' salvia (*Salvia nemorosa* 'East Friesland')

5. Bowles' golden sedge (*Carex elata* 'Aurea')

6. Chartreuse-leaved coleus (*Solenostemon scutellariodes*, also sold as *Coleus blumei* var. *verschaffeltii*) (9 plants)

Planting

Planting annual seeds in a lasagna bed is so simple. If you're going to plant seeds in a brand-new bed, build the bed at least 6 inches tall (and make sure that bottom layer is newspaper!). In the area you want to seed, lay your palm flat on the bed surface and press gently to form a slight depression. Sprinkle seed in that area and top it with a thin sprinkle of fine compost. Then press the planted area again to ensure that the seeds make contact with the soil. Water seeded areas daily with a fine spray of water to keep them moist. Mark the area with a label detailing what was planted and when.

Setting out bedding plants is even easier than planting annual seeds. Just pop the annuals out of the plastic six-pack, pull back the layers of the lasagna bed, set the plants in place, and snug them in by pressing the soil around them lightly with your hands.

Some annuals, including snapdragons and pansies, can withstand cold weather, but most annuals are quite tender and shouldn't be planted outside until all danger of frosty nights is past.

Care During the Season

Annuals need little care during the growing season beyond watering when the weather is dry. Flowering annuals are not heavy feeders. Once you've planted your garden, all you need to do is add a thin top layer of compost to feed the soil. Annuals actually do better without extra nitrogen. Too much nitrogen will produce all foliage and no flowers.

Container-grown annuals do need feeding periodically to encourage maximum bloom. I start them out right by sprinkling small amounts of alfalfa meal, bloodmeal, or organic cottonseed meal among the layers when I fill my containers. I also feed container annuals every 2 weeks with a dilute solution of fish emulsion.

You can encourage your annuals to keep producing new blooms by deadheading (cutting off dead flowers) or by pinching back plant stems that have spent flowers to stimulate new flowering sideshoots. Some annuals tend to drop their blossoms and continue to form new ones without deadheading. This "self-cleaning" feature is very desirable if

Deadhead your annuals to stimulate new flowers to form. If the plants have leafy stems, pinch off only the fading flowers. If the stems are bare below the flower, cut the stem back to a pair of leaves.

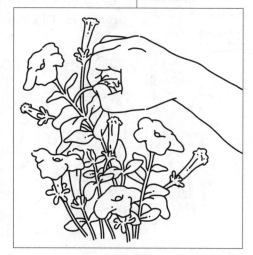

Cut the Quantity, Not the Size

Even though you're planting a small garden, don't shy away from tall or bushy annuals—just buy fewer of them. You'll do fine with a single four-pack or six-pack of each type of annual you plan to grow.

you're lazy about garden maintenance, so watch for it in plant descriptions.

At the end of the season, pull the spent annuals out of beds and containers and toss them on your compost pile. Be sure to cover the bare areas of soil with a protective mulch for winter.

Mixing Old and New Annuals

With annuals, there's always something new to try and something old to rediscover. One of the great joys of growing annuals is that each year presents a fresh slate. You can choose to grow annuals you know and love, or you can try something completely different.

I plant a few new annuals every year just for fun. 'Velour Blue Bronze' violets (*below left*), osteospermum (*below center*), and the Bravo Hybrids of Swan River daisies (*below right*) are three of my best new discoveries.

A Few of the New

I've had fun with some of the new annuals that have appeared in catalogs and garden centers over the past several years. (This is another benefit of continuing to learn about plants, new and old.) One of the new annuals I've learned to love for its masses of bright purple, rose, and white flowers is osteospermum. It's quite hardy, and it's naturally compact and drought tolerant. It brings a passionate response from visitors to The Potager, whether it's planted in a bed or a container in full sun. If you haven't tried osteospermum yet, I recommend 'Passion Mixed' as a good one to start with.

Growing violets isn't new, but the color of *Viola* 'Velour Blue Bronze' is. This hardy annual grows in sun to partial shade. It produces an amazing pattern of magical blue-mauve on the upper petals and a striking bronze on the lower petals. Bushy plants are compact and free flowering.

If you're looking to stop traffic, plant a sunny bed or patio planter with the Bravo Hybrids of Swan River daisies (*Brachycome iberidifolia*). They produce a stunning mixture of white, blue, and violet flowers with black centers.

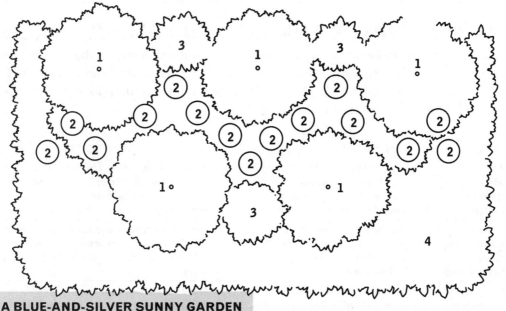

A BLUE-AND-SILVER SUNNY GARDEN

1. 'Johnson's Blue' geranium
   (*Geranium* 'Johnson's Blue')

2. Dwarf yellow-flowered
   Asiatic lily (*Lilium* Asiatic
   hybrid cultivar)

3. Flat sea holly (*Eryngium planum*)

4. 'Strata' mealycup sage
   (*Salvia farinacea* 'Strata')
   (24 plants)

Scale: 1" = 14"

Lilies and sea holly flowers mix in this sunny garden. As the lily foliage dies back, mealycup sage flowers and mounds of geranium foliage will fill the gaps.

A Trio of Old-Time Favorites

When I made the switch from large-scale to small-scale gardening, I rediscovered the pleasures of three old-time annuals: sweet peas, portulaca, and lantana. This trio is important in small gardens because sweet peas grow vertically, portulaca fills small nooks and crannies, and cantara is spectacular in hanging baskets. Sweet pea (*Lathyrus odoratus*) is one of the best annuals for "growing up." In full sun, it produces vines that climb from 5 to 10 feet, and the flowers are wonderfully fragrant. Try 'Fragrantissima', which blooms in all the colors in the spectrum.

(continued on page 76)

73

PAT'S FAVORITE ANNUALS FOR SMALL SPACES

Most annuals will do well in small spaces and containers. Many of the annuals I describe here are actually tender perennials, but they behave like annuals in most of North America. You could also add to this list two edible annual flowers: calendula (see page 166) and nasturtium (see page 180).

PLANT NAME	DESCRIPTION	SMALL-SPACE GROWING TIPS
Wax begonias (*Begonia Semperflorens-Cultorum hybrids*)	White, pink, or red flowers and bright green or bronze, rounded foliage. Masses of blooms form on mounded plants. 8 to 12 inches tall.	Grow and bloom best in shade (bronze-leaved types will tolerate sun) and moist soil. Set plants on 4-inch centers or plant six plants in a 10-inch pot.
Cleome, spider flower (*Cleome hassleriana*)	White, pink, or purple ball-shaped blooms attract butterflies. Stems and leaf undersides are thorny. To 5 feet tall.	Set out transplants in spring as soon as frost is past, or sow seed in fall. Best in full sun. Deadhead to prevent self-sowing.
Cosmos (*Cosmos bipinnatus*)	Upright branching stems support large, daisylike flowers in pink, white, and purple. 3 to 4 feet tall.	Needs full sun. Plant seeds or plants in late spring or broadcast seed in fall for next-summer bloom. Dwarf 'Diablo' is only 12 to 16 inches tall. Grow tall varieties, too. They'll do fine even in a small bed.
Pinks (*Dianthus* species and hybrids)	A large group of biennials and short-lived perennials generally grown as annuals, including sweet William (*D. barbatus*) and China pinks (*D. chinensis*). Most are low-growing, with narrow leaves and five-petaled flowers in pink, red, white, and bicolored. Most species are 6 to 12 inches tall.	Buy started plants, and plant in full sun and well-drained soil. Pinks tolerate partial shade in hot southern regions. Cut back after flowering to prolong blooming. I love 'Bath's Pink', with soft pink spring flowers, and 'Tiny Rubies', which has double pink, fragrant flowers. I grow 'Spotty' in window boxes. It has lovely blue-gray foliage and red-and-white flowers.
Impatiens (*Impatiens walleriana*)	These are bushy, spreading plants with oval leaves, succulent stems, and flat flowers in a range of colors to match any planting scheme. To 3 feet tall in ideal conditions.	Grow best in partial shade. Buy started plants. In a container planting, one plant will be plenty. Impatiens will do well in window boxes and hanging baskets as long as you water them regularly.
Edging lobelia (*Lobelia erinus*)	Compact mounded or trailing plants with slender stems and narrow leaves. Delicate, five-petaled flowers in blue, rose-pink, red, and white. Only 6 inches tall.	Can take full sun, but partial shade makes the flowers appear to glow. Cool nights encourage abundant bloom. Buy started plants and use them for edging small beds and large containers.
Sweet alyssum (*Lobularia maritima*)	Low mounding or spreading habit. Masses of tiny flowers in white, pink, or purple completely hide foliage. To 6 inches tall.	Does best in full sun. Buy plants or sow seeds in midspring. Self-sows in following years. The *best* plant for edging window boxes and other containers. They're also great to naturally soften the edges of a path.

PLANT NAME	DESCRIPTION	SMALL-SPACE GROWING TIPS
Zonal geranium (*Pelargonium* × *hortorum*)	Erect plants have rounded leaves with ruffled edges. Flowers are borne on slender stems above foliage. Flowers may be white; shades of red, pink, or salmon; or bicolored. 12 to 24 inches tall.	It's almost un-American not to grow a few containers of zonal geraniums! They're easy to grow in full sun, and it's possible to overwinter them indoors. Root cuttings in spring for planting outside.
Petunia (*Petunia* × *hybrida*)	Trumpet-shaped flowers in many colors on mounded plants or long, trailing stems. Multiflora types sport small, numerous flowers, and grandifloras have large, ruffled flowers. To 12 inches tall.	Plant in full sun in hanging baskets, containers, and garden beds. Buy started plants. I like to use petunias as a flowering groundcover under upright specimen plants such as ornamental grasses.
Coleus (*Solenostemon scutellariodes*, also sold as *Coleus* × *hybridus*)	Patterned leaves in many unexpected and vibrant color combinations. 6 to 24 inches tall.	Likes moist conditions and partly shady sites—too much sun can damage leaves. In a large planting tub, combine several varieties in many shades of green, plus accents of lime green, hot pink, mahogany, and bronze to brighten a shady nook.
Marigolds (*Tagetes* species and hybrids)	French marigolds (*T. patula*) form low mounds (to 12 inches tall) with small orange, red, or yellow flowers. Signet marigolds (*T. tenuifolia*) also form mounds (to 12 inches tall) of fine, ferny foliage. Colors include yellow, such as 'Lemon Gem', orange, and rusty red 'Paprika'.	Marigolds need full sun. They're easy to start from seed, and started plants are widely available, too. I like to buy several different varieties for a mixed all-marigold bed. For the same effect in containers, plant several pots, each with a different variety, and group them together.
Garden verbena (*Verbena* × *hybrida*)	Tender perennial with upright or spreading habit. Flowers are primrose look-alikes in bright colors: red, purple with white centers, pink, blue, and white. 8 to 12 inches tall.	Plant in full sun and well-drained soil. Buy started plants. Garden verbena is a cheery edging plant for a small bed, and it's an excellent choice for window boxes. Other species of verbena are hardier than the tender hybrids, and I use them, too.
Pansy (*Viola* × *wittrockiana*)	Low, mounded plants have narrow leaves with scalloped edges and flat, five-petaled flowers. They're spring bloomers, but may rebloom in fall. They're available in red, white, blue, yellow, and orange. To 8 inches tall.	Plant in full sun or partial shade and keep moist. They usually suffer when conditions turn hot in summer. Charming pansies supply early color in containers and window boxes. Flowers are edible.
Zinnias (*Zinnia* spp.)	Common zinnias (*Z. elegans*) sport single or double flowers in a variety of shapes, sizes, and colors. From 12 to 36 inches tall. Narrow-leaved zinnia (*Z. angustifolia*) forms low mounds covered with daisylike orange, yellow, or white flowers; grows to 12 inches tall.	Give zinnias full sun. Sow seeds in place or buy started plants. Choose low-growing varieties of common zinnias, such as 'Peter Pan' or 'Pom Pom', to edge a bed or plant in containers. Narrow-leaved zinnias are perfect for hanging baskets and window boxes.

Remembering portulaca growing in my grandmother's garden, I tried it in my small gardens and found that it was a natural. The spreading stems fill in nooks and crannies perfectly, and it's great for containers, too. 'Kariba Mixed' resembles the type my grandmother grew but has double flowers that look like minature roses.

Lantana is actually a tender perennial, but unless you live in Zone 9 or farther south, it won't overwinter. No matter, there's nothing more sensational than a hanging basket or window box of blooming lantana. Give it full sun. 'Camera Mixed' will delight you in combinations of red and yellow, rose and yellow, and lilac and white. Lantana is perfect for my current living situation in a second-floor apartment with an outdoor deck. I attached permanent hooks to the deck railing from which I hang baskets of lantana. The stems spill down 3 to 4 feet above the heads of people climbing the stairs to the deck.

Growing Bulbs

Bulbs bring us colorful flowers when we need them most: in early spring, when the weather still seems more wintry than warm. I'll tell you, though, bulbs aren't just for spring. I plant bulbs for summer and fall color, too. Bulbs are wonderfully efficient for small gardens because you can plant them in layers—bulbs several inches deep, with annuals and perennials set above them at the surface.

Bulbs are easy to grow, too. They come packaged with their own food, need little fussing over, and generally have few pest problems.

Planting Bulbs

Advance planning is a must if you want to grow bulbs. For example, to enjoy a spring show of crocuses, daffodils, hyacinths, and tulips, you need to order and plant your bulbs in fall. The same principle holds true for other bulbs, too. For fall and summer bloom from bulbs such as agapanthus, dahlias, and gladiolus, you'll need to plant in spring as soon as the ground is warm and danger of frost is past.

You can buy bulbs at garden centers, but for practically unlimited choices of colors, shapes, and sizes of flowers, I recommend that you discover the world of mail-order bulb buying. Mail-order nurseries that specialize in bulbs offer hundreds of choices. For addresses and Web sites of some suppliers, turn to "Resources for Lasagna Gardeners" on page 271.

Because bulbs are planted below soil level—as much as 8 inches deep—traditional planting techniques can involve a lot of labor. But when you garden lasagna-style, planting bulbs couldn't be simpler. Pull the layers aside to the proper depth, and set the bulbs in place. You can go as deep as needed, even setting the bulbs directly on top of the newspaper layer at the bottom of the bed. There's no need for special bulb-planting tools and no tough digging. I use my favorite tool, a Ho Mi or Korean hand plow, to open planting holes for bulbs in the loose, friable soil of my gardens.

Some bulbs will even plant themselves! I've scattered hundreds of daffodils bulbs in the woods behind my house. They nestle themselves into Mother Nature's natural lasagna beds and bloom the following spring.

To figure roughly how deep to set a bulb, measure the height of the bulb. Multiply that measurement by 2 or 3 to determine how deep you need to set the bulb. For example, crocus bulbs are about 1 inch high, so you should plant them with the base of the bulb 2 to 3 inches below the bed surface.

As your bed settles, you may see the tops of the bulbs peeking out. The fix for this is to keep on layering—adding leaves, grass clippings,

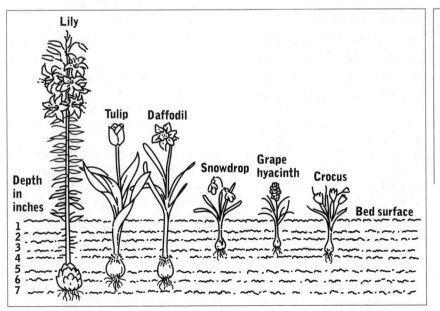

Plant bulbs at a depth that's proportional to the height of the bulbs. You'll plant tulip bulbs much deeper than you would dainty crocus bulbs.

compost, or whatever else you have on hand as the seasons come and go. This protects the bulbs and renews soil fertility at the same time.

Planting depths are the same for bulbs in containers. You can set the bulbs in place at the appropriate depth as you add layers to the container. Or, fill your containers, and then use a hand tool to pull open a hole of the right depth for the bulb. Either way, it takes very little effort.

I like to plant a half-barrel with a mixture of bulbs that bloom at different seasons. To start, I put in a base layer of newspaper and fill the barrel half-full with compost, potting mix, and shredded leaves. I set in the tulip bulbs and layer on 4 more inches of material. Next I settle daffodil and large hyacinth bulbs in place, and I add 3 inches worth of layering. The final step is to add the tiny bulbs like crocuses, grape hyacinths, and squill, topped by an inch or two of compost.

Care During the Season

As soon as I see bulb foliage pushing up through the soil, I give those bulbs a meal to help stimulate the best growth and bloom. I just walk through the garden with a container of granular organic fertilizer and sprinkle a scoopful around each cluster of bulb foliage. It's also a good idea to water bulbs while they're actively growing. Water container bulbs well, too, but check that the containers are draining properly—bulbs don't like to sit in waterlogged soil.

Spring-blooming bulbs are self-supporting, but some summer- and fall-blooming bulbs have tall stems that need support. You can stake tall bulbs such as lilies individually with bamboo stakes or create a grid of stakes and string for gladioli and dahlias.

SHRUBBY SHELTER FOR FORCING BULBS

Early containers of spring-blooming bulbs are a delight, but providing the right conditions for forcing the bulbs can be a pain. Chances are there's a great natural storage area for a few containers right outside your front door. Plant containers of daffodil, hyacinth, and tulip bulbs in late fall and push the containers well under the spreading shelter of the shrubs in your foundation planting. Nestle the pots into the loose mulch of fallen leaves or needles. The containers will be protected but will receive the chilling needed to stimulate flowering. In 2 to 3 months, the foliage should be poking out of the pots, and you can bring the containers indoors to a sunny window.

Dealing with bulb foliage after the plants finish blooming can pose a dilemma. Bulb experts will tell you to leave the foliage alone until it turns yellow or brown in early summer. That's the right thing to do because the foliage needs time to produce food to recharge the bulb for the following year's bloom. But in a small garden, those clumps of foliage—particularly long-lasting daffodil leaves—can become very messy as they sprawl across the garden. It's tempting to cut the foliage off altogether, but I resist the urge, and you should, too. I compromise by gathering the stems into a bunch and fastening them with a rubber band. This technique robs the bulbs of some of their food-producing power, but they seem to tolerate it, and they bloom beautifully year after year.

Once bulb foliage turns yellow or brown, it's fine to cut it off at ground level and add it to the compost pile. After that, hardy bulbs should be self-sufficient until the following spring.

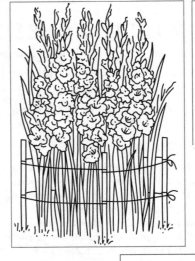

Plants with tall flowerstalks, such as gladioli, will stay upright and in place if you support them with stakes and string.

Preparing Bulbs for Winter

When fall comes, it's time to dig up tender bulbs to store over winter. After the foliage fades, cut the stems back to about 6 inches. Then use a hand tool to loosen the soil around the plants; this won't take much effort in a nice, loose lasagna bed. Lift the bulbs out and brush off as much soil as you can. Spread the bulbs on newspaper in a cool, shady place, and jot notes on the newspaper so you'll know which bulbs are which. Let the bulbs dry for several days.

Put the dried bulbs in paper bags, mesh bags, or boxes of peat moss, and label the containers. Store the bulbs in a dark place where the temperature is about 50° to 60°F. Check the bulbs once a month during winter and throw out any that are rotting. If the bulbs look shriveled, sprinkle a little water on them.

GIVE YOURSELF THE GIFT OF FLOWERS

Flowers renew the spirit, and as a way of renewing my spirit, I give myself a gift of special new flowers for my garden each year. One year I began a collection of lilies that I've continued to add to each year. My first lily was a hybrid Asiatic, 'Apeldoorn', which has clear orange flowers with outward-facing petals. In 9 years, I have added many different colors and some with fragrance, too. Lately I've discovered dwarf oriental lilies. They are perfect in my small gardens and well suited to growing in containers. My gift program must be working because despite many challenges and changes in my life, my spirit is whole. So give yourself the gift of flowers—I know you're worth it.

PAT'S FAVORITE BULBS FOR SMALL SPACES

Here's a list of my top 10 bulbs for small gardens, but the truth is, almost any flowering bulb is appropriate for a small garden. I hope you'll try all of these and then some! While the bulbs below bloom in a variety of seasons, colors, and shapes, they have one thing in common: All of them need well-drained soil.

PLANT NAME	DESCRIPTION	SMALL-SPACE GROWING TIPS
Agapanthus (*Agapanthus* spp.)	The day I saw my first heavenly blue agapanthus I knew they were special. Related to lilies, they have evergreen, straplike leaves surrounding tall stems topped with clusters of deep blue flowers from midsummer to early fall. 24 to 28 inches tall. Zones 8–11.	Like a sunny location and deep, fertile, well-drained soil. Plant in spring with crowns about 2 inches below soil level. In winter, cut stems to ground level and mulch with leaves or straw. Will grow well in containers in areas where they're not hardy. Move containers inside each winter, and repot them each year in spring.
Alliums (*Allium* spp.)	A large group of easy-to-grow ornamental onions, with straplike leaves and clusters of tiny white, purplish, or yellow flowers in late spring or early summer. Leaves only reach about 1 foot tall, but flower stems of some species can reach 5 feet tall. Hardiness varies with species.	Give alliums full sun. Even tall alliums don't take up much garden space, so try tucking these tiny bulbs among perennials or annuals. My favorite is drumstick allium (*A. sphaerocephalon*), with wandlike flower stems about 3 feet tall topped by a ball of purple flowers. Great for fresh arrangements and drying.
Crocuses (*Crocus* spp.)	There are versions of these low-growing goblet-shaped flowers for both spring and fall color. Beloved Dutch crocuses (*C. vernus*) bloom in February or March in lavender, purple, white, or yellow. 4 inches tall. Zones 3–8. Showy crocus (*C. speciosus*) foliage shows in early summer and then goes dormant. The lilac flowers emerge in September. 4 to 6 inches tall. Zones 5–9.	Crocuses need full sun. Plant Dutch crocuses along the path to the door you use most to boost your spirits in the last days of winter. Plant autumn crocuses where they can poke through the foliage of a groundcover such as lamb's-ears. When the blooms emerge through the lush gray foliage, the combination is a traffic stopper.
Dahlias (*Dahlia* hybrids)	Dahlias come in all sizes, from giant dinner-plate blooms to tiny pom-poms that bloom in window boxes. Flowers may resemble cactus blossoms, mums, or giant powder puffs. Bloom begins in early August and continues until frost. 1 to 5 feet tall. Hardy in Zones 9–11.	Plant in full sun after all chance of frost is past, and keep constantly moist. Plant large dahlia bulbs at the backs of flowerbeds, and fill window boxes with miniatures. Small dahlias include the Dahlinova Hybrids that are ideal for patio planters, borders, and pots. Pair them with sweet alyssum in window boxes. Great flowers for cutting. I fill every vase in the Potager café many times over with dahlias in late summer, and they always draw "oohs" and "aahs" from my customers.

PLANT NAME	DESCRIPTION	SMALL-SPACE GROWING TIPS
Snowdrops (*Galanthus* spp.)	Small clumps of narrow green leaves emerge as early as midwinter. Nodding white flowers bloom in late winter or early spring. To 6 inches tall. Zones 3–9.	Plant bulbs in fall, 3 to 4 inches deep in moist soil in partial shade. Try to find a spot close to a stone that will reflect heat to encourage earliest bloom. Snowdrops provide early color in dormant gardens. As perennials emerge, they will overshadow the snowdrop foliage, which goes dormant by midsummer.
Gladiolus (*Gladiolus* species and hybrids)	Fans of swordlike leaves and tall flowerstalks that bear several funnel-shaped flowers each in summer to early fall. Colors range from basic red, yellow, and white to "I see it but I can't believe it" shades. 2 to 5 feet tall. Zones 8–11.	Glads are easy to grow in any good soil in full sun. Start planting in early spring and continue planting every 2 weeks until mid-June for continuous bloom. Replant new bulbs every year, or dig them each fall and store them over winter. Glads usually need staking or tying. Gladiolus are favorite cut flowers. Cut stems before flowers are completely open and immediately place stems in warm water.
Lilies (*Lilium* hybrids)	Upright single stems with narrow leaves grow in spring; dramatic flat or funnel-shape flowers open in early to late summer. Flower colors include lilac, orange, pink, red, yellow, and white. 2 to 5 feet tall. Zones 4–8.	Plant lilies between shrubs, in beds, and even in containers. They will grow in partial shade but do best in full sun. Protect lilies from wind, which can cause the heavy stems to topple. It's a good idea to dig and divide lilies each year in late summer—give the extra bulblets to your friends. Try 'Stargazer' lily in a large container placed where you can enjoy its unique fragrance and upturned flowers.
Grape hyacinth (*Muscari armeniacum*)	These little bulbs produce spikes of fragrant globes in deep cobalt blue in midspring. 6 to 8 inches tall. Zones 3–8.	Plant in sun or partial shade. Easy to tuck into rock gardens, beds, containers, and window boxes. Grape hyacinths are inexpensive, so I buy lots and plant them along walkways and at the feet of daffodils and tulips for bright spring color.
Daffodils, jonquils (*Narcissus* species and hybrids)	A large group of bulbs with straplike leaves and trumpetlike flowers that bloom in spring. Flowers may be yellow, white, or bicolored. Varieties are available with a wide range of bloom times. 6 to 20 inches tall. Most are hardy in Zones 4–8; some are hardy to Zone 2.	Plant in full sun or partial shade; they will bloom for years. Try 'Minnow' for prolific bloom during early to midspring; it has white blossoms with yellow centers. Hoop petticoat daffodil (*N. bulbocodium*) is a miniature that produces several deep yellow flowers from each bulb. Try these two in rock gardens, pots, or in drifts in a lawn.
Tulips (*Tulipa* species and hybrids)	Tulips are famous for their cup-shape flowers available in an incredible array of colors, sizes, and forms. The leaves are broad and the flowers bloom on slender, upright stems. 6 to 30 inches tall. Hardiness varies with species.	Plant tulip bulbs 6 to 8 inches below the bed or container surface. Smaller species tulips can be planted nearer the surface. I plant new bulbs each fall to keep my beds full. Plant tulips in the foreground of beds alongside a path or in containers.

Growing Perennials

Perennials are easy, low-maintenance plants for large gardens, and the same is true for small gardens. When you're working in small spaces, though, it's important to research the plants before you buy, because some perennials can form huge clumps up to 8 feet tall, while others spread rapidly year after year and can engulf a small bed. Plant breeders are coming up with new, compact varieties of many favorite perennials these days, so you'll find plenty of choices for your small gardens.

Planting Perennials

Starting perennials from seed generally takes more time and effort than starting annuals does. Frankly, I don't bother. I buy potted plants at the garden center or order dormant bareroot plants from mail-order nurseries when I want something special.

When you plant a potted perennial, conditioning the plant is as important as conditioning the soil. You may find that the perennial has been growing in that pot a *long* time, and the roots may be compacted or coiled into the shape of the container. You need to free up the roots so they can spread through the soil. Water the plant well (or stick the pot in a bucket of water to soak for an hour), then remove

---

SMALL SECRETS FOR BIG SUCCESS

The Perfect Hand Tool

About 10 years ago, I met a man on the steps of the National Herb Garden in Washington, D.C. We were taking a rest before continuing our tour of gardens. Our conversation turned to tools and he introduced me to the Ho Mi, or Korean hand plow. I placed my first order with his company and began to use and sell this wonderful tool.

It's thousands of hand tools later, and I still haven't found another hand tool that surpasses it. When I spot a weed in one of my gardens, I flick it out easily with the wicked point of the hand plow. It's great for pulling apart compacted and matted roots of potted perennials and shrubs before planting. The best use for the Ho Mi is lifting and dividing perennials. I work the roots loose on one side of a clump of perennials, and then I thrust the tool's tip into the soil on the opposite side of the clump and lift. The entire clump pops up in one motion. I also use the tool to hack the clump into divisions. (See "Resources for Lasagna Gardeners" on page 271 for mail-order companies that sell Ho Mis.)

it from the container and place it on a flat surface. With your fingers or a hand tool, work the roots to loosen and separate them. In some cases, you'll need to cut through the roots with a knife. To do this, score the roots from top to bottom of the rootball in four spots around the edges, then work on each section of roots.

Once you've set the plant's roots free, open a planting hole in your lasagna bed. Set the plant in place, and check that it is sitting at the same level as it was growing in the pot. Fan out the roots as best as you can, and cover them with soil.

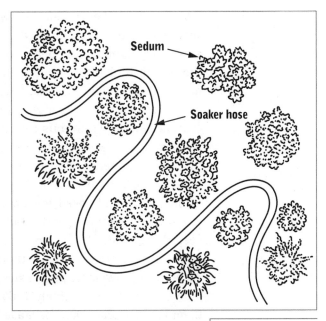

Water deeply and thoroughly, and mulch around the plant. Press the soil surface with your palms to bring the roots in contact with the soil. It's important to keep the soil moist while the plants are getting established. Using a soaker hose can be helpful for this, as shown in the illustration on this page.

Snake a soaker hose among perennials for easy watering during dry spells. Keep the hose away from perennials that like dry conditions, such as sedums.

You can plant potted perennials from spring through fall, but early spring and fall are the best times. In spring, container-grown plants have time to become well established before the heat of summer sets in. Fall is also a good time to divide and transplant most types of perennials. Each fall I move plants that have outgrown their space. It's also a good time to pull out any unwanted self-sown plants, or to pot them up to give to friends.

Care During the Season

Lasagna gardens are naturally rich and friable. Each time you add a layer of material to the top, it becomes food for both the soil and for earthworms, who in turn leave worm castings. The castings are food for the soil, too. Each spring, I supplement the worms' efforts by adding a ½-inch layer of compost to my perennials; in the South, put on 1 inch yearly. (I give a few plants some special treatment, such as my roses. They receive a special application of organic rose food twice during the growing season.)

Most established perennials won't need any watering if you keep them well mulched, unless you have a long dry spell or you live in a very dry climate. To check soil moisture, stick your hand through the mulch and into the soil. Remember that different perennials have different water needs. Some like constantly moist soil, while others stand up to drought conditions without flinching. Check "Pat's Favorite Perennials for Small Spaces" on page 86 for tips on the water needs of specific perennials, or consult a good perennials encyclopedia. Perennials in containers will need more frequent watering, of course.

Some perennials need to be divided regularly to promote vigorous growth, while others grow a tad too vigorously and need dividing to keep them small. Other perennials, such as daylilies, hostas, and peonies, live for generations without ever being divided.

I tend to grow some aggressive perennials because I love them too much to live without them. I divide these plants every year to keep them in their place (and because I own a garden center, I can always use more plants to sell). 'Coronation Gold' yarrow grows in one of my 2-foot gardens, and it would definitely conquer the bed if I didn't divide it each year. I can lift it in early spring or fall and it still blooms every year.

I grow a combination of favorite perennials—Siberian irises, 'Bergarten' sage, lemon daylilies, and lupines—in a bed that's just 2 feet deep.

Dividing perennials is easy, so don't be nervous about it. Lift the entire plant from the soil and gently tug on stems around the base until you feel them begin to loosen from the mass. Keep tugging and each plant will divide into many separate plants. Replant the largest division in the garden bed. The rest you can pot up for your gardening friends, plant elsewhere in your yard, or throw on the compost pile.

Preparing Perennials for Winter

Some gardeners faithfully cut down perennial foliage and seedheads as soon as they turn brown in the fall, but not me. That's partly because I'm a lazy gardener, but it's also because I love wildlife. I know that my gardens can provide shelter over the winter for beneficial insects, small mammals, and birds. Seedheads also provide food for the birds, so my garden stays put. Sometimes the dried foliage becomes an artistic part of the winter scene, too, as snow accentuates the lines of the foliage or mounds up on flat seedheads of yarrow and sedum.

I do mulch my garden with shredded leaves in fall, to continue feeding the soil and to protect the perennials from heaving out of the soil as it freezes and thaws.

In late winter or early spring, I clear away dead foliage and stems to reveal the exciting new shoots that are pushing up from underground. The dead plant material works well as a coarse base layer for a new lasagna bed. Or, if you're maxed out on bed space, you can add the spent plant matter to your compost pile.

Groundcovers in Small-Space Gardens

Groundcovers are perennials that do just what their name says—they spread and cover the ground. Gardeners usually plant groundcovers as a way to fill lots of garden space quickly, so you may be wondering why I'm mentioning them in this book on small-space gardening. The answer is that many groundcovers are too lovely not to include—even in small gardens—and if you handle them wisely, they don't have to be space hogs.

For example, I can't imagine a garden without lady's mantle (*Alchemilla mollis*). It forms beautiful mounds of large, scalloped leaves with sprays of yellow-green flowers in spring and early summer. The flowers add color and texture to fresh or dried bouquets.

(continued on page 91)

PAT'S FAVORITE PERENNIALS FOR SMALL SPACES

It was torture to limit myself to a list of only 25 perennials. I could have listed 25 favorite perennials for shade, 25 perennials for white blooms, 25 perennials for long-season bloom—you name the category, there are plenty of great perennials to fill it. So use this list as a jumping-off point, and realize that every year you garden, you may discover 25 new favorite perennials of your own.

PLANT NAME	DESCRIPTION	SMALL-SPACE GROWING TIPS
Yarrows (*Achillea* spp.)	Large, flat flower heads rise above ferny foliage. Blooms in shades of yellow, pink, red, and white. Some types will spread rapidly. 8 inches to 4 feet tall. Hardiness varies with species.	Require full sun and well-drained soil; does well in hot, dry locations. Yarrow may flop in rich soil, so plant it in a bed that's on the lean side. Frequent cutting encourages all-summer bloom; use the blooms in arrangements, or cut the flowers before they open fully for drying. Compact (15- to 18-inch) 'Kamtscha-ticum' has pretty pink flowers; 'Schwellen-burg' sports gold blooms and silver-gray foliage. Divide plants yearly and replant small pieces to keep them under control. Woolly yarrow (*A. tomentosa*), a fuzzy, compact groundcover with gold blooms, works well under taller perennials or in a saucerlike container.
Artemisias (*Artemisia* spp.)	Shrubby plants with silvery-gray foliage in a wide range of heights and textures. Flowers form in fall but are barely noticeable. Choose plants carefully because some spread rapidly. 1 to 6 feet tall. Hardiness varies with species.	Plant in full sun and well-drained soil; heat- and drought-tolerant. Try *A. absinthium* 'Lambrook Silver' or *A. schmidtiana* 'Silver Mound' in a container on your deck or patio. Pair artemisias with hot-colored perennials and annuals for contrast. I think that the artemisias planted near my roses repel pests.
Asters (*Aster* spp.)	Alpine aster (*A. alpinus*) forms mounding plants with purple, white, or pink flowers with yellow centers. It blooms in early summer. 6 to 12 inches tall. Zones 2–7. New York aster (*A. novi-belgii*) is a fall-bloomer with abundant white or blue flowers with yellow centers. 1 to 6 feet tall. Zones 3–8. Other aster species are generally too large for small gardens.	Alpine aster grows best in cool climates but is dependable for only 3 to 4 years. It needs full sun and very good drainage. Divide plants in spring or fall and replant only the outer sections of the clump, or take stem cuttings to root. Plant in rock gardens or in containers. New York asters need full sun, moist soil, and frequent dividing to keep them neat. Try one (or more) of these: 'Audrey' (single lilac flowers); 'Jenny' (single red flowers); 'Snow-sprite' (semidouble white flowers); 'Professor Anton Kippenburg' (lavender-blue semi-double flowers).

PLANT NAME	DESCRIPTION	SMALL-SPACE GROWING TIPS
Chinese astilbe (*Astilbe chinensis*)	Fluffy pink flower plumes bloom in summer and early fall on low stems with divided leaves. The dried plumes look beautiful in the winter garden. They stay erect a long time and change color for winter interest. 8 to 24 inches tall. Zones 4–8.	Plant in sun or shade, but beware—astilbes need constantly moist soil or the foliage will blacken and they'll grow very slowly. Divide them every 3 years. Try one in a large pot as a centerpiece for a container grouping in the shade. I like these small cultivars: 'Christian' (lilac-pink flowers); 'Finale' (light pink flowers); and 'Serenade' (late-blooming rose-red flowers).
Boltonia (*Boltonia asteroides*)	Tall, billowing clouds of small, daisylike flowers that appear in late summer to early fall. 4 to 6 feet tall. Zones 3–9.	Plant in full sun or light shade. Cut plants back by half in early summer for bushier growth and more bloom. Divide clumps and replant every 3 years. 'Snowbank' boltonia softens the spiky foliage of ornamental grasses beautifully. In a container, use a tomato cage to support boltonia so it won't topple over.
Fringed bleeding heart (*Dicentra eximia*)	Classic heart-shaped flowers in spring and summer over ferny foliage. 12 to 18 inches tall. Zones 3–9.	Thrives in shade but can also do well in sun as long as its soil is constantly moist. I buy one container-grown plant and divide it immediately before planting it in my garden or containers. Divide every 3 years after. Bleeding heart foliage contrasts beautifully with tulips in a sunny bed or with hostas in shade.
Purple coneflower (*Echinacea purpurea*)	Wonderful, dark pink flowers with prominent, bright orange centers on upright stems covered with coarse, lance-shaped leaves. Butterflies love the blossoms. 2 to 4 feet tall. Zones 3–8.	Needs full sun and good drainage. Cut flower heads before they set seed to prevent self-sowing. Choose small cultivars, such as 'White Swan', which has white petals around an orange-bronze center cone, or 'Kim's Knee High', which bears rose-colored 2- to 3-inch flowers. Purple coneflowers are taprooted, so root-prune plants in containers to keep them going.
Spurges (*Euphorbia* spp.)	Cushion spurge (*E. polychroma*) has bright yellow bracts (modified leaves) in early spring and colorful fall foliage. To 18 inches tall. Zones 3–8. Myrtle spurge (*E. myrsinites*) has long stems of blue-gray leaves that end in bright yellow bracts in spring. It grows only 6 to 10 inches tall. Zones 5–9.	Easy to grow in full sun and well-drained soil. Cushion spurge takes the place of shrubs in gardens short on space, and it looks beautiful in a container, too. Myrtle spurge foliage offers cool contrast to spring-flowering bulbs in a small garden bed.
Gaura (*Gaura lindheimeri*)	Loose sprays of white flowers with light pink centers on long, thin stems. Blooms for several weeks in summer. Zones 5–9.	Withstands drought and poor soil. Takes no more room than many larger plants that give far less in return. 'Whirling Butterflies' flutters like butterflies in the slightest breeze. No in-ground space? Plant in a deep pot (at least 24 inches). It's taprooted, so if it declines, try lifting it and root-pruning.

(continued)

PAT'S FAVORITE PERENNIALS FOR SMALL SPACES—CONTINUED

PLANT NAME	DESCRIPTION	SMALL-SPACE GROWING TIPS
Cranesbills, hardy geraniums (*Geranium* spp.)	Mounded plants with lobed leaves and five-petaled, saucer-shaped flowers that stand above the foliage. Blooms may be blue, pink, purple, rose, or white, and they appear in late spring or early summer. Ask before you buy, because while some stay neat and tidy in one spot, other species spread rapidly. 4 inches to 2 feet tall. Most species hardy in Zones 4–8.	Grow in full sun or partial shade in well-drained soil. Plant cranesbills at the edge of a small garden bed or in a rock garden. Their mounded form is just made for containers, too, and the foliage remains attractive even when the plants aren't blooming. One of my favorites is *G. sanguineum* 'Shepherd's Warning', which grows only 4 to 6 inches tall and has deep rose-pink flowers.
Daylilies (*Hemerocallis* species and hybrids)	Clumps of straplike foliage and lilylike flowers in an almost unending variety of sizes and colors. Some species are invasive, so research before you buy. 1 to 6 feet tall. Hardiness varies with species.	Plant in sun to partial shade in well-drained soil. Feed lightly with compost each spring to encourage heavier flowering. In large gardens, daylilies are grand in a wide sweep or to cover a bank. But they also have a place in small gardens, either as a groundcover or a focal point. You can plant small daylilies in rock gardens and containers, too. I like these small daylilies: 'Stella de Oro' (clear gold flowers), 'Eenie Weenie' (small yellow flowers), 'Eenie Allegro' (creamy apricot flowers), and 'Little Grapette' (purple flowers).
Hostas (*Hosta* species and cultivars)	Bold, heart-shaped leaves are hostas' best feature. Foliage may be green, yellow-green, blue-green, or variegated. Mauve or white flowers bloom on tall stalks above the foliage in summer or fall. 6 inches to 3 feet tall. Hardiness varies with species.	Easy to grow in partial to full shade. Like rich, moist, but well-drained soil, but will even grow in dry shade. 'Golden Tiara', 6 to 8 inches tall, has rich gold leaves with bright gold margins. 'Pacific Blue Edger' is about 8 inches tall and has blue-gray leaves with dusty white undersides. 'Moonlight' has leaves that change from green to golden yellow and then creamy yellow when the plants get morning sun. I use hostas to edge shade gardens, fill spaces in rubble walls, and for combinations in planters along shady paths.
Candytufts (*Iberis* spp.)	A star of the spring garden, with bright white blooms covering spreading mats of foliage. 12 inches tall. Zones 4–8.	Like full sun and well-drained soil. Cut plants back with hedge shears after blooming, and they may rebloom in summer. Mulch over winter with evergreen branches in cold-winter areas. Plant candytuft to cascade over rock walls or as a groundcover. Set containers of candytuft near hot-colored flowers to cool them down.

PLANT NAME	DESCRIPTION	SMALL-SPACE GROWING TIPS
Irises (*Iris* spp.)	Sword-shaped leaves and exotic blooms in a rainbow of colors. Bloom time ranges from spring to fall. 4 inches to 4 feet tall. Hardiness varies with species.	Plant in moist soil and full to partial sun. To keep bearded irises blooming, lift and divide the plants every 3 or 4 years after flowering in early summer, or in early fall. Break away the old rhizomes and discard. Replant the rhizome half exposed to light and air. Divide other irises if they seem crowded or if bloom declines. Spring-blooming crested iris (*I. cristata*) grows 4 to 8 inches tall and has blue flowers with a yellow-and-white blaze. Use it as a groundcover under trees, in a rock garden, or in a container. Also try hybrid cultivars of Japanese iris (*I. ensata*) in containers.
Rose campion (*Lychnis coronaria*)	Branching flower stems emerge from rosettes of soft gray foliage. Bright magenta flowers bloom throughout summer. 2 to 3 feet tall. Zones 4–8.	Easy to grow from seed, but you can also buy one or two plants, and once established they will reseed. Requires full sun and well-drained soil. You can tuck this plant into an opening just 6 inches wide, because the foliage stays compact and the flowerstalks suspend the blooms well above the foliage. For a blazingly colorful container, plant three rose campion plants in a 10-inch pot.
Peonies (*Paeonia* species and hybrids)	Single or double bowl-like blooms in May on shrubby plants with dark green foliage. Many colors available. 1 to 3 feet tall. Most are hardy in Zones 3–8.	Plant in fall. Start with bare woody roots and position the eyes (buds) 1 to 2 inches below the bed surface. Plant each clump 3 feet apart because they will increase in spread as they mature. Some peonies tend to flop when they bloom; to prevent this, support the plants early with a peony ring or stakes and string. Peonies will live as long as 100 years with little care.
Oriental poppy (*Papaver orientale*)	Dark green, hairy foliage and bold flowers with crepe-papery petals in orange, pink, red, or white in late spring. Foliage goes dormant and dies away after the flowers fade. 2 to 3 feet tall. Zones 2–7.	Plant in light, well-drained soil and full sun. Plan for a spreading companion that will cover the space left behind when the poppies die back. Combine daffodils, poppies, and a hardy rose bush. The poppies hide the fading daffodil foliage, and after the poppies die back, the rose blossoms take center stage. Plant poppies in pots; after the foliage fades, remove the pots to an out-of-the-way spot.
Russian sages (*Perovskia atriplicifolia* and cultivars)	Shrubby perennial with graceful upright stems covered with silvery-gray foliage. Sprays of lavender-blue flowers bloom in summer. 2 to 4 feet tall. Zones 4–9.	Need full sun and good drainage. Don't let the size of this plant scare you; I grow it in a tiny spot between the sidewalk and the street. Try compact 'Little Spire', which grows about 2 feet tall. Prune Russian sage back each spring for a fresh, tidy display.

(continued)

PAT'S FAVORITE PERENNIALS FOR SMALL SPACES—CONTINUED

PLANT NAME	DESCRIPTION	SMALL-SPACE GROWING TIPS
Creeping phlox, moss phlox (*Phlox subulata*)	Small blue, magenta, pink, or white flowers cover carpets of spreading stems in spring. To 6 inches tall. Zones 2–9.	Needs full sun and light, well-drained soil. Cut back after flowering to encourage side growth. A great edging plant, groundcover, or container plant for a dry, sunny site.
Primroses (*Primula* spp.)	Showy spring flowers in branching clusters or on upright stalks over broad leaves. Many color choices. Blooms last up to 5 weeks. To 1 foot tall. Hardiness varies with species.	Plant in cool, moist soil in light to partial shade. In the South, treat primroses as annuals. A natural to combine with bulbs. I plant them in rock gardens and in an old basket that I've "planted" in my shady garden border.
Rudbeckia, orange coneflower (*Rudbeckia fulgida*)	Daisylike, orange-yellow flowers top upright stems with hairy, lance-shaped leaves. Provides a long display of color in mid- to late summer. 1 to 3 feet tall. Zones 3–9.	Plant in a warm, sunny spot with rich, moist soil. Seek out dwarf varieties such as 'Pot of Gold' and 'Viette's Little Suzy', which only reach about 1 foot tall. They'll grow well in a large container or planter on a patio, too.
Salvias (*Salvia* spp.)	Spikes of blue or purple flowers in summer and fall atop mounded or upright plants with branching stems. 1 to 4 feet tall. Hardiness varies with species.	Need full sun and good drainage. Fairly drought tolerant and will bloom all summer if deadheaded. 'May Night' is my favorite hardy salvia. Other cultivars good for small spaces include 'East Friesland' and 'Blue Queen'.
Pincushion flowers (*Scabiosa* spp.)	Round, flat, blue or pink flowers are held aloft on long slender stems emerging from a rosette of green foliage. Flowers are very attractive to butterflies. 18 to 24 inches tall. Zones 3–9.	Need full sun and well-drained soil. Added organic material will ensure good performance. Keep new flowers coming by cutting off spent blooms. The most compact variety is 'Butterfly Blue'. Use it as an edging plant or in a container of butterfly-attracting flowers.
Sedums (*Sedum* spp.)	Many species and varieties of fleshy, succulent plants, from low evergreen mat-formers to taller border types. Clusters of small, starry flowers in pink, red, yellow, and white. 2 inches to 2 feet tall. Hardiness varies with species.	Need sun and good drainage; drought tolerant. A perennial favorite with rock gardeners and alpine enthusiasts. Golden moss stonecrop (*Sedum acre*) is a creeping type with golden yellow flowers that will fill in around stepping stones. Try upright sedums like 'Autumn Joy' in a container with a peony ring to support the stems.
Speedwells, veronicas (*Veronica* spp.)	Showy, dependable, long-blooming perennials. Most have upright spikes of blue, pink, or white flowers; some species have upright stems, while others are low and spreading. 3 inches to 4 feet tall. Most are hardy in Zones 3–8.	Will grow well in well-drained, average to poor soil. Plant in full sun in the North and partial shade in the South. Cut back hard after flowering to produce fuller plants. As a groundcover, try *V. prostrata* 'Trehane', which has yellow foliage and blue flowers. For garden beds, plant *V. spicata* 'Red Fox', 15 inches tall with rosy red flowers, and 'Snow White', 18 inches tall with white blooms.

I use it as an edging for my small shade gardens, and because I cut so many of the flowers for arrangements, it doesn't self-sow.

Another way to grow groundcovers on a small scale is as a living mulch in a large container that holds a potted tree. Heartleaf brunnera (*Brunnera macrophylla*) is a good choice for this. This lovely, understated, shade-loving perennial has heart-shaped leaves and bears small, blue, spring flowers that resemble forget-me-nots. I buy one large potted brunnera and divide it into several small plants to fill a large container. You can also plant it in a hanging basket and hang it from a tree limb in the shade.

Sweet woodruff (*Galium odoratum*) is a well-known groundcover that can be invasive, but here's an idea: Plant it around the bases of shrubs or trees planted in or beside a lawn instead of using bark mulch. Mowing the grass will stop the sweet woodruff from spreading, and the groundcover will be a buffer to prevent you from accidentally ramming the tree or shrub with your lawnmower. It will be covered with clusters of tiny white flowers just in time for May Day celebrations (I cut the flowers and float them in cups of wine when I celebrate my birthday in May.)

One of my most successful groundcover experiments was with foamflower (*Tiarella cordifolia*). I planted this shade lover in interesting containers set in various shady spots around the garden. The plants put out runners that spilled over the sides and rooted themselves into the surrounding garden beds. When the plants bloomed in spring, there were ribbons of foamy white flowers trailing from the containers. To keep the plants in check, I cut back the runners as needed.

Ornamental Grasses in Small Spaces

When I talk about growing ornamental grasses in small spaces, people always look doubtful. They're probably picturing a vast clump of miscanthus or switch grass (*Panicum virgatum*). Giant grasses like those certainly can't be squeezed into a small bed. Plus, it's hard to use the trick of frequent division to keep a vigorous ornamental grass small, because dividing a large grass is a heavy-duty project that can require a hefty saw and a crew of three people.

Not all grasses grow on such a grand scale, though, and I've discovered some excellent midsize grasses for small gardens and containers. I like the contrast their foliage and fountainlike shapes can lend to a garden. Plus the dried foliage stays attractive through the winter, so your garden still has interest and movement in the off-season. The dried foliage is an elegant addition to dried flower arrangements, too.

Most grasses are tough characters that don't need pampering. In general, plant them in well-drained soil and full sun, and don't worry about fertilizing or pest control. They rarely suffer from pest problems—another plus in my opinion. I've only experimented with a few ornamental grasses, but based on my success with them, I know that I'll try more.

Pink ribbon grass (*Phalaris arundinacea* 'Feesey') is one of my personal favorites. I grow it as an accent plant in the garden and for bunches of foliage to add to fresh flower arrangements. The stems are pink and the long, soft leaves are green and white. It's a great partner for white-flowered perennials. This grass can spread aggressively, so be cautious if you plant it.

Blue fescue (*Festuca amethystina*) has blue-green, spiky foliage that complements spring bulbs beautifully. In midsummer, it puts out bloom stalks that persist until the following spring. Not a plant for a solo performance, try planting it in a group of three.

You can create an impressive garden show in a small area by grouping large containers planted with ornamental grasses and perennials.

Also try a trio of Japanese blood grass (*Imperata cylindrica* 'Red Baron'), which has flat leaf blades that turn blood red to green tinged with red, and then orange-brown with the first hard frost.

An ornamental grass in a container adds elegance to an entry or patio. For a partly shaded site, try bulbous oat grass (*Arrhenatherum elatius* subsp. *bulbosum*), a truly petite grass with variegated foliage. In hot regions, this grass dies out in summer and then comes back in fall. I move the pot out of sight when this happens and bring it back to a prominent location when it regrows.

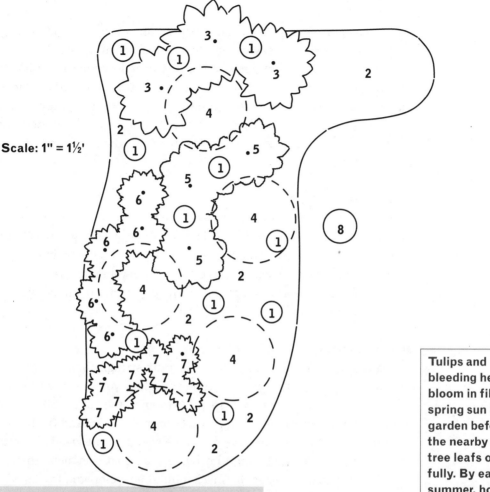

Scale: 1" = 1½'

HOSTAS AND BLEEDING HEARTS IN THE SHADE

1. Tulip

2. Labrador violet (*V. labradorica*) (22 plants)

3. 'Bright Lights' hosta (*Hosta* 'Bright Lights')

4. Fringed bleeding heart (*Dicentra eximia*)

5. 'Blue Cadet' hosta (*Hosta* 'Blue Cadet')

6. 'Kabitan' hosta (*Hosta* 'Kabitan')

7. *Hosta longissima*

8. Trunk of shade tree

Tulips and bleeding hearts bloom in filtered spring sun in this garden before the nearby shade tree leafs out fully. By early summer, hosta foliage will dominate the shady scene.

Another container grass that I like is variegated Japanese sedge (*Carex morrowii* 'Aurea-Variegata'). It's evergreen, and the arching blades have a central creamy stripe. It forms low mounds with inconspicuous flowers. It grows best in light sun to full shade in moist locations. Cut it to the ground in late winter to allow a new flush of growth to come through. I worry that it's too tender to remain outdoors in my area, so I keep it in an unheated greenhouse over winter.

Growing Vines

The care and feeding of vines depends on whether they're annuals or perennials. Growing annual vines is a simple project. If growing vines is new to you, start with one of the annual vines like morning glories or sweet peas that are easy to grow from seed. When you're ready for something more challenging, move up to perennial vines such as clematis or maypop.

Annual Vines

Planting and caring for annual vines is quite straightforward. Just set up your trellis or support at the time you plant your seeds or plants. As the vines begin to stretch, help guide them to the support if needed. Water them if conditions are dry, and keep the area around the base of the vines mulched to conserve moisture and prevent weeds. Annual vines may need extra feeding to provide the boost they need to grow and bloom in just one season. Check a plant encyclopedia for the specific requirements of the vine you're growing before fertilizing, though. For example, nasturtiums need no extra food and will do best in unimproved soil.

Perennial Vines

Planting perennial vines is a much more permanent decision. While it's easy to transplant most herbaceous perennials, it's not easy to move a perennial vine. Plan carefully: This is one choice you really do want to get right the first time.

Do some research about your vine of choice. How large will it grow? How much pruning will it need? What kind of care and feeding will you have to provide? Is it right for your zone? Does it have tenacious, adhesive stems that will pull paint off a fence or house?

Once the choice is made, give the vine the best possible growing conditions while it establishes itself. I like planting vines in fall, because that allows them to get a head start on establishing roots before sending out topgrowth. Like most gardening tasks, though, it's okay to plant vines whenever you find the time. Spring and summer may be when you have the most choices; some mail-order nurseries will ship vines almost all year long.

Even though vines take very little in-ground space, that soil should be the best you can provide. I like to plant in an established lasagna bed where those earthworm tilling machines have loosened the top 10 to 12 inches of soil. Planting perennial vines is like planting other perennials: Open a hole that's the right depth for the plant and about twice as wide, so that the roots can spread laterally. Adjust the depth of the hole as needed, set the roots in place, and fill the hole with soil. Water thoroughly and add a top mulch right away to keep the soil moist and the roots cool. The improved soil and attention to water and mulch will be good for new root production.

Supporting and Training Vines

Most vines need a little boost to help them climb on the support or even in the right direction. Once they take hold, they can usually get along without your help. In fact, a vine may take off seemingly with a mind of its own.

PAT'S SMALL SPACE STORIES

Eva's Perennial Sweet Peas

Sometimes our gardens contain undiscovered treasures at our feet. A great example of this is the perennial sweet pea (*Lathyrus latifolius*) vines growing alongside the house next door to The Potager. For 25 years, my neighbor Eva had noticed purple flowers among a tumble of foliage on the ground and wondered what they were. When she mentioned them to me, I had to investigate and I identified her treasure for her.

We set up a series of strings on the side of Eva's house. Once the vines clambered up them, their beautiful blue-green foliage and purple blooms were a joy to behold. Although perennial sweet peas aren't fragrant like their annual cousins are, the vines bloom from June through September in average soil. The vines will grow up to 9 feet long. The plants need little care and are hardy in Zones 5 through 9. I persuaded Eva to let me collect some seed from her vines, and now the same lovely purple blooms grace the fence at The Potager.

Last year I grew morning glories in the softened soil near an old doghouse at The Potager. I intended for them to grow over a short section of fence, but when I wasn't looking, they clambered over the doghouse and then over a decorative wishing well sitting next to it. I'd intended to transport both the doghouse and wishing well from The Potager to my house in Westbrookville, but needless to say, the doghouse and well stayed put for that summer. They certainly looked beautiful, and they showed me that there are plenty of nontraditional supports for vines. The well looked especially nice with vines entwining themselves up the side supports and roof. I think I'll plant more morning glories around it—after I move it to Westbrookville.

If an annual vine outgrows its space, there's no crisis, just a temporary change of plans. But with perennial vines, pruning to keep the vines inbounds is usually essential. The basic techniques you'll use when making pruning cuts are the same as for pruning fruit trees (see page 196). Cut away any dead wood you spot at any time of year. In general, prune vines that bloom in spring just after they finish flowering. Prune summer-blooming vines between late fall and late winter.

Vines in Containers

With proper care, container-grown vines will grow and bloom just as well as vines grown in the ground. Plants in containers will need supplemental feeding with a solution of fish emulsion to support production of those long vines. If your vines seem to stop growing, they may be pot-bound. If this happens, carefully remove the root mass from the container, untangle the roots, and trim off about one-third of the root system. Replant the vine in a larger pot with fresh potting soil and compost. You can prune the vine back before doing this so that you can manipulate the pot more easily. Or, if someone can assist you, you can perform the root surgery without detaching the vine topgrowth from the trellis.

Preparing Vines for Winter

I don't do anything special to my vines at the end of the season, other than to apply a winter mulch about 6 to 8 inches deep to protect the crowns from frost-heaving. The leafy vines provide places for birds to hide in bad weather, and the seedheads of some vines are food for songbirds. The vines add winter interest in the garden, especially when they're coated with fluffy snow. In spring, when my gardening energy is renewed, pruning vines is one of the first things I do.

GROWING THE QUEEN OF VINES

Undisputed queen of the climbers, clematis offers more flowers over a longer period of time, in more varieties, than any other single flowering climbing plant. Exciting? You bet! You'll jump up and down when you see 'Nelly Moser' with its plate-size, pink-and-purple stripe blooms, climbing the sides of the old shed and a post in the garden.

Clematis species and hybrids bear flowers in all sizes and many wonderful colors. The vines can grow from 8 to 25 feet in a season. Clematis is perfect for small gardens because you can plant it in very little space or in a container. It will grow up, over, through, and onto anything. Plant it in an existing tree or shrub. Plant more than one variety together for a longer season of bloom. Plant two flashy colors together for a funky style. Love white? Plant 'Henryi', and the blooms will dazzle you.

I grow sweet autumn clematis in a 2-foot-wide garden beside the ramp leading to the entrance of The Potager. The ramp has a railing with window boxes attached to the top. The clematis begins to grow up the ramp railings in early spring. In early summer, I chop off vines threatening to cover the ramp and train the remaining vines to cling to the rail and flower boxes.

In five easy steps, here's the rundown for growing clematis.

1. Choose a site in full sun, and 3 to 4 weeks before you plan to plant, layer up a small lasagna bed on the site. At that time, install the trellis or other supports. The actual planting hole should be 12 inches away from the wall or trellis to allow room for air circulation around the vine.

2. On planting day, remove your nursery-grown clematis plant from the container and submerge the roots in water. Keep them underwater until bubbles stop coming to the surface.

3. Open a planting hole and set the plant in place. Make sure the plant sits at the same level relative to the soil as it was growing in the pot. Firm soil around plant roots and water again.

4. Clematis grow best with their roots in the shade, so plant a shallow-rooted, hardy perennial or small shrub at the foot of the clematis. Surround the roots with mulch.

5. Prune at the right time. Spring-flowering clematis bloom on the previous year's wood, so they should be pruned lightly right after flowering (or not at all). Fall-blooming types flower on young wood produced the same year. They require pruning every year in late winter or early spring. If you're not sure when your clematis blooms, wait and watch. Once you know what its bloom time is, you'll know how and when to prune it.

PAT'S FAVORITE VINES FOR SMALL SPACES

If you're new to growing vines, take advantage of my experience and start with a few of the ones I recommend here. Some vines can become aggressive monsters that aren't suitable for small spaces, so I've avoided mentioning those, even though they're beautiful and popular in large garden situations. For more information on vines, see the growing instructions for clematis on page 97, grapes on page 209, and nasturtiums on page 180.

PLANT NAME	DESCRIPTION	SMALL-SPACE GROWING TIPS
Bougainvilleas (*Bougainvillea* spp.)	Bougainvilleas are a central part of the southern scene. Their flowerlike bracts are brilliant shades of bright pinks and purples over a long bloom season. Handle with care—the stems may be very thorny. 20 to 30 feet long. Tender perennials hardy in Zones 9–11.	Bougainvilleas love it hot and are at their best in full sun. If you don't live in the deep South, try growing it in a container and bringing it inside during winter. (Keep the container on a wheeled plant stand so it's easy to move). Provide a trellis for support, and prune back hard after flowering to keep it in control. Bougainvillea also looks beautiful cascading out of a large hanging basket. Some new varieties have spectacular variegated foliage; ask your local supplier about them.
English ivy (*Hedera helix*)	There are several hundred varieties in different shapes, colors, and sizes. White or yellow coloring gives this ivy a special look, and combined with all-purpose green, it creates an interesting color pattern. 30 to 40 feet long. Zones 5–11.	It would surprise you to know how little space (about 8 inches) the ivy that covers my daughter's house grows in. All ivies prefer alkaline soil and shade. My garden offers both, so our ivy is very happy. Choose a site for English ivy with an eye to future growth. English ivy clings to surfaces, and removing the clinging roots from walls or fences is a tough job. It's easy to train potted ivy to cover a wire frame for a pretty garden accent.
Hops (*Humulus lupulus*)	Large leaves with three to five heart-shaped lobes. Flowers aren't very showy, but female plants form conelike seedpods. To 30 feet long. Zones 3–8.	One hop plant can be grown in a half-barrel, trained up a lath strip, and—left to its natural course—will cover a 12 × 48-foot lath ceiling to provide summer shade for a deck or patio.

PLANT NAME	DESCRIPTION	SMALL-SPACE GROWING TIPS
Moonflower (*Ipomoea alba*)	This annual vine fills your garden with bloom and fragrance long after the sun goes down. Sweet-scented white flowers, 6 inches wide and long, open in early evening and are like beacons of light at night. To 10 feet long. Tender perennial hardy in Zones 10–11.	Easy to start from seed in full sun. Moonflower will climb on a trellis or porch railing. Plant it by your deck or patio. Seedpods have an interesting shape and add to the visual appeal of this vine.
Morning glories (*Ipomoea purpurea* and *I. tricolor*)	These old-fashioned, fun plants bloom in blue, white, pink, and red from summer to early fall. To 15 feet long. Tender perennials hardy only in Zones 10–11.	Plant from seed in spring and keep well watered. You can grow morning glories in containers, train them up string trellises in smallgardens, or plant them to clamber over a structure in your yard. Best grown from seed.
Jasmines (*Jasminum* spp.)	Jasmine vines have lancelike leaves and starry flowers with narrow or rounded white petals that bloom in spring to summer. Some species have fragrant flowers. To 30 feet long. Hardiness varies with species.	Plant in full sun to partial shade. Prune after flowering to control size. My son-in-law Steve discovered yellow jasmine (*J. nudiflorum*) on a trip with me to the Atlanta Botanical Gardens. I was glad I was there to tell him what it was so he could rush out and buy it to train over his arbor. My favorite is evergreen *J. polyanthum*, which has wonderful white flowers and that lovely jasmine scent. It needs to be pruned hard, but it's a small price to pay.
Sweet peas (*Lathyrus odoratus*)	Leafy vines sport fragrant flowers with ruffled petals in many colors (but not yellow). To 6 feet long. Annual.	Another super-easy climber, with the bonus of lovely fragrance. Sow seeds in fall for early-spring bloom. Plants will reseed, giving the impression that they're perennial. Perennial sweet peas (*L. latifolius*) have the same beautiful flowers, but no fragrance.
Honeysuckle (*Lonicera* × *americana*)	A medium-size climber with oval leaves and highly fragrant pink and cream flowers in summer. Red berries form after flowers fade. To 22 feet long. Zones 6–9.	Honeysuckles need little room for their roots and fill vertical spaces with lovely vines and flowers. Plant in well-drained soil or in a large tub and train it onto a narrow trellis. *Caution:* Some species of honeysuckle are extremely invasive, so be sure you buy the proper type.

(continued)

PAT'S FAVORITE VINES
FOR SMALL SPACES—CONTINUED

PLANT NAME	DESCRIPTION	SMALL-SPACE GROWING TIPS
Mandevillas (*Mandevilla* spp.)	Originating in the rain forests of South America, mandevillas are grown as annuals in most parts of North America. They have woody, twining stems and broad, heart-shaped leaves. The most widely available cultivar is 'Alice du Pont', a hybrid with rich pink flowers. *M. splendens* has wonderful, funnel-shaped pink flowers with yellow eyes. 10 to 20 feet long.	North of Zone 10, grow mandevilla in a container so you can move it inside in fall. In late spring or early summer, when temperatures are above 50°F, move the plant outside. Once bloom starts, keep well watered and equally well drained. In fall, prune stems back to 2 inches and keep lightly watered.
Maypop (*Passiflora incarnata*)	Also called wild passionflower, maypop is the state flower of my home state of Tennessee. It's an excellent climber with beautiful white flowers that have showy blue stamens. The fruit is edible, too! To 6 feet long. Zones 6–8.	Plant maypop in full sun or light shade in well-drained soil. It may die back to the ground in winter, but it will regrow the following year. Because of its compact size and lovely flowers, this vine is a natural for growing on a trellis in a small garden.
Scarlet runner bean (*Phaseolus coccineus*)	Relatives of pole beans with bright orange-red flowers. To 8 feet long. Annual.	One of the easiest climbers to grow. I always plant my scarlet runner beans in planters in a spot where the flowers and beans are easy to harvest (I use the flowers in salads.) The vines cover an arbor or trellis in a very short time.
Black-eyed Susan vine (*Thunbergia alata*)	Daisylike orange, yellow, or white flowers with black centers and triangular leaves. Blooms June through October. To 6 feet long. Hardy in Zones 9–11.	Treat this vine like an annual, planting after all danger of frost is past. Black-eyed Susan vine is easy to grow from seed, taking just 8 weeks from seed to bloom, but I never have room or time, so I buy fully mature, blooming vines. Support them on a trellis or let them spill over a hanging basket. In fall, bring the plant inside and mist it regularly to provide humidity. It may live almost all winter before dying away. The Suzy Hybrids are dwarf versions and are best for hanging baskets or window boxes.

CHAPTER 4

VEGETABLES FOR SMALL SPACES

How much room does it take to grow vegetables? Less than you'd think! Choose compact varieties, grow plants vertically, and plant crops in containers. You can enjoy plenty of fresh produce from small-space gardens. With that first bite of a spicy radish, tender spinach leaf, or sweet, ripe tomato comes the heady feeling of success.

The Sky's the Limit!

If you garden in small spaces, does that mean you can only grow miniature vegetables? Certainly not! I've grown full-size vegetables in a garden that was only 1 foot wide. My 1-foot garden was 30 feet long and ran along the side of my house just outside the roof overhang. I used the rain gutters as anchors for wires so I could train plenty of crops vertically, with short crops filling in around them. (You may want to install L-brackets to support gutters if you try this.) A rain barrel provided lots of water to keep the garden growing strong.

When you think about growing vegetables in small spaces, break the rules. You don't have to plant vegetables in rows. Look for unconventional opportunities. Could you build a small triangular lasagna bed at the corner of your lawn? If so, you can grow a zucchini plant or two, plus pole beans or cucumbers trained up a tepee-style support. You don't even need a garden plot to grow vegetables—most vegetables grow very well in containers. By using your imagination and by growing *up*, you can know the pleasure of growing some of your own flavorful food in even the smallest of spaces.

When your kitchen garden space is limited, use wall space to grow cucumbers, runner beans, and sweet peas on trellises. Plant shallow-rooted crops in containers, leaving valuable ground space for deep-rooted crops such as tomatoes.

Vegetable Gardening Basics

The most important requirement for a vegetable garden is adequate sun, so scout your yard for the sunniest spots available. At a minimum, look for an area that receives 6 hours of sun each day. Morning-long sun with late-afternoon shade is preferable to morning shade and afternoon sun. Don't worry if the soil in that sunny patch is dense clay, loose sand, rock, or hardpan. Your vegetables will grow in nutrient-rich layers *on top* of those problematic soils.

If you have a choice, it's also nice to build your vegetable garden close to your house. That way, harvesting is convenient and close to a source of water. With a small-space garden, watering isn't a big chore. Chances are that on a small property, your garden will be close to a faucet and certainly within the reach of a standard garden hose.

Building a Bed for Vegetables

Many vegetable crops like rich soil, so a lasagna bed is a dream come true to these plants. Build beds for vegetables with plenty of rich materials such as compost, grass clippings, and leaf mold, and of course, always start with a base layer of thick pads of newspaper. If you're building a bed in fall to plant the following spring, I recommend that you build a nitrogen-rich pile and cover it with black plastic (see page 20 for more about this method). You'll have perfect planting conditions when you remove the plastic in spring.

Vegetables also need good drainage or they'll fall victim to root rots and general malaise. Because of this, build your bed at least 3 inches higher than the minimum needed to cover up the roots of transplants. This will ensure that roots will stay high and dry.

When you're laying out a lasagna bed for vegetables, make it 3 feet wide at the most. That way it will be easy for you to reach the center of the bed to harvest without straining your back or being tempted to step on the bed. (Don't smash those healthy roots!)

SMALL SECRETS FOR BIG SUCCESS

An Accent on Greens

Don't limit your veggies to the vegetable garden. Many vegetable plants these days have unusual and beautiful foliage and can be great accents for ornamental gardens or container plantings. For example, lettuce, mustard, kale, and spinach are all well suited to small ornamental gardens. Try 'Nagoya Garnish Red' flowering kale among perennials. The frilly, fan-shaped leaves are red with green edges, and they look stunning in a garden or in a container. 'Fizz E' endive produces heads with finely cut lacy leaves and cream-colored interiors. It looks terrific as a border to a foundation bed and can tolerate warm weather. 'Red Bor' kale has magenta leaves and grows only 18 to 24 inches. Try this flashy plant on your patio in a terra-cotta pot—it's a real attention-getter!

Buying Seeds and Plants

Packets of vegetable seeds are everywhere these days: garden centers, hardware stores, home centers, even in the grocery store and drugstore. When you're gardening on a small scale, though, it really pays not to buy seed on impulse. Instead, check some mail-order catalogs for varieties especially developed for compact growth and fast yields.

Many vegetable crops are easy to grow because they can be seeded directly into your lasagna beds; these include beans, carrots, lettuce, peas, and spinach. A few, such as peppers and tomatoes, require some dedication to start from seed because you need to start them

INDOOR SEED-STARTING: HIGH-TECH VERSUS LOW-TECH

I confess: I don't have to start my own vegetable or flower seedlings indoors. Because I own a business that requires so many transplants, I work with a grower who starts seeds of the varieties I want especially for me and sends them to me ready to go in six-packs.

It's a good thing, too, because my apartment is jammed with a 200-book garden library, computers, printers, fax, scanner, phones, and a tableful of cameras, projectors, and slide storage, plus cabinets of notes and reference tools. Not to mention that I travel to give 30 to 40 lectures a year and never put away my bags. Little pots of seedlings wouldn't stand a chance at my place!

That said, what about you, the gardener who doesn't have his or her own supplier but who wants to plant special small-space varieties available only by seed? I'll offer you two options: high-tech or homemade.

For high-tech seed-starting, there are a range of commercial products that include growing trays, a cover, and an automatic watering stand. If you follow the directions that come with this type of system, you

can't go wrong. I find the **APS** system sold by **Gardener's Supply Company** just about foolproof. I recommend this to people trying seed-starting for the first time and to gardeners who are too busy to tend seedlings every day. I still use it with a few things I start at home for fun. It's so easy to care for seedlings with this system, especially if you travel a lot. I take my system to a friend who plant-sits while I'm away. A unit that holds 30 to 40 plants will cost about $7 to $10.

For those of you who prefer the low-cost recycled approach, it's easy enough to find containers. The woman who delivers our mail often buys premade salads for lunch in the deli section of the local market. She's discovered that the large, clear plastic salad containers with attached lids serve beautifully as a simple seed-starting system. She punches some holes in the bottom and sides of the container, sets it on a plastic tray, fills it with seed-starting mix, and keeps it in a sunny window.

If you find yourself bitten by the seed-starting bug, check "Pat's Picks (Recommended Reading)" on page 274 for books with complete information on starting seeds and raising transplants indoors.

indoors on a sunny window or under lights. Before you make the decision to buy seeds and start these plants indoors, try shopping for transplants at your local garden center or nursery. Again, choose varieties with compact growth whenever you can—if you're not sure, ask someone on the staff for advice or check out my "Pat's Picks" lists later in this chapter. If you want to grow those specific varieties, you may need to start the seeds yourself. For tips on seed-starting, see "Indoor Seed-Starting: High-Tech versus Low-Tech" on the opposite page.

You probably won't have space to grow all the crops I describe in this chapter, so let your taste buds guide your choices—plant your favorite things to eat!

A Fresh Feast from Containers

Watching and waiting for harvest is a big part of the fun of growing vegetables, and when you grow vegetables in containers on your deck, balcony, or patio, you can enjoy the anticipation up close. Cucumbers growing in a self-watering pot with a twig trellis supporting the vines are a delight to look at and easy to pick. A patio tomato bordered by leaf lettuce in a planter box on a deck supplies fresh salad every day. Fast-growing radishes and slow-growing carrots are great companions for a sunny window box.

I've grown nearly every vegetable imaginable (except asparagus) in containers, and I've almost always been happy with the results. These are my secrets for successful vegetable production in containers:

- Choose varieties suitable for container growing.
- Match the crop to the right size container.
- Be sure the containers you use have plenty of drainage holes.
- Provide plenty of nutrients in the lasagna layers.
- Be sure your containers get plenty of sun.
- Never let your containers dry out.

When you plant veggies in containers, follow the directions on page 50 for planting con-

Pole beans, a patio tomato, and leaf lettuce share space happily in a large, deep container. Position the planter in full sun, and rotate it every few days if needed so all plants get their share of light.

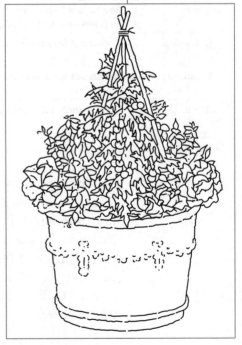

MIX-AND-MATCH CONTAINERS

Growing vegetables in containers may not take as much space as you think! The secret is knowing which crops need lots of root space and which ones can get by with less. Here are some guidelines for matching crops to the right size containers.

CROP	MINIMUM CONTAINER SIZE	GROWING TIPS
Beans, bush	8-inch pot for one to three plants.	A 2-foot-long window box will hold eight to ten bush bean plants.
Beans, pole	20-inch pot for a three-pole tepee with three to six plants.	Combine pole beans, a patio tomato, and leaf lettuce in a 24-inch container.
Beets	24-inch-long window box for eight plants.	Combine leaf lettuce, radishes, and beets in a 24- to 36-inch window box. Plant beets as the center row, spacing plants 6 inches apart.
Celery	10-inch pot for three plants.	Harvest leaves for seasoning or 3-inch baby stalks for snacking.
Carrots	36-inch window box with middle row of plants 2 inches apart.	Choose short, early-maturing variety for baby carrots. Plant radishes at same time for early harvest.
Chard, 'Bright Lights'	18-inch pot for five plants.	Harvest outside leaves. Beautiful!
Corn	Two to four 24-inch containers with six plants each for good pollination.	Plant small, early-maturing variety and pick ears when baby size.
Cucumbers	18-inch pot for four plants.	Choose variety with short vines and provide support.
Eggplant	12-inch pot for one plant.	For an interesting effect, plant two pots with varieties that bear fruits of different colors.
Garlic	10- to 12-inch pot for six plants.	In cold climates, plant pots in fall, leave buried in mulch, and uncover in early spring.

tainers lasagna-style. As far as I'm concerned, there's no such thing as too much compost when you're making lasagna layers in containers for vegetables. If I'm short on compost, I'll supercharge my containers as described on page 52. Some crops, such as beans, are light feeders and will do fine without extra fertility. If you're not sure whether a crop you're planting is a heavy or light feeder, check my recommendations in the crop descriptions later in this chapter.

CROP	MINIMUM CONTAINER SIZE	GROWING TIPS
Kale	8- to 10-inch pot for one plant.	If you use 'Dwarf Blue Curled Scotch', you can put three or four plants in a single 12-inch pot.
Leeks	10-inch pot for one plant.	For blanched stems, plant in bottom of pot in 2 inches of soil and fill in with soil as the plant grows.
Lettuce	12-inch pot for six plants.	Buy several varieties and plant three or four pots at once.
Melon	20-inch pot for one plant.	Train vine onto lattice or trellis. 'Early Dew' is a small, early melon.
Peas	18-inch pot for ten to twelve plants. Plant 1 inch apart.	Snap peas are fast, easy, and you eat the whole pod. Provide support.
Peppers	12-inch pot for one plant.	'Jingle Bells' is a mini sweet pepper with 2-inch fruits. 'Senorita' is my pick for a potted jalapeño.
Potatoes	20-inch pots, barrels, or baskets hold three plants each.	Place newspaper and 2 inches soil on bottom. Place potato pieces on soil and cover with 2 inches soil. As plants grow, cover with more soil.
Pumpkins	24-inch pot for one plant.	Provide strong support and choose small fruited variety.
Radishes	24-inch window box holds 20 plants.	Sow early spring and late summer. Try growing 'Easter Egg' for fun colors.
Spinach	10-inch pot for five plants.	Start a new pot every 10 days for extended harvest.
Squash, summer	20-inch pot for one plant.	Pick fruit when 6 to 10 inches long. Provide a water reservoir.
Tomatoes, determinate	15-inch pot for one plant; provide short stake.	Try an extra-early variety, 'Ruby Cluster,' and eat tomatoes in 58 days.
Tomatoes, indeterminate	12- to 15-inch pot with tall stake or trellis for training.	Lots of room around bottom of plant for intercropping.
Tomatoes, patio	10-inch pot for one plant.	Great for combination container plantings.

I also keep a close eye on my container vegetables, and if they're not performing as well as I think they should, I'll feed them with a dilute solution of liquid seaweed every 2 weeks. Keep track of these feedings so that you don't overdo it. Too much fertilizer may give you plants with incredibly lush foliage but not much fruit. Also, plants with too much lush, leafy growth may become the victims of insect pests such as aphids. It's a balancing act, but if you keep a close eye on your plants, you'll get it right.

Plant a Theme Garden

I think it's great fun to plant a small vegetable garden around a special theme, such as "My Top Crop." If you're a real tomato lover, you'd plant a cornucopia of tomatoes, including yellow and orange patio bush varieties, cherry tomatoes, and grape tomatoes. Have a passion for peppers? Plant everything from sweet frying peppers to a rainbow of colorful bell peppers accented with a sampling of exotic hot peppers. After all, with a small-space garden, your goal won't be to stock your pantry or freezer with a winter's worth of produce. So why not try something a little crazy—indulge your taste buds!

If you're a salad lover, you're in luck, because many salad crops take very little space. In my salad garden, I fit in assorted carrots, chives, cucumbers, lettuces, nasturtiums, radishes, spinach, and tomatoes. Plan your salad garden around the salad ingredients that you like best. Grow a variety of colored lettuces in a collection of unusual containers for a striking effect.

Ethnic themes are a great inspiration for creative small gardens. You can grow just the ingredients you need for a fresh, flavorful meal featuring your own produce. I've put together three great examples to get you started: a Tex-Mex garden, an Italian garden, and a French garden. I've included instructions on what to plant and how to plant it, and I've even thrown in some delicious recipes. Plant a garden with an ethnic theme, and then start experimenting. Pretty soon, you'll be sending me your terrific garden and recipe ideas!

A Tex-Mex Garden

Do you love spicy salsa and all those great dishes served at Tex-Mex restaurants? In a small garden, or even in and around a backyard patio, you can grow basil, bell peppers, cilantro, chile peppers, garlic, onions, oregano, thyme, and tomatoes. These are the main ingredients in fresh food with a Mexican flavor.

Making the Garden

If your patio is made of flagstone or patio block, you can use a pry bar to lift out stones or blocks to create three small openings, each one about 2 × 2 feet. Then build a mini lasagna bed on each opening. Start with wet newspaper, and layer on about 12 inches of organic materials: compost, shredded leaves, topsoil, grass clippings, and peat moss. In one bed, plant a full-size tomato plant. (Hammer a sturdy stake through the lasagna bed and into the soil below at planting time, so you can support the plant as it grows.) In another opening, plant a bell pepper, and in the third, plant several garlic bulbs and a handful of onion sets. Plant the chile pepper and the herbs in pots or in a narrow bed at the edge of the patio.

It won't be so easy to create planting spaces right on a concrete patio. Instead, you'll have to rely on narrow planting beds along the edges of your patio, or you'll have to plant all your ingredients in large containers or planter boxes. (See "Planting Containers" on page 50 for instructions on creating lasagna layers in a planter.)

To add vertical interest, place some of your pots of herbs and chile peppers on upturned pots to raise them to a higher level. This effect works especially well for the thyme: As it grows, the trailing stems will cascade over the side of its container.

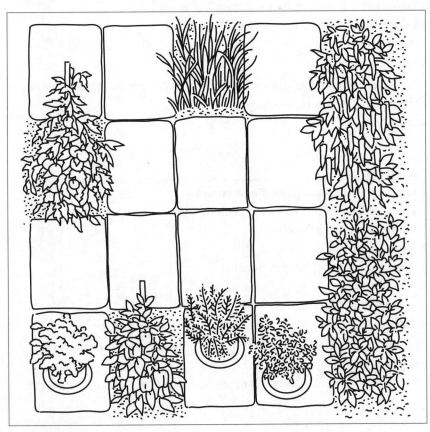

Plant tomatoes, peppers, onions, and herbs in and around your patio to create a Tex-Mex garden.

Making the Recipes

Yum! What could be better than salsa made with entirely fresh and flavorful veggies and herbs? Bring on the chips! I also enjoy serving both of these salsas over hot pasta. I bring the salsa to a boil in a small saucepan just before serving it.

Salsa Cruda

4 medium tomatoes, peeled and chopped
½ cup chopped onion
½ cup chopped celery
¼ cup chopped green bell pepper
¼ cup olive oil
1 or 2 green chile peppers, roasted, peeled, and chopped
1 teaspoon mustard seed
1 teaspoon crushed coriander seed
2 tablespoons red wine vinegar
Dash pepper
Salt

Combine all ingredients in a large bowl. Add salt to taste. Cover and chill several hours or overnight.

Makes 3 cups

Salsa Verde

2 medium tomatoes, peeled and cubed
1 green chile pepper, roasted, peeled, and chopped
1 medium onion, minced
2 large garlic cloves, minced
½ cup chopped parsley or cilantro
¼ cup olive oil
1 teaspoon salt
Pepper

Combine all ingredients in blender and blend until smooth. Add pepper to taste.

Makes about 16 ounces; serves 4 as a main course or 6 to 8 as a side dish

A Linguine Garden

All you need is a narrow garden bed along your foundation or shed to grow an Italian "linguine" garden filled with basil, garlic, onion, oregano, tomatoes, sweet frying peppers, zucchini, and parsley.

Making the Garden

To set up this garden, put trellises in place first to support the tomato vines. Then prepare the lasagna bed, using wet newspaper as the base layer and topping it with layers of organic ingredients. The bed can be as narrow as 1 foot and shouldn't be any wider than 3 feet. My linguine garden is 30 feet long and 1 foot wide. Plant a tomato plant at the base of each trellis, and fill in the bed with garlic, onions, pepper plants. Two zucchini plants will be all you need. Pot up basil, oregano, and parsley plants in large pots and set them in open spots between the tomato trellises.

Making the Recipes

These sauces are perfect for pasta. The herb and olive oil sauce is also delicious for dipping bread.

Herb and Olive Oil Sauce

½ cup olive oil
4 cloves garlic, minced
1 medium onion, chopped
¼ cup chopped parsley
¼ cup chopped basil

Combine all the ingredients in a food processor and pulse briefly at high speed. Serve over hot pasta.

Yields 6 ounces; serves 2 to 4

Long and narrow, a linguine garden produces a bounty of fresh vegetables and herbs for your favorite pasta sauces and Italian dishes.

Fresh Tomato Sauce

¼ cup olive oil

2 large cloves garlic, crushed

1 small onion, diced

6 medium tomatoes, peeled and cubed

Leaves from 1 stem parsley, minced

Leaves from 1 stem oregano, minced

Salt and pepper

Heat oil in a saucepan on medium heat. Add the garlic and onion and cook until clear. Add the tomatoes, parsley, oregano, and salt and pepper to taste. Cook on medium heat for 30 minutes. Serve over hot pasta.

Yields 18 to 24 ounces, depending on size of tomatoes; serves 4 to 6

A Taste of France

Vertical gardening is the key to growing tender peas and beans for a garden with a French theme.

Find a bit of room to grow petits pois (peas), haricots verts (filet beans), baby carrots, rosemary, parsley, tarragon, French sorrel, and garlic. Then you'll be ready to serve la belle cuisine. This garden can be planted against a foundation or fence, or in a free-standing bed.

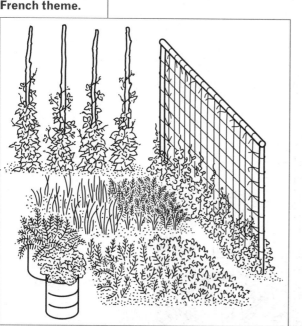

Making the Garden

The first step is to set up supports for the peas and beans. The peas can grow on a net trellis strung between two posts, while the beans can wind their way up bamboo or sapling poles set near the back of the garden. If you have enough space, plant the other crops in front of the tall beans and peas. If you're short on in-ground planting room, you can mount a window box for the baby carrots. Plant the rosemary and parsley in pots; that way you'll be able to bring them indoors for the winter, too. Use the lasagna bed space for the tarragon, sorrel, and garlic.

Baked Garlic and Tarragon Chicken with Petits Pois

1 whole roasting chicken

5 tarragon stems

4 garlic cloves

¼ cup olive oil

Salt and pepper

Petits pois

Remove any giblets from the cavity of the chicken. Rinse the chicken, inside and out, under running water, and pat dry. Stuff the chicken with 3 tarragon stems and 2 cloves of garlic. Crush the remaining 2 garlic cloves. Make a paste from the olive oil, the leaves from the remaining 2 tarragon stems, and the crushed garlic cloves. Add salt and pepper to taste. Brush the skin with the paste, and place the chicken on a rack in an open baking dish. Bake at 475°F for 1 hour. Remove from the oven and discard the stems and garlic from inside. Serve with freshly steamed petits pois.

Serves 4 to 6

Rosemary Lamb with Glazed Baby Carrots

12 baby carrots

¼ cup olive oil

2 garlic cloves, crushed

4 rosemary stems, bruised

12 baby lamb chops

Salt and pepper

¼ cup sugar

2 ounces butter

Leaves from 4 stems flat leaf parsley, chopped

Place carrots in a small saucepan in enough water to cover. Cook on medium heat until just tender. Heat the olive oil in a large, heavy skillet. Place the garlic and rosemary stems in the oil for 2 to 3 minutes to release their flavors. Remove the garlic and rosemary to a small dish. Place the lamb chops in the flavored oil in the skillet. Season with salt and pepper to taste. Lay the garlic cloves and rosemary on top of chops and cook until one side is brown. Turn the chops and remove from heat when meat is still pink. When carrots are fork-tender, drain and return to heat. Toss the carrots with sugar and butter, and cook until the sugar liquefies. Add the chopped fresh parsley.

Serves 4

Baked Cod with Sorrel Sauce and Haricots Verts

4 dozen haricots verts

2 tablespoons melted butter

1 tablespoons flour

1 cup half-and-half

1 cup fresh-picked sorrel leaves, chopped

Salt and pepper

Cod, four 6-ounce pieces

Scallion flowers

1 red pepper, cut into strips

Cook the beans in enough salted water to cover until fork-tender. In a heavy saucepan, combine melted butter and flour. Stir over medium heat until the flour is incorporated into the butter. Add half-and-half and sorrel leaves, stirring continuously with a wire whisk. To thin, add small amounts of water and continue whisking. Add salt and pepper to taste. Season cod to taste and bake at 425°F until flaky. Remove the fish to warm plates and serve with the sorrel sauce. Add scallion flowers and strips of red pepper for garnish.
Serves 4

Best Vegetables for Small Spaces

It's often said that knowledge is power, and this is certainly the case when it comes to choosing plants for your vegetable garden. The more you know about what a particular crop needs in order to thrive, the more likely you'll be happy with your harvest.

When you're gardening in small spaces, it's even more important to know all you can about plants because you don't have room, literally, for trial and error. Seed catalogs from reputable companies are good sources of information about timing your planting and other growing tips. In this section, I'll share my insights and ideas for getting the most from vegetables in small spaces.

BEANS

You can't buy the "just-picked" flavor of homegrown beans. Beans are fun to grow and take less space than you would imagine. You can produce enough fresh snap beans from a planting in a large pot or up a single pole to be able to serve beans with dinner once a week. I don't recommend growing dry beans in a small garden, however. You need to plant a considerable patch of dry beans to reap a worthwhile harvest, and I'd much rather devote that precious space to crops that I can enjoy freshly picked.

A bush bean border for a bed of annuals looks pretty and puts the plants in easy reach for harvesting. Try a colorful mixed planting of purple beans, green beans, and yellow wax beans.

Bush Beans

Bush beans are ideal for small spaces. You can plant them in a strip just 3 inches wide at the edge of the garden, in a window box, or in a double row in a narrow garden. You can even tuck them here and there in a flower garden. These pretty plants grow about 12 inches high and bear purple, yellow, or green beans. Pick a variety that matures in a short time, and make the most of your space by planting small patches every 2 weeks for an extended harvest.

PAT'S PICKS ~ BUSH BEANS

'Brittle Wax' (52 days from seed to harvest): Huge, early crops. Slightly curved, round yellow pods grow to 7 inches.

'Burpee's Stringless Green Pod' (50 days): Exceptional flavor and entirely stringless green bean. Very high yield.

'Bush Blue Lake' (55 days): The standard by which other beans are judged. An improved green bean from an old variety, it has few problems and continues producing pods as long as you keep beans picked.

'Gold Mine' (55 days): Unusually upright plants are great for small gardens. High yields of clusters of 5-inch-long yellow wax beans.

'Golden Rocky' (65 days): A longer wait for full maturity pays off with the increased harvest time. You get an abundance of wonderful-tasting golden yellow beans on 25-inch plants.

'Jade' (60 days): Pencil-straight green pods with a long season of production.

'Nugget' (52 days): A sturdy bush plant growing 15 to 20 inches tall with impressive yields of round, bright yellow beans with a rich, buttery taste.

'Royal Burgundy' (60 days): A good producer in cool-summer areas. The beautiful purple pods turn green when cooked.

'Sequoia' (53 days): Delicious, stringless, 5-inch purple Romano type that cooks to bright green. Tolerates cool weather.

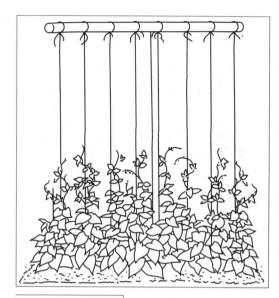

If there's a metal clothesline support in your yard, build a narrow lasagna bed beneath it, use stakes and strings for a trellis, and plant pole beans.

Pole Beans

Plant pole beans at the base of a fence, trellis, or other support at the back of an existing garden. Or, you can create a minibed just 6 inches wide especially for your beans. I grow mine on tepees made of 6- to 8-foot bamboo poles tied together at the top. You can even grow pole beans up the side of your house with the support of a simple trellis. Buy two or three different kinds of pole beans and mix the seeds in one planting. If you grow scarlet runner beans, you can eat the flowers *and* the beans!

French (Filet) Beans

French beans are varieties of snap beans that should be picked when they're very slender. If you let them grow to normal snap bean size, they become tough. But catch them young, and they're the tastiest, most tender beans you'll ever eat.

Site and Soil. Beans need at least half a day of sun, and they like full sun best. Good drainage is important, so don't skimp on bed height if the soil under the bed is heavy or poorly drained. Beans will do well in rich or poor soil conditions, so a lasagna bed should provide everything they need.

Planting. It's best to plant beans from seed. They won't germinate well in cold soil, so be patient. Wait until the danger of frost is past

PAT'S PICKS ~ POLE BEANS

'Kentucky Blue' (73 days from seed to harvest): A cross between 'Kentucky Wonder' (my grandmother's favorite) and 'Blue Lake', combining the best qualities of both. Produces large (6- to 7-inch), straight pods on vines that can reach 8 feet. Great in the back of the garden on a tepee or a trellis.
'Romano' (60 days): Long, flat pods with rich flavor. A stringless variety that freezes well.

'Selma-Zebra' (51 days): Delicious and eye-catching green-and-purple pods that come up quickly.
'Violet Podded Stringless' (70 days): Germinates well in cool soil with a very abundant harvest. Purple pods turn green when cooked.
'Spanish Musica' (62 days): Vigorous vines that bear broad, flat, meaty pods with rich taste and a nice crunch.

and the soil is warm (at least 60°F). Sow seeds 1 to 2 inches deep, spaced 2 to 3 inches apart. (Simply push them into the soft soil of your lasagna garden.) Space pole beans at least 4 inches apart, and set up your trellis or other support before you plant. The seeds will germinate in 6 to 10 days.

Growing Tips. Beans in a rich lasagna bed need little care. Bean plants have shallow roots, so keep the soil constantly moist. Don't overwater, though, because too much water may cause pods to drop. Once seedlings emerge, add an extra top mulch to conserve moisture and suppress weeds.

Don't touch your plants when the leaves are wet from rain or dew, because this can spread disease problems. If you've had problems in the past with bean leaf beetles, flea beetles, or other bean pests, cover the plants with floating row cover as soon as seedlings emerge, and leave it on until it's time to start harvesting. Tuck the edges of the cover into the soil so there are no openings where insects could sneak through.

Harvesting. Pick snap beans when they're about as thick as a pencil. Keep picking every 2 or 3 days, or the plants will tend to stop

---

PAT'S PICKS — FILET BEANS

'Astrel' (65 days from seed to harvest): A slim, stringless baby filet with unstoppable production and high yields.

'Maxibel' (50 days): A stringless, tender, firm-textured high yielder. Produces slender, 7-inch beans.

'Triumph de Farcy' (48 days): Slender, crunchy pods with a distinct flavor. Early-bearing, productive, and can be harvested often. Pods grow 3 to 6 inches long.

PAT'S SMALL SPACE STORIES

Budge's Bean Brainstorms

My friend Budge Loakley was both a fly-fishing expert and a great vegetable gardener. My favorites were his "one-pole pole beans." In a sunny spot at the side of his yard, Budge had erected a single 12-foot stake and planted a few pole bean seeds at the base. It was that simple—just a single pole of beans, taking up virtually no garden space. (I'm not sure how he harvested the beans at the very top, though!)

Budge made good use of his fly-tying skills to create other bean supports, as well. One that can work well in a small garden is his bent-pipe support. Using copper pipe and elbow fittings to make two horseshoe-shaped supports, he tied long lengths of twine about 6 inches apart to each support for his climbers. Budge harvested excellent beans all summer from his two curtains of pole beans, in a minimum of space.

producing new pods. If you can see seeds bulging inside the pods, you've waited too long! Pick filet beans when they're very skinny. Pinch pods off with your fingers. Don't pull on the pods or you may break off whole sections of the plant.

In the Kitchen. Beans are always best when you cook them right after picking. Wash the beans and leave them whole, or slice them lengthwise into long strips or crosswise into 1-inch pieces. Place in a saucepan with water to cover. Bring to a gentle boil and cook until just tender. Leave the lid off for the first 5 minutes of cooking for best color. Then cover and check every 5 minutes until they're as tender as you like. (After you've done this once, you'll know the right amount of time for the future, too.) Here are my tips for dressing up beans: Add a little butter, salt, and pepper; spritz them with lemon juice and sprinkle with minced fresh parsley; top beans with crisp bacon pieces; or sprinkle beans with minced fresh basil, marjoram, dill weed, savory, or thyme.

BEETS

Homegrown beets are unexpectedly sweet and rich-tasting. We beet-lovers use both beet greens and roots for cooking. Borscht is my favorite beet dish, and my daughter Mickey is a proud winner of the "Borscht Belt" from a local farmer's market contest for the best recipe for borscht (see "In the Kitchen" on the opposite page). Now I know that not everyone likes beets. If you're not bullish on beets, don't grow them. Mickey won't mind!

Site and Soil. Beets grow best in full sun, but you can also try them in light shade. Plant them in a mature, well-drained lasagna bed, or grow them in containers.

Planting. Plant beet seeds in early spring. Sow seeds ½ inch deep and 4 inches apart. Mix in a little radish seed, and the fast-germinating radishes will serve as row markers until the beets appear—beets take a week or two to germinate. Keep the soil consistently moist. Don't sow seeds

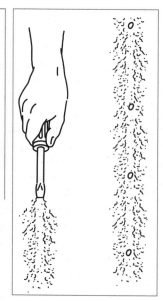

A pointed tool such as an old screwdriver or a claw-type weeder works well for scratching shallow furrows in which to plant seeds of beets or other root crops.

too thickly; beet seeds are unusual in that each knobby "seed" you plant will produce a cluster of seedlings. Thin each cluster to a single plant when the seedlings are 2 to 3 inches tall. Get an early start by starting seeds inside in peat pots. Where I live, plants started in February indoors are ready to set out in the garden in April, with a late-May or early-June harvest. Here in my Zone 5 garden, I also sow a crop in late June or early July to harvest in late August or September.

Growing Tips. If flea beetles like to feast in your garden, cover beet plants with floating row cover as soon as seedlings emerge, and leave it on until it's time to start harvesting. Tuck the edges of the cover into the soil so there are no openings where insects could sneak through. Take the cover off when the weather heats up, because beets exposed to high temperatures may form light-colored roots or roots with internal rings.

Harvesting. Pick the tasty beet greens while you're waiting for the beets to mature. Harvest the roots when they are about 2 inches wide for the best flavor and texture.

In the Kitchen. Beet greens are wonderful steamed or boiled in salted water with a little olive oil added. When I began growing beets, I didn't even eat the roots, only the tops. I used to boil the roots and use the beet water to dye eggs for Easter, muslin for decorating, and eggs for pickling. Now I've learned to love beet salad. To prepare it, combine shredded raw beets with a dressing of olive oil, red wine vinegar, and sugar. (For each cup of shredded beets, use 1 tablespoon of oil, 1 tablespoon of vinegar, 1 teaspoon of sugar, and salt to taste.) If you like a bit of bite in your beets, add a few drops of hot pepper sauce. And of course you'll want to know Mickey's recipe for her prize-winning soup: Peel and chop 4 to 6 tender beets and boil them until they're fork-tender. At the same time, sauté 2 tablespoons of diced celery and 2 tablespoons of onion in 1 tablespoon of butter. Let the beets and the celery and onion mixture cool, and then add them to a food processor with 2 cups of chicken broth. Puree until smooth. Add salt and pepper to taste. You can serve this borscht hot or cold.

PAT'S PICKS — BEETS

'Chicago Red Hybrid' (49 days from seed to harvest): Most hybrids mature to a uniform size all at once, but this variety will produce roots of several different sizes, so you can enjoy baby beets very early and continue the harvest.

'Little Ball' (56 days): Tasty, smooth, and dark red. A tiny, tender gourmet baby beet that's hard to beat.

'Monogram Globe' (60 days): Each seed produces only one seedling, so thinning is a thing of the past. Baby 'Globe' beets can be picked early.

'Red Ace Hybrid' (54 days): Has the best color with dark red roots. Does well in most soils and especially good in dry seasons.

A PLACE FOR ASPARAGUS

Think growing asparagus is impossible in a small space? You don't need as much space as you might think. My asparagus bed is 4 × 10 feet and it produces enough for two people to eat as much as they want, plus a little extra to freeze or give to the neighbors. I think it's worth the space it takes up for the rewarding experience of eating tender raw asparagus spears or steamed or grilled asparagus with fresh lemon.

Yes, you can plant asparagus lasagna-style, without digging, tilling, or weeding. Mark your site (be sure it will get at least 6 hours of sun per day), making it 4 feet wide by as long as you can afford. Cover it with a thick layer of wet newspaper, followed by other organic ingredients with alternating layers of peat moss or compost until the bed is 10 to 12 inches deep. Let the bed rest over winter. Order crowns from a reputable mail-order supplier, and opt for 2- and 3-year-old crowns—they'll produce a better first harvest than 1-year-old crowns will. Plant the crowns in rows 2 feet apart, setting crowns 18 inches apart. To prepare a row, open two shallow trenches 3 inches apart along the bed. This leaves a little ridge down the center of the row. Place the crowns on the ridge, spreading their roots evenly into the trenches. Cover the crowns with 2 to 3 inches of a soil-and-compost mix. As shoots grow the first year, keep adding more mix until the crowns are 4 inches below the surface of the soil.

To get the most from your small-space asparagus bed, after you harvest the main crop, broadcast some leaf lettuce seed over the bed. Make several cuttings from the lettuce, and then allow it to go to seed. I've also broadcast flower seeds over the bed— tall zinnias, marigolds, and cosmos. They produced wonderful splashes of color among the ferny asparagus stems. Be sure to mulch any open areas of the bed with grass clippings during summer to keep weeds at bay.

In fall, cut the asparagus fronds back after they die. Every fall I feed the bed with a 1-inch layer of composted manure topped with chipped leaves, and I think that's the secret to the bed's strong production. In cold-winter areas, mulch the bed with straw for the first few winters to protect the crowns. This is important when the bed is young because the crowns aren't too far below the soil surface. I don't bother with the straw mulch on my established bed.

BROCCOLI

One large head of broccoli is sufficient for preparing a nice side dish for the dinner table. The plants will keep producing small side heads after the first cutting, so even a small broccoli planting can keep you supplied with fresh broccoli for many weeks.

Site and Soil. Save a spot in full sun for broccoli. A 1- or 2-year-old lasagna bed should supply plenty of fertility. When planting broccoli in older beds, layer on 2 to 3 inches of compost before planting.

Planting. Start seed indoors 6 to 8 weeks before your last expected frost date, or buy transplants. Harden off transplants for 2 weeks before planting. In the South, plant broccoli in fall, because it doesn't do well in hot conditions.

Growing Tips. I set out each transplant with a cutworm collar like the one shown in the illustration at right to prevent those pesky caterpillars from chomping on the stems. I also apply mulch right away to keep the soil cool. If you have a long spell of cold, rainy weather, the heads on your broccoli may rot. If they do, cut off the main head and watch for a new flush of small side heads.

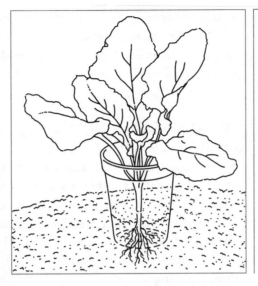

Protect broccoli and other transplants with a cutworm collar—a paper cup with the bottom cut out. Carefully slip a collar over each transplant as soon as you plant it. Push the collar into the soil so that the bottom inch is below the soil surface.

Harvesting. Check your plants daily once you notice that heads have formed. Don't hold out for huge heads: Broccoli has the best flavor and texture before the flower heads begin to open. Use a sharp knife to cut the stem on an angle 4 to 6 inches below the head. (Cutting on an angle is important because this will allow water to run off the cut stem. Otherwise, the stem may stay wet from rain or dew and start to rot.) Keep watering after the main harvest, to stimulate the growth of smaller side heads.

In the Kitchen. For a colorful, crunchy salad, combine chopped raw broccoli flowers with diced red peppers and your favorite Italian dressing. To stretch it when unexpected guests arrive, add anything

PAT'S PICKS ~ BROCCOLI

'Rosilind' (60 to 65 days from transplant to harvest): Early maturing, with a purple head. My neighbor, Jerry Seigle, grows this pretty broccoli in his small garden. 'Rosilind' is so lovely that you'll be tempted to leave it in the garden to go to seed, but don't—it's truly delicious. Once you cut the main head, side shoots will continue developing well into fall.

'Small Miracle' (56 days): Territorial Seed Company developed this little broccoli plant especially for small gardens. Each 12-inch plant produces a small round flower head, and plants can be spaced 8 inches apart. The finely beaded and dark green heads measure 6 to 8 inches and have an exceptionally mild flavor.

else that crunches: celery, carrots, cucumbers, green or yellow summer squash, radishes, scallions, snow peas, or raw snap beans. How about chopped nuts, raisins, or dates? Open a can of bamboo shoots, bean sprouts, or water chestnuts—drain and rinse them, then chop and toss.

CABBAGE

As a rule, it takes a lot of bed space to grow cabbage. However, if you want to experience the pleasure of growing this interesting vegetable in a small garden, try a compact variety that forms firm little heads. Or try Chinese cabbage: It forms an upright head, so you can space plants more tightly than regular cabbage.

Site and Soil. Choose a sunny, well-drained spot for cabbage. If you're planting cabbage in a mature bed, add a layer of extra compost before planting.

Planting. I recommend buying cabbage transplants at the garden center in spring, or you can start seeds inside 8 to 10 weeks before planting time. You can start planting cabbage about 4 weeks before your last expected spring frost. If you want to grow cabbage for a fall crop, sow seed directly in the garden by midsummer. Cover the seeded area with a board or a light scattering of straw to keep the seedbed moist and cool. Check frequently, and when the seed germinates, remove the covering.

Growing Tips. Use cutworm collars to protect transplants from cutworms (see the illustration on page 121). Cover plants with a floating row cover to protect against cold nights and to keep out flea beetles and cabbage maggot flies. Tuck the edges of the cover into the soil so there are no openings where insects could sneak through. Mulch around roots to keep soil moist. In the first few weeks after transplanting you can water your plants with a dilute solution of fish emulsion for an extra nutrient boost.

Harvesting. Once heads are fully formed, you can begin harvesting by cutting the stem just above the lowest leaves. If you want to spread out your

Chinese cabbage fits compactly into a garden bed behind a border of bushy annuals such as dwarf zinnias or marigolds.

PAT'S PICKS ~ CABBAGE

'Dynamo' (70 days from transplant to harvest): Round blue-green heads average half the size of normal early varieties. Space plants 8 to 12 inches apart. Once the heads mature, they can remain in the garden for up to 2 months without splitting. Flavor improves with age.

'Early Jersey Wakefield' (65 days): An heirloom variety with conical, solid, 1-pound heads. Matures in only 2 months.

'Gonzales' (55 days): This early cabbage produces firm, small heads.

After the head is harvested, you'll get a second harvest of cabbages the size of tennis balls.

'Minuet' (48 days): A Chinese cabbage that produces heads only 9 inches tall and 7 inches wide and has a light, sweet taste. Space 12 inches apart.

'Red Express' (63 days): A super-early cabbage that produces small but solid heads on compact plants. Can be planted 8 inches apart to produce single-serving minicabbages.

harvest, twist some of the cabbage heads a half-turn and leave them in place. This breaks some of the roots, so the plants won't be prone to taking up too much water and splitting open. You can then leave the heads for about a week before harvesting.

If you cut the stems of the cabbage plants high, leaving at least 2 inches of stem, the plants may form small side heads that will be fine to harvest and eat as well.

In the Kitchen. Cabbage is a unique vegetable in that it can be stored for long periods of time, either in the garden or under refrigeration. It can be eaten raw, cooked, or pickled. It's indispensable in coleslaw, sauerkraut, and egg rolls, not to mention stir-fry, cabbage rolls, and soup.

I will travel miles out of my way for good coleslaw. The coleslaw we serve at The Potager is so good that I eat it every time my daughter Mickey prepares it. And my personal favorite coleslaw dressing is a mixture of 1 cup of mayonnaise, 1 tablespoon of cider vinegar, and ¼ cup of milk. Whisk the mixture until it's smooth and fluffy. Then finely grate 2 cups of cabbage and 1 carrot, season to taste with salt and pepper, mix in the dressing, and chill before serving. Other options: Add sugar, minced onion, green pepper, celery seed, or poppy seed to suit your taste. This recipe is the closest I can come to the coleslaw my mother made. I've almost duplicated that flavor I remember, but something is missing. Perhaps the perfect slaw will have to remain just a fond memory from my youth.

CARROTS

Baby carrots are the only type of carrots I bother to grow. I don't like the work involved in tending a crop of full-size carrots through the season—thinning, weeding, mulching for winter. It's easy to tuck baby carrots into lasagna beds, containers, or even a window box, and you only have to wait a couple of months from seeding to delicious harvest.

Site and Soil. Carrots like full sun and loose, sandy soil. It's best to plant them in a mature, fairly deep lasagna bed. I use layers of sand and peat moss in addition to other organic materials in a bed where I plan to grow carrots to help ensure that the bed will be very loose and open. If you grow long carrots, it's important that they will be able to stretch their roots without coming in contact with rocks and heavy soil. Obstacles like these result in crooked, distorted carrots. For small gardens, be sure to choose a carrot variety that takes up little space. If you don't have any space in a mature bed, try growing baby carrots in containers.

Planting. Plant seed in spring as soon as your beds are thawed and crumbly. Carrots are a cool-season crop, and they'll produce bitter, woody roots in hot weather. Carrot seed is tiny, but it's important not to overseed; otherwise you'll end up stuck with the painstaking task of thinning the flimsy seedlings. Before planting, water the bed thoroughly. Mix sand with the seed and broadcast it lightly over the bed or container to get an even sowing. Because carrots are slow to germinate, mix some radish seeds in also. The radishes will pop up in a day or two, marking the area and

PAT'S PICKS ~ CARROTS

'Little Finger' (60 days from seed to harvest): A true baby carrot bred to be eaten young. This is one of the best carrots for small gardens, and it does well in containers. You can have several crops coming along at different times by planting them 2 weeks apart.

'Scarlet Nantes' (68 days if you let them mature to 5 to 6 inches): I can't resist eating them early because they are the sweetest variety. The tops on 'Nantes' are short, which is good for small gardens.

'Short and Sweet' (68 days): 4-inch roots with bright color to the core. Bred for heavy or poor soil.

'Thumbelina' (60 days): The whole carrot only measures 1 to 1½ inches at maturity, so one carrot is one bite. 'Thumbelina' is suited to close plantings, container growing, and growing in heavy soils.

breaking the surface crust for the delicate carrot seedlings. Carrot seedlings may not appear for 2 weeks, and they'll still be quite small when the radishes are ready to pick, so you'll get two crops from the same growing space. In cool summer areas, sow seed every 3 weeks for an extended harvest. If you live in an area with hot summers, stop sowing in midspring and start again in

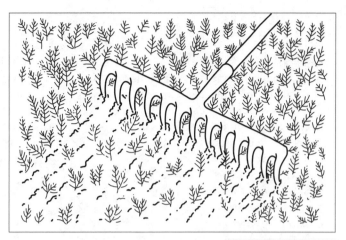

midsummer for a fall crop. Wherever you live, stop sowing about 2 months before your first predicted frost.

Growing Tips. After sowing seed, mist the bed lightly to keep it moist. Even a normal sprinkling from a hose can wash the light carrot seed out of place. Standard recommendations for thinning carrots say to space the plants 2 to 3 inches apart, but I think that leaves too much open space for weeds to invade. I thin seedlings to stand ½ inch apart. When the roots have grown to about 1 inch long, pull and eat some to allow space for the rest of the crop to expand.

Harvesting. Harvest begins as soon as carrots are 1 to 2 inches long. These first tiny carrots will not be a deep, rich orange—that color develops later. As soon as carrots have a deep orange color, it's time to harvest the rest of the crop. Loosen the soil around roots with a garden fork (or with an old meat fork, if you're growing carrots in a container) so you don't break off the tops.

In the Kitchen. I'll rub the soil off and eat carrots right in the garden, but carrots truly shine in the kitchen. They liven up salads, soups, stews, and cakes. I like them as a side dish with most meats, and I can make a meal of carrot sticks.

I use a clean plastic scrubber to wash my carrots and thus avoid peeling them. Cook carrots until they're tender in just enough water to cover. Add salt to the cooking water if desired, or add a tablespoon of sugar for a sweeter taste. For sweet glazed carrots, drain the cooking water from 2 cups of sliced, cooked carrots and add ¼ cup of white or brown sugar and ½ stick of butter. Continue cooking over low to medium heat until the butter melts and the sugar dissolves.

It's a common mistake to oversow carrots. To open up a dense forest of carrot seedlings, draw a rake or hand cultivator gently through the stand for a first, quick thinning. Follow up with hand thinning until the plants are 2 to 3 inches apart.

Compact Corn

If you thought that only gardeners with plenty of wide-open spaces could grow corn, I've got the news you've been waiting to hear—there's a new corn that fits in a small-space garden. Territorial Seed Company has come out with 'Bonus', a baby-corn variety that grows only 5 feet tall and puts out as many as four 2- to 4-inch cobs per plant.

Planting corn in raised "hills" is a good idea, and with a lasagna garden, the whole bed is a hill! If you're planting corn in a new bed, add extra layers to the area where you plan to plant the corn (an extra 5 to 6 inches is good).

Corn is a nutrient-hungry crop, so use lots of compost or add some fish meal to the planting area. Plant three to five seeds in a circle, keeping seeds about 4 inches apart. Make hills of seeds 8 to 12 inches apart.

If you want an early corn with regular-size cobs on short plants, try Territorial's 'Earlivee'. Sow seeds 8 inches apart in four short rows that are 12 inches apart. You'll need four rows for pollination. Stokes also offers 'Fresh Start', an early corn for small gardens. It germinates well in cool soil and is ready to eat in 62 to 67 days.

I've also planted regular-size corn in half-barrels and 24-inch pots. As long as I planted four containers' worth, pollination was very good.

Although I don't reap a big crop from my small corn plantings, I think corn is so much fun to grow that I don't care. I plant something around the base of the stalks that will climb, because I love this "living support" idea; pole beans, baby cucumbers, and vining nasturtium all work well. If you plant a vigorous pole bean like 'Kentucky Blue', it will climb up one side of the stalks and down the other. 'Smart Pickle' cucumber isn't so prolific, but at 3 to 5 feet, it's the perfect size for a small cornstalk. I also use the cornstalks for decorations in October and November.

CUCUMBERS

So easy and quick to plant and grow, cucumbers are also natural space savers in both bush and vine form. I like to grow mine on a bean tower mixed with other vining crops. You can also plant them on an A-frame trellis made from scrap lumber or bamboo strung with twine, or on a vertical trellis made from wire strung between fence posts. You can even nail netting to a fence to support cukes. Use your imagination!

Site and Soil. Cucumbers need lots of sun, good drainage, and rich soil, whether they're grown in the ground or in a container. Full sun is best, but you can get by with a site that is shady for a couple of hours in the afternoon as long as it receives full morning sun. You can also grow a cucumber in a 6-inch pot and train it up a support.

Planting. Cucumbers are very tender, so wait to plant seeds or plants until the soil is warm and all chance of frost is past. Sow seeds about 1 inch deep, 6 to 8 inches apart. Two plants will produce enough slicing cukes to feed four people. Provide protection from wind by planting cucumbers against a sheltering fence or wall. For earlier cukes, start seeds indoors in peat pots about 3 weeks before you plan to plant them outdoors. To extend your harvest in the other direction, sow a second crop outdoors about 5 weeks after you plant the first seeds or transplants outside.

I like to grow cucumbers in containers, too. I plant two seeds in a 6-inch pot, and if both seeds germinate, I snip off the weaker seedling with scissors. I train the vine up a support. Self-watering pots are great for thirsty cucumbers.

Growing Tips. Keep the bed evenly moist until true leaves appear. Consistent watering is important to prevent the fruits from becoming bitter. Water cucumbers growing in pots daily. I rely on regular mulching to keep the roots cool and moist. Mulch with compost that includes some composted manure to feed the soil at the same time.

Harvesting. Use scissors to clip the fruits from the vine. Keep cucumbers picked, and they keep on coming. Let fruits sit on the vine, and you'll end up with big, overripe, unappealing cucumbers, and the vine will stop producing.

In the Kitchen. Refrigerate young cucumbers immediately after picking and they'll keep for up to 3 weeks. One of my favorite cucumber recipes comes from my friend Doug Bury. To prepare this terrific dish, slice and salt 3 cups of cucumbers in a bowl. Place a heavy weight on the slices and wait 1 to 2 hours.

PAT'S PICKS ~ CUCUMBERS

'Jade' (54 days from seed to harvest): Early, slender Asian cucumber. Great in small spaces on a trellis. These cucumbers have vigorous vines and a gourmet-quality taste. It's a nonbitter variety with thin-skinned fruit and fresh flavor. **'Orient Express'** (64 days): My favorite. Its long, slim fruit grows well on small trellises. You can pick this cucumber at any stage. **'Salad Bush'** (56 days): A real space saver, this compact, bush-type plant is perfect for containers or to tuck into the front of the border. Each fruit is 8 inches long and has dark green skin. The taste is unbeatable.

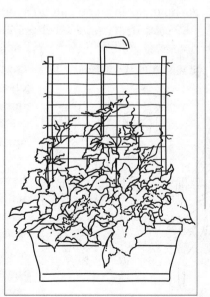

My golfing days are over, so I've turned my golf clubs into plant supports. Potted cucumbers supported by a grid of string can use the extra support a 9-iron has to offer.

Drain the liquid from the bowl. Rinse the cucumbers with water and drain again. Stir together about ½ cup each of sour cream, heavy cream, and mayonnaise. Then add 3 tablespoons each of chopped fresh chives and dill. Mix the creamy sauce into the cucumbers, add salt and pepper to taste, and chill before serving. For a different taste, add 1 tablespoon each of white wine vinegar and sugar to the cream mixture. A third variation: Add rings of sweet onion or green and red pepper strips.

GARLIC

Garlic is a fascinating crop, planted in fall in most areas for harvest the following summer. Because it ties up bed space for such a long time, some small-space gardeners don't bother growing their own garlic. I wouldn't be without it, though, in The Potager kitchen.

Site and Soil. Garlic needs full sun and a well-drained site, or it will rot during the wet spring thaw. A mature, rich lasagna bed is the best choice; a bed started in spring will be ready for garlic planting in fall.

Planting. For best results in cold climates, plant individual cloves in fall, pushing them 1 to 2 inches into the soil and about 6 inches apart. Choose a hard-neck type, and select large, firm cloves with undamaged skins for planting. The cloves will send out roots in the fall, which will help hold them in place when the soil freezes and thaws in winter and spring. Topgrowth starts in early spring. If you plant your garlic in spring, you can do so as soon as the ground has thawed.

Growing Tips. In early summer, garlic plants will produce a thin flowering stalk topped by a pointed flower head. This stem is called the scape, and it's a good idea to cut it off so the plant will focus its energy on enlarging the bulb. Water garlic well until late June, then cut back on watering.

Garlic and carrots make good companions when planted together in early spring. You can harvest garlic greens as desired. The garlic bulbs won't grow very large, so they won't interfere with the developing carrots.

Harvesting. If you planted garlic in spring, it won't form large bulbs because it wasn't exposed to winter chilling. So harvest the greens as you need them, using scissors to trim the leaves.

For fall-planted garlic, uproot one bulb and break it open when the leaves start to turn brown in midsummer. If the cloves haven't formed separate segments yet, your garlic isn't ready to harvest. Wait

PAT'S PICKS ~ GARLIC

'Russian Red' (midseason): I buy my garlic bulbs directly from growers and this is my favorite for its spicy, hot flavor.

'Italian White' (midseason): This New York State hardneck is for all of the Northeast and cold regions of the country.

another week or two, and check another bulb. Don't leave your garlic in the ground too long or the skin will begin to break down. Hang the bulbs in a dark, airy place for a few weeks to cure. Then trim the leaves and roots, and store the garlic in a mesh bag.

In the Kitchen. Garlic is now welcome even in the most timid cook's kitchen. Once you learn how to roast a head of garlic and spread the sweet pulp on a crust of bread, you'll be hooked. I love garlic in pasta dishes. To prepare one of my favorite dishes, cook 1 pound of your favorite pasta, drain it, place it back in the pot, and add 2 tablespoons of olive oil. Toss the pasta and oil to coat, and set it aside to cool. In a heavy skillet, place 2 tablespoons of olive oil, 4 cloves of crushed garlic, and ½ cup of minced onion. Cook and stir until the onion is transparent. Add 1 pound of fresh spinach, salt and pepper to taste, and ¼ cup of water. Cover the mixture and let it steam for 1 minute. Remove the lid and stir. The spinach should be wilted. Add the contents of the skillet to the pasta and toss. Serve with grated Parmesan. This will serve four hungry people.

If you grow garlic for greens, they'll make a nice garnish—use them in place of chives. Or add them to sauces and pasta. You can even whip up a garlic-greens pesto by blending the greens with olive oil, Parmesan, and walnuts or pine nuts in a blender.

KALE FROM RUSSIA WITH LOVE

Kale is a hearty plant that you might not think of for a small garden, but I plant one particular variety of kale in all of my small vegetable gardens. My kale of choice is 'Red Russian', a delicate, colorful kale with purple stems and deep gray-green, non-curled leaves that have purple leaf veins and toothed edges. With 'Red Russian', you'll be cutting baby leaves to add to salads or stir-fry a mere 25 days after seeding. In 50 days, mature leaves are ready to be picked for steaming or using in salads. Besides its delicious taste, 'Red Russian' is a beautiful edging plant and a unique container plant.

Plant kale in full sun or in light shade in hot-summer regions. Thin plants to 6 inches apart in very small spaces or to 12 inches apart if you have some wiggle room.

Blanching leeks produces the most tender, whitest stems, and in a lasagna bed, it's easy to do. Just push the loose soil of the bed up around the stems two or three times during the season as the stem elongates.

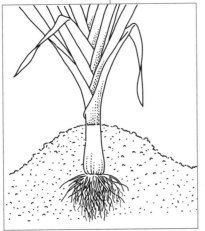

LEEKS

I don't grow onions in my small gardens, but I do find space for their cousins the leeks. Leeks don't form bulbs; instead we eat the thick white stems. Leeks are milder and sweeter tasting than onions and are best known for the fabulous flavor they lend to potato soup. Leeks make a good companion for beans and grow best in cold regions.

Site and Soil. Leeks need full sun and loose, moist, but well-drained soil with added organic material—a lasagna bed is perfect. Because you'll be "hilling" soil around the leeks as they grow, it's best to plant them in a mature bed where the lasagna layers have had a chance to break down. Leeks also like lots of nitrogen, so add some alfalfa meal or pesticide-free cottonseed meal to the soil before planting.

Planting. Leek seedlings are delicate, and the plants need to grow for a long season. For best results, start seeds indoors in peat pots 4 to 6 weeks before your last expected frost. Don't rush transplanting—allow the seedlings to reach at least 4 inches tall indoors. To plant leek seedlings, open a trench 2 inches deep in the top of the lasagna bed. Then scoop out individual planting holes in the trench for each transplant, setting the plants 6 inches apart.

Growing Tips. As the leeks grow, hill soil up around the lower two-thirds of the plants. I do this two or three times during the season. Hilling blanches the stem, and the white stem is the edible part of the plant.

Harvesting. Leeks can stay in the garden until you are ready to use them. To harvest, use a garden fork to loosen the soil around the plant. Grasp the leaves and uproot the entire plant.

In the Kitchen. To prepare leeks for cooking, cut off the roots and the coarse green tops. Use only the white stalks, and clean them thoroughly by slitting the stalks and washing them several times with water.

Oven-roasted leeks are a savory addition to other roasted vegetables like carrots, celery, and parsnips. Potato-leek soup is a favorite. Start with ¼ cup of olive oil in a large soup pot. Brown 1 cup of chopped onion in the oil, then add 3

PAT'S PICKS ~ LEEKS

'Dawn Giant' (98 days from seed to harvest): This variety has truly huge stems, and it can be sown directly in soil in early spring.
'King Richard' (75 days): Remarkable early maturity and stem length.
'Laura' (115 days): Extra-hardy leeks for late fall harvest or to overwinter in the garden. Upright leaves are a deep bluish color and stems are medium length.

quarts of chicken stock. Peel and dice 2 pounds of white potatoes and add them to the pot. Cut 4 or 5 cleaned leeks into 1-inch pieces and add them to the pot. Cook until the potatoes are tender. Season with salt and white pepper to taste. Garnish with chopped fresh dill weed.

LETTUCE

Lettuce, especially leaf lettuce, is the perfect crop to tuck here and there in small beds and containers all season long. There are cold-resistant varieties for early and late sowing and heat-tolerant varieties for summer crops. Leaf lettuce is great for planting in pots, window boxes, at the bases of other plants, and as an edging for flower gardens.

Site and Soil. Lettuce prefers cool weather and consistent moisture. It will grow well in full sun in cool conditions, but it does best when shaded from mid-day sun in hot weather. Plant it in a new or mature lasagna bed or in a container with plenty of organic material that will hold moisture.

SCAVENGE SOME SPACE FOR SCALLIONS

Onions are so inexpensive and abundant at the grocery store that I don't bother growing them in my small gardens. The one exception is scallions. I use 'Southport White' bunching onions for scallions. Each bulb that you stick into the soil will produce a small cluster of bulbs with juicy green tops. Plant them in spring, tucking the sets into open corners or spaces between other plants. The plants rarely suffer from any problems, and they'll be ready to harvest in about 68 days. Pull them as needed and use them in salads and soups, or as garnishes.

PAT'S PICKS — LETTUCE

'Baby Green' (60 days to maturity): A miniature Bibb crossed with a butterhead. Grows only 5 to 6 inches tall and produces bright green heads with tender texture.

'Black Seeded Simpson' (26 days from seed to baby leaf stage; 48 days to maturity): Early, curly, light green leaves. Tender and sweet at all stages.

'Freckles' (28 days to baby leaf stage, 55 days to maturity): A gorgeous, red-spotted romaine.

'French Nicoise' (30 days): A very spicy mesclun blend that includes wild onion, 'Broadleaf Batavian' endive,

'Treviso' chicory, garden cress, and arugula.

'Integratia Red' (25 days to baby leaf stage, 55 days to maturity): Medium, upright head with frilly, red leaves for clipping. Well adapted for spring and fall crops. Wonderful for winter production in mild areas.

Italian Saladini blend (28 days): A mild mesclun mix that includes loose leaf and butterhead lettuces, chicory, and salad burnet.

'Royal Oakleaf' (28 days to baby leaf stage, 49 days to maturity): Deep green and deeply lobed leaves.

Planting. You can start sowing lettuce seed outdoors as soon as the soil is workable. Lettuce seed needs light to germinate, so gently sprinkle the seed over the area you want to plant and then lightly rake the area, or spread one sheet of wet newspaper over the seeds, and remove the paper when the seeds germinate.

Don't plant too much at one time. A standard packet of lettuce seed contains about 800 seeds. Sowing 15 to 20 leaf lettuce plants per person is plenty if you make plantings every 2 weeks.

For an extra-early harvest, start one set of plants indoors 5 to 6 weeks before you plan to plant it outdoors. For summer sowings, try putting the lettuce seed in the refrigerator for 5 days before planting, to speed up germination.

Growing Tips. It's okay to let leaf lettuce grow densely, but if the plants seem overcrowded, uproot some (remember, you can use these thinned plants in salad). Thin butterhead types to 10 to 12 inches apart. Suppress weeds by adding loose layers of a fine mulch around the young plants. Keep soil evenly moist, watering early in the day so the foliage dries quickly (wet lettuce is more prone to disease problems). During hot conditions, supply some shade by setting a lawn chair over your lettuce patch.

Harvesting. Use scissors to snip baby lettuce about 1 inch above ground level, or pick off individual leaves by hand. Pick outside leaves for continued harvests.

In the Kitchen. Always wash lettuce well in cold water to remove grit. Using a salad spinner is the best way to remove water

Extend your harvest by sowing two or three varieties of lettuce that mature at different times. You'll harvest baby greens one week, mature leaf lettuce the following week, and butterhead the next.

from the leaves. Or you can place washed leaves on a towel, loosely roll it up, and let it sit for 15 to 20 minutes. A simple vinaigrette is best for delicate greens, but when eating one of the spicy mesclun mixes, try spritzing the leaves with lemon.

PEAS

A small patch of snow peas or snap peas is always worth planting for the incomparable sweet taste of fresh-picked pea pods. I don't recommend shelling peas because the harvest is so much greater from snap peas and snow peas, where you can eat the pods as well as the peas. Peas are a space-efficient crop because you can harvest and pull out the vines in time to plant warm-weather crops such as peppers.

Site and Soil. Full sun and raised lasagna beds are perfect for peas. Plan ahead and build a bed with plenty of compost to provide rich, well-drained conditions. I also add a very thin layer of bonemeal to a bed where I plan to plant peas. Don't add high-nitrogen material like grass clippings or you'll have all leaves and no peas.

Planting. Here in the Catskill region of New York State, we plant peas from March to April. In Southern gardens, plant peas in early to late winter. If you plan to grow peas vertically, set up the support before planting. Sow two rows of seed 6 inches apart, along either side of the trellis.

Some snow pea and snap pea varieties have vines that stretch to 5 feet or taller. Plant tall varieties at the base of a trellis. A pea netting trellis like this one is easy to set up and can hold a heavy crop of vines.

There are plenty of choices for pea trellises. Prunings from fruit trees or other hardwood trees make easy supports. Just push the prunings about 1 foot into the ground, about 6 inches apart. Or set steel fence posts at either end of the row and string commercial pea netting or weave nylon cord between them.

Soak seed in water overnight to get a head start on germination. For a really early start, you can start seeds inside in individual peat pots. Let the plants grow up to 4 inches tall before

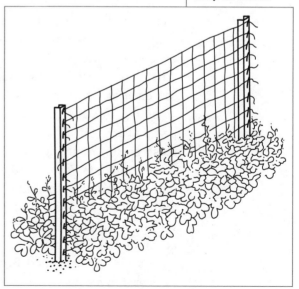

PAT'S PICKS ~ PEAS

'Oregon Sugar Pod' (65 days from seed to harvest): A snow pea with vines that grow only 24 to 28 inches tall. No trellising is necessary, but when you grow these vertically you can fit more in a small space, so I plant two rows 3 inches apart with a short fence between them. My family eats these sweet peas like candy.

'Sugar Ann' (66 days): Needs no trellising; the snap pea of choice for containers and window boxes. Its compact, 18- to 24-inch vines cascade over container edges for easy picking.

'Super Sugar Snap' (58 days): Needs a trellis because the vines grow 5 to 6 feet tall. Try it at the back of a garden bed.

planting outside. To sow seeds directly outdoors, use your finger to push seeds about 1 inch into the surface of the bed. Firm the soil over the peas by pressing down on the bed with the back of a rake or hoe.

Growing Tips. Keep soil evenly moist until peas emerge, then lay off watering until flowers start to appear. Once you spot flowers, water the plants thoroughly every week. Apply mulch to keep soil cool around the roots.

Harvesting. Once pods form on the vines, check daily to catch them at their prime. Pick snow peas when the flat pods are about 3 inches long but before they start to swell. Pick snap peas when they are bulging with seeds but before they lose any of their bright green color. Handle the vines gently as you harvest. Use scissors to cut the pods free, or pinch them off gently with one hand while you support the vine with the other. Harvest every day or two so plants keep producing.

In the Kitchen. Edible podded peas are a treat to eat raw in salads or all by themselves. You can also cook them by lightly boiling, steaming, or stir-frying. For a divine appetizer, I prepare shrimp and pea pod scampi. In a large sauté pan, combine 2 crushed cloves of fresh garlic, 2 chopped scallions, and ¼ cup of olive oil. Sauté for 1 minute and add ½ pound of edible pea pods. Toss the pea pods in the pan for 5 minutes, then add 1 pound of cleaned shrimp, 1 cup of dry white wine, and salt and pepper to taste. Continue cooking and tossing until the shrimp turn pink. Add 2 tablespoons of butter and continue heating until the butter melts. Serve in individual bowls with white or seasoned brown and wild rice. Garnish with fresh parsley. Serves two.

PEPPERS

Peppers aren't just for large gardens. Hot peppers grow on bushy, compact plants that can fit into any small garden scheme. I've even found a few bell pepper varieties that don't take up too much space. The critical factor with peppers is heat. If you have enough sunny, protected spots to go around, or if you garden in the South where there are plenty of garden hot spots, have a little fun with peppers.

At The Potager, I grow six different kinds of hot peppers, and in my garden shop, I sell six-packs containing one plant each of the six varieties. This is a great way to encourage gardeners to try new things, and it's perfect for people who are gardening on a small scale. Convince your local garden center to try it!

Site and Soil. Peppers are definitely a warm-weather, long-season crop. Choose a spot in full sun that's protected from cooling winds. Prepare a bed for peppers in fall; add a thin layer of bonemeal as you build the bed. Don't go too heavy on nitrogen, or you may get all foliage and little fruit.

Planting. Peppers can be slow to start from seed, so I recommend buying transplants. If you can't find transplants of the varieties I've listed below, don't be too concerned. There are plenty of great hot pepper varieties available. Harden off the plants you buy by setting the plants outside during the day and bringing them into a sheltered area at night for about 1 week before planting them in the garden.

PAT'S PICKS ~ PEPPERS

'Bananarama' (70 days from transplanting to yellow fruit): Produces large sweet peppers on small plants. Peppers start out yellow and turn red, and they can be picked at any stage. They're 8 inches long when fully grown and are great for grilling.

Jalapeño (60 days to green fruit; 80 days to red fruit): Thick-walled and hot.

'Jingle Bells' (45 days to green fruit; 65 days to red fruit): A miniature sweet pepper and the earliest variety to turn red. This is the cherry tomato of peppers and my choice for a container or small-space garden. The 1½-foot-tall plants support a large crop of blocky, 1½-inch square fruit.

'Senorita' (80 days to ripe fruit): A jalapeño with great flavor, but milder than others.

'Thai Hot' (50 days to green fruit; 70 days to red fruit): Produces large numbers of tiny "firecrackers" for flavor that is hot, Hot, HOT!

Don't plant peppers outdoors until all danger of frost has passed. Water well and surround roots with mulch to keep the soil moist. Peppers will grow well in containers, too.

Growing Tips. If nights in your area tend to drop below 60°F in summer, help your plants get extra heat by mulching the bed with black plastic or red paper mulch and covering the plants with floating row cover at night. Bring container peppers indoors overnight if cool temperatures are predicted. Peppers need nighttime temperatures of about 70°F or their blossoms will not set fruit.

Peppers are perennials, so if you're growing a pepper plant in a container, you can bring it indoors for the winter. Set it in the hottest, sunniest indoor spot you can find. Treat it as you would any houseplant over winter. It won't produce new fruit, but it may continue to ripen fruit that is already set. The following spring, either set the pot back outside or transplant the plant right into your garden bed. Water it well with a liquid organic fertilizer to stimulate new growth. It won't take long for new blooms to appear.

Harvesting. You can pick peppers when they're green, or you can let them ripen fully to red, yellow, orange, or another mature color (which depends on the type and variety you're growing). Pick mature peppers promptly to encourage new blooms. Cut peppers from the main stem rather than pulling them off, which can injure the plants.

In the Kitchen. Eat bell peppers right from the garden by coring and seeding, then cutting them in half and dipping them in an olive oil–based marinade with your choice of fresh herbs: basil, sweet marjoram, sage, and thyme are all good choices. Or place peppers on a vegetable grilling tray on a hot grill. Brown them on each side and serve hot.

I use hot peppers to add some zip to a variety of dishes, but most of my crop goes into bottles of vinegar or is dried. To dry hot peppers, thread a needle with heavy-duty thread and string the peppers together, passing the needle through the stem, not the fruit. Hang the pepper string in a sunny window to dry, then move it out of the sun so it won't fade.

Grow fresh chile peppers in a chile pepper can! When you make lasagna layers in the container, include a thin layer of bonemeal to help ensure good fruit set.

CHILES

JALAPEÑOS

POTATOES

You can buy potatoes cheaply at the supermarket year-round, so why bother growing them? Well, for one thing, your choice is only three or four varieties at the market, but when you order seed potatoes from specialty growers, you can grow a rainbow of colored potatoes. (See "Pat's Picks" below for a hint at the range of choices.) Most important, though, is that you'll know that your homegrown tubers are completely free of sprout-inhibiting chemicals and pesticide residues.

While potatoes grown traditionally can take up a lot of room, you can grow them in even a small garden by planting them in containers. You can also interplant potatoes in a bed with other crops. I grow shallow-rooted lettuce, herbs, and edible flowers in my potato beds.

There are potato varieties that mature quickly and others that take more time to mature. Early-maturing varieties are good for warm regions because potatoes only grow well in cool temperatures. If you live in a cool-summer area, choose slow-maturing, late-season varieties.

Site and Soil. Potatoes do best in full sun, and a lasagna bed is perfect for providing the well-drained conditions that help prevent tubers from rotting.

Planting. You can plant potatoes in a mature bed, but that means digging into the bed to plant. So I build my beds or fill my containers right as I plant.

One way to grow potatoes is in a hay bed. Start as always by covering the ground with a thick layer of wet newspaper. Scatter the seed potatoes over the newspaper and cover them with about 10 inches of hay or straw. As the vines poke up through the hay, add another layer. When it's time to harvest, fork the hay aside to reveal the tubers.

Now that I'm limited to small gardens, I don't tend to use my hay-bed method for potatoes. Instead, I've adapted the method to create a bed that does double-duty, producing potatoes and other crops in one space. To do this, I start the same way, putting my seed potatoes right on top of the newspaper. Then I cover the seed potatoes with 6 to 8 inches of lasagna layers. I plant lettuce or spinach, radishes, dill, and sometimes even edible flowers in the sur-

PAT'S PICKS ~ POTATOES

'All Blue' (Late-season): Skin and flesh are deep purple and add color and flavor to the dinner plate.
'Nordonna' (Mid-season): Oval to round potatoes with bright red skin and white flesh. Good both for new and full-size potatoes.
'Russian Banana' (Late-season): Large, finger-shaped tubers with thin skin over pale golden flesh. Superb flavor.
'Yellow Finn' (Late-season): The "flavor potato" with deep yellow skin and buttery yellow flesh.

face layer of the bed. As the season progresses, I harvest the lettuce, spinach, and radishes, and the potato foliage grows up through the bed to fill the space. The dill rises up over the potatoes until I harvest it, and I layer on hay or straw as the potatoes grow.

Still another option is to grow potatoes in one-half of a garbage can. Cut a 30-gallon garbage can in half crossways. Cut out the whole bottom of the bottom half, or cut several holes in the bottom. Set the half-can in a garden bed, or even on a gravel patio or driveway—any surface that will allow good drainage. Put a layer of newspaper on the ground surface inside the half-can. Then put in your seed potatoes and light lasagna layers on top. Keep adding more mulch as the potatoes grow.

Growing Tips. Potatoes need water on a regular basis to produce a good yield. Lasagna garden beds are naturally cooler around the roots and conserve water, but if conditions are dry and the bed has dried out, water it thoroughly.

Harvesting. You can pick early new potatoes without uprooting your plants. Simply push your hand in under the plant and feel around to find some tubers. Grab the tubers and pull them out. When you grow potatoes in lasagna layers, it's easy!

Plant seed potatoes as you build a lasagna bed, and then plant fast-growing crops like lettuce and radishes on top. Harvest the top crops as the potato shoots emerge, and then mulch your potato crop until the potato tubers are ready to harvest.

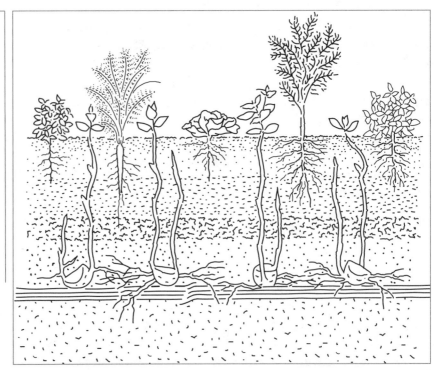

For the main harvest, wait until the plants start to die down. Loosen soil by carefully inserting a garden fork and turning it. Dig the potatoes as you need them for fresh use, but be sure to unearth all potatoes before the first frost. If you have extra potatoes at the end of the season, you'll need to cure them before storing them. To cure them, spread them on newspaper in a dark place where the temperature is between 50° and 60°F for 2 weeks. Then store the potatoes in a dark, cool place in a box or basket.

In the Kitchen. Boil potatoes until tender, then add salt, butter, and chopped fresh parsley. For fried potatoes, slice and place in ice water for 10 minutes, then pat dry. Cook slices in heated oil in a large skillet until tender and brown. Drain on paper towels and add salt and pepper or seasoned salt to taste. Boil small red potatoes whole and leave the skins on for potato salad.

PUMPKINS

Pumpkins and melons don't come to mind first when you're thinking about what to plant in a small garden. But I'm here to tell you that you should give one (or both) a try. I do believe the eating is sweeter when you've grown it yourself. You can grow pumpkins up a fence, screw hooks with a screw eye into the fence, and suspend a fabric sling or net bag from each hook to support the developing fruit. Or do what I do and grow one of the space-saving varieties in a container on your patio.

PAT'S PICKS ~ PUMPKINS

'Baby Bear' (105 days from seed to harvest): Has short vines and produces 8 to 10 fruits per plant, making it the perfect choice for small-space gardeners. This miniature pumpkin is a deep orange color with a long, sturdy handle. Cooks love its moist, sweet taste when it's baked. The semihulless seeds are delicious roasted. Weighing in at about 2 pounds, the fruits can be grown on a trellis without individual support.

'Baby Boo' (90 days): Grows on vigorous vines 10 to 12 feet long, but the pumpkins themselves are child-size and pure white. Perfect for decorations, painting, or pies.

'Jack Be Little' (90 days): Grow on a fence or trellis. Each vine will produce about 6 pumpkins. Children love these tiny pumpkins, which look wonderful on the vine and as house decorations in fall.

Site and Soil. Pumpkins will grow well in full sun or partial shade in well-drained, rich soil.

Planting. Sow seed outside after all chance of frost is past. Or, 3 to 4 weeks before your last frost, start seeds indoors in peat pots. Plant them, pot and all, outside after your last frost date. Plant varieties that produce long vines in a spot where you can train them up a fence or trellis. Bush varieties can be planted in large containers or in garden beds.

Growing Tips. Add a cup of compost to the planting area when you sow seeds, and topdress with more compost when plants have four to six leaves. Pumpkins need lots of water to keep those big vines hydrated, so water deeply, especially when the weather is dry. If the plants wilt a little on a hot day, don't panic. If plants wilt suddenly and drastically, it could be a sign that they've contracted bacterial wilt. Water well, and see if the plants recover. If not, you may have lost your crop. A good way to lessen the chance of bacterial wilt is to keep plants covered with floating row cover from the time they're seedings until they start to flower, or until the vines spread too much to keep covered. Tuck the edges of the cover into the soil so there are no openings where insects could sneak through. This protects the young plants from being fed on by insects that transmit bacterial wilt. Pumpkins require 15 to 20 inches of water during the growing season.

> Train pumpkins on an angled wood-and-wire-mesh trellis and you'll create a shaded area underneath that can be perfect for growing salad crops such as lettuce and spinach throughout summer.

Harvesting. Pumpkins can be harvested after their rinds are hard and their skin turns its mature color. Use a sharp knife or pruners to cut the pumpkins free, leaving 3 to 4 inches of stem attached to each pumpkin. Be sure to harvest all your pumpkins and bring them inside before the first hard frost. Cure them in the sun or in an airy room at room temperature for 10 days.

In the Kitchen. Everyone should bake a pie using fresh pumpkin once in their life. (*Caution:* It's a long process and after you've done it once, you may never do it again!) You will certainly gain a healthy appreciation for the beauty of canned pumpkin. You can also bake pumpkins whole, scoop out the seeds, add some maple syrup and butter, and serve as a side dish with dinner. Lead a pumpkin-carving session with your children and grandchildren using one of those fancy decorating kits. Or wash small decorative pumpkins, and use them as part of a table centerpiece.

RADISHES

Radishes are an undemanding crop that will produce in a diverse range of growing conditions. Because they germinate and grow so quickly, they're a great crop to plant with children to show them the miracle of what seeds can do.

Site and Soil. Radishes like loose, improved soil that drains well, and they'll do well in either a lasagna bed or a container. You'll have to thin once they come up, so don't overseed.

Planting. Radishes like cool weather, so they grow best when sown in spring and late summer. Start planting as early as you can in spring. Cover the beds with row cover if you expect a hard frost overnight. If you're sowing seed in rows, make the rows about 2 inches apart, or 3 to 4 inches apart for large roots like 'French Breakfast'. You

For winter salad, grow leaf lettuce and radishes on a sunny windowsill inside your house.

PAT'S PICKS ~ RADISHES

'Cherry Belle' (22 days from seed to harvest): These little round, red-skinned, crisp radishes will be the first crop on the table.

'Easter Egg' (28 days): A rainbow of colors—red, white, purple, and violet—are produced from one packet of seed. I love these so much that I make successive plantings both in spring and fall.

'French Breakfast' (25 days): Carmine-colored 3- to 4-inch roots with white bottoms. They grow well in spring and into early summer and have a mild taste.

can also broadcast the seed lightly over the bed. If you're a radish lover, sow more seed about every 10 days for a constant supply. Stop sowing in late spring because summer radishes are usually woody and have poor flavor.

Growing Tips. Keep soil evenly moist—if it dries out, the radishes will be woody and have a very hot taste that is not pleasant. Thin to 2 inches apart when the plants have two to four leaves. Mulch small plants with grass clippings to keep the soil moist.

Harvesting. Begin harvesting as soon as you see the shoulders of the radishes peeking out of the soil. The roots should slip easily out of the loose lasagna-bed soil when you pull on the tops. Don't delay harvesting or the roots will become woody.

In the Kitchen. I brush radishes clean and eat them right in the garden. If you must wash them, add a bit of salt when serving. For a super-spicy slaw, either put radishes through a food processor or slice them by hand into small strips. For each cup of sliced radishes, add 1 tablespoon of white vinegar, 1 tablespoon of olive oil, 1 teaspoon of sugar, and salt and pepper to taste. Chill and serve the slaw on a bed of homegrown lettuce.

SPINACH

Spinach is lots of fun to grow because it's so easy, as long as conditions are fairly cool. You can plant it every 2 weeks in spring or fall to enjoy a long harvest. Undemanding and delicious, spinach planted later in fall will overwinter if kept mulched, and it will be ready for picking early in spring. And you don't need much space—try growing spinach as a border for other crops.

PAT'S PICKS ~ SPINACH

'Bloomsdale Savoy' (50 days from seed to harvest): Thick, succulent, dark green leaves are very wrinkled and curled and very sweet in salads.

'Steadfast' (50 days): Make successive sowings from late April to early summer. Sow again in fall for an early spring crop.

'Teton' (45 days): Very dark green smooth oval leaves with erect plant habit. Slow to bolt and can be planted for spring, summer, and fall crops.

'Tyee' (45 days): Has dark green, somewhat crinkled leaves that resist downy mildew. Grows up to 10 inches tall, which helps keep leaves clean.

Site and Soil. A lasagna bed that has loose soil to a depth of 12 inches is perfect for spinach. I like to add some bonemeal and compost to the planting area.

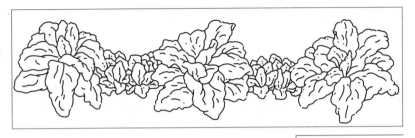

Upright varieties of spinach like 'Tyee' are perfect for small gardens because you can tuck a low-growing crop like leaf lettuce near the base of the spinach plants.

Planting. Spinach is a crop that really benefits from a lasagna bed, because you can plant seeds in very early spring, well before the regular soil in your garden would be ready to work. Sow seeds ½ inch deep and about 1 inch apart. After mid-spring, sow 'Steadfast' or 'Tyee', which are less likely to bolt during early hot spells. If you're a devoted spinach eater, you can try growing it through the summer by seeding it in the shade of trellised pole beans or other small crops. In late summer, sow seeds again to harvest a fall crop.

Growing Tips. Thin plants to 3 or 4 inches apart. Mulch as needed with grass clippings or another fine mulch to keep weeds from becoming a problem.

Harvesting. Pick individual spinach leaves from the outsides of the plants—the centers will keep producing new leaves. I start harvesting as soon as I can get 1 to 2 cups of leaves at one picking.

In the Kitchen. Wash the leaves well. Baby spinach leaves are tender and don't need cooking; toss them with other salad greens. Cook larger leaves in salted water just until wilted. Serve with butter or olive oil. At The Potager, warm pasta salad with spinach is our most popular dish. Here's the recipe: Pile 2 cups of washed baby spinach leaves on an ovenproof platter. Add 1 small tomato, cut into cubes, and ¼ cup of raw mushroom slices. Heat 1 cup of cooked pasta and put it on top of the spinach. Top with ¼ cup of shredded Swiss cheese. Heat in the oven at 400°F for about 5 minutes, or until the cheese melts. In a pan, sauté an 8-ounce boned and skinned chicken breast, cut into strips, and add it to the top of the salad. Garnish with rings of red onion. Serve with your favorite dressing. Serves one.

Spinach is also a tasty addition to a quiche, especially when you make the quiche with blue cheese. Just use your own favorite quiche recipe, and add 1 cup of chopped fresh spinach and ½ cup of crumbled blue cheese to the filling. You'll want to use a deep-dish pie pan to accommodate the extra filling.

SQUASH, SUMMER

The old adage "Be careful what you wish for" comes to mind when I think about growing summer squash in a small garden. Sure, you could find room for four plants, but if you do, you'll be giving away squash to your entire neighborhood. I plant just one zucchini plant and one yellow gooseneck, but even so, I've sometimes thought about opening a vegetable stand.

Site and Soil. Choose a spot with full sun for your summer squash. Prepare a lasagna bed with lots of nitrogen-rich ingredients, or if you're planting in a mature bed, you may want to scoop out a well and fill it with rich compost enriched with organic fertilizer (1 cup per 5-gallon bucket of compost). You can even plant summer squash directly in a compost pile!

Planting. Wait until all chance of frost is past. Plant two or three seeds 1 inch deep, or set out one transplant. If you had to buy a four-pack of plants, don't plant them all—give some to your friends or neighbors. Some summer squash plants grow on stout vines that you can train to a fence or trellis. If you have room for a squash vine to climb, sow three seeds in a hill at the base of the support. Start vines up the support when they are young and pick fruit before it gets heavy.

Growing Tips. Keep soil evenly moist and provide irrigation for dry spells. Squash plants don't like to have their roots disturbed, so don't cultivate around the plants. Instead, keep renewing mulch around the plants to suppress weeds.

PAT'S PICKS ~ SUMMER SQUASH

'Patty Pan', 'Peter Pan', and 'Sunburst' (60 days from seed to harvest): Small, saucer-shaped squashes that grow on bush-type plants.

'Sun Drops' (48 days): Compact, bushy, heavy-yielding plants will furnish the garden early with lots of tender minisquash. Fruits are yellow, 3-inch ovals.

'Eight Ball' (40 days): An All-American Selections Winner, and you'll see why when you grow it. This dark green zucchini is ball-shaped. It will grow well in a medium-size planter or a very small garden.

'Spacemiser' (55 days): Traditional zucchini flavor in 33 percent less space! Has smaller, space-saving bush habit that's open for easy harvest. Big yield on small plants makes this a must-have.

'Yellow Crookneck' (65 days): My grandmother planted this squash, and though I've tried all the rest, I keep coming back to it. It grows beautifully in a container and is delicious when lightly steamed.

Harvesting. Pick summer squash when they're 4 to 6 inches long, and they'll be very tender and delicious. Check plants daily so you don't miss the fruits when they're young—they can become monster-size in only a few days. Use a knife or pruners to cut fruit from main stems instead of pulling them off, which can damage the vine.

In the Kitchen. Summer squash makes a quick and easy side dish. Just dip slices of different summer squashes in olive oil or Italian dressing, place them on a vegetable grilling tray, and grill until tender. Or try my recipe to prepare squash indoors: Mix 4 cups of thinly sliced summer squash with 1 cup of sliced onion and 2 to 3 cloves of crushed garlic. Sauté in a small amount of olive oil or vegetable spray until just tender. With either cooking method, add salt and pepper to taste.

It's important to attract pollinators to squash plants, especially when you're only growing one or two. Plant basil as a companion and let it go to flower—bees love basil blossoms, and they'll visit your squash blossoms, too.

SQUASH, WINTER

Growing winter squash in a small garden is a challenge, but it's certainly not impossible. The secret is to train these wonderful vines on a fence or a sturdy trellis.

Site and Soil. Winter squashes are heavy feeders that need rich, well-drained soil, so they love lasagna beds! I plant winter squash at the base of a fence in a lasagna bed that's only 2 feet wide. I also plant winter squash in a half-barrel and at the base of a sapling trellis. (See page 46 to learn how to make a twig trellis.) All three methods work, so take your pick and be sure to choose a site with full sun. The main ingredient for success is choosing varieties with a compact growth habit.

Planting. Once the soil is warm and the danger of frost is past, plant seeds 1 inch deep and about 8 inches apart. Three plants will yield plenty of fruit. To be sure you'll get three good plants, plant nine seeds in clusters of three and thin each cluster to the best plant.

PAT'S PICKS ~ WINTER SQUASH

'Autumn Cup' (95 days from seed to harvest): Small spaces are no problem with this green buttercup squash that grows on space-saving semibush plants, perfect for a space-squeezed garden. Concentrated fruit set means more produce in a smaller space.

'Gold Nugget' (85 days): So sweet it's a great substitute for sweet potatoes in

casseroles and pies. The compact bush plants will yield three to five 1- to 1½-pound fruits that melt in your mouth and have a sweet flavor.

'Sweet Dumpling' (110 days): If you can find room to trellis a medium-size vine, give this one a try. It's an acorn-shaped fruit with unusual coloring and is perfect for single servings.

Growing Tips. Winter squash need little more than lots of sunshine and consistent moisture. During cool summers, I place black plastic under plants to absorb heat. To do this, cut a 2 × 2-foot square of black plastic, slit it to the center, and cut an opening for the plant stem. Slip the plastic in place and weight the edges with rocks or soil.

Winter squash keep better in storage when the stem is attached to the fruit, so cut fruits off the vine rather than pulling them off. And don't carry winter squash by the stem, or it may break off.

If squash vine borers are a serious problem in your area, cover the planting site with floating row cover immediately after planting. Tuck the edges of the cover into the soil so there are no openings where insects could sneak through. Leave the cover in place until you need to train the vines up a trellis or fence, or until flowers appear on the vines. This will give the plants a strong start and help forestall problems from bacterial wilt disease transmitted by the borers.

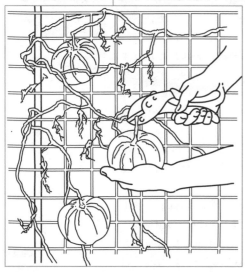

If you train winter squash on a fence, be prepared to support the fruits, or their weight may cause them to tear free of the vines. I like to use the net bags used to package lemons, garlic, and other produce from the supermarket. I wrap the bag around the fruit, secure the top with a rubber band, and attach it to the fence with a hook with a screw eye.

Harvesting. Allow winter squash time to ripen thoroughly in the garden until the shell is quite hard. When the weather turns colder and the vines die, cut the fruits from the vine. (A pair of hand pruners works well for cutting through the tough stems.) Winter squash needs to cure so it will last well in storage. To cure, put it in a dark place at 80° to 85°F for about 10 days. Then store it in a cool, dry place (50° to 55°F).

In the Kitchen. I love baked winter squash. To prepare it, cut the squash in half, scoop out the seeds, and place the halves (cut side down) in a baking dish. Add 1 inch of water to the bottom of the dish. Cover and bake at 350°F until tender. If you're cooking in a microwave, use a glass dish and cover it with plastic wrap. Once the squash is tender, turn the halves over and fill the cavities with your choice of brown sugar and butter, honey and butter, or maple syrup and butter. Enjoy!

TOMATOES

Top choice on most gardeners' "what to grow" list is tomatoes. After all, summer wouldn't be complete without that first taste of a ripe tomato. What would you do to harvest the first ripe tomato on your block? The hardest part of growing tomatoes may be deciding what to grow—some seed catalogs devote as many as eight pages to tomatoes. Three classic varieties for small gardens or containers are 'Sweet Million', a cherry tomato; 'Patio', a small slicing tomato that's perfect for containers; and 'Early Girl', a standard slicing tomato. You may have your own tried-and-true favorites. For a little adventure, try one or two of the varieties listed in "Pat's Picks" on page 148. I've recommended some ultra-early varieties that are ideally suited for small gardens. The fruit is smaller on these plants, but it's still very flavorful.

A note about tomatoes: You'll see tomatoes described as "determinate" or "indeterminate." Determinate tomatoes are bushy plants, 1 to 3 feet tall. Once these plants produce flowers at the vine tips, they stop growing and concentrate on developing all their fruit quickly. Indeterminate plants are the traditional lanky tomato vines that stretch from 6 to 20 feet long. The vines grow and produce new flowers and fruit all season. In general, determinate types are easier to manage in small-space gardens, but you can control the growth of indeterminate tomatoes by training them on a trellis and pruning sideshoots.

Train vigorous tomato vines to a trellis made of concrete reinforcing wire supported by sturdy posts. Tie the vines to wire with heavy-duty twist-ties, or weave twine through the wire and stems.

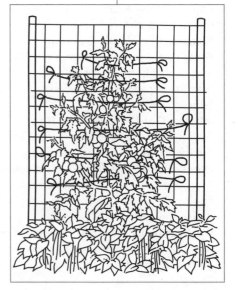

Site and Soil. Tomatoes like heat, so plant them in a protected spot in full sun, or position containers where they'll be out of strong winds. Tomatoes like moderately rich soil, so if you're planting them in a brand new lasagna bed, create a "well" of compost in the bed for each transplant. In containers, use generous layers of compost to supply nutrients and also to hold plenty of moisture. Tomatoes won't produce well and may have problems with blossom end rot (a blackening of the blossom end of the tomato) when they don't receive a steady supply of water.

Planting. Tomatoes won't do well when soil temperatures are less than 50°F. Harden off transplants for 2 weeks before planting. You can set out transplants 2 weeks before the last frost date, but be prepared to protect the plants from cold nights or unexpected cold spells. You can cover plants with floating row cover (which will protect plants to 26°F) or set rose cones over the plants. (These have to be taken off during the day.) Overturned baskets also work when weighted down with heavy stones. If the transplants are leggy, strip off the lower leaves and lay the stems horizontally in a

PAT'S PICKS ~ TOMATOES

'Chello' (80 days from transplant to harvest): A small, determinate tomato that ripens before all others. It has a bright yellow color and its sweet flavor is superior to other cherry types.

'Glacier' (55 days): Developed in Sweden for postage-stamp gardens and raised beds, 'Glacier' is a compact plant that produces salad-size 2½- to 3-inch fruit.

'Husky Gold' and **'Husky Red'** (70 days): My picks for pot culture. These husky plants have the sturdiest stems I've ever seen and they bear fruit all season. They are semidwarf but need staking or caging or the weight of the fruits may cause the stems to break.

'Italian Gold' (75 days): A compact determinate with high yields, it produces huge amounts of 3-ounce fruit.

'Juliet' (60 days): A small plum type with an aggressive vine, but it can be kept pruned to stay in place. You'll love the delicious little fruits in salads or for cooking.

'Northern Delight' (65 days): Bred in North Dakota for the short seasons of the far north. Its 2-inch, slightly oval fruit is every bit as sweet as tomatoes grown further south.

'Oregon Eleven' (60 to 65 days): Tidy, determinate vines loaded with 1½- to 2-inch fruit with thin skin. Another good choice for containers.

'Prairie Fire' (60 to 65 days): Great for containers and small gardens, with 1½- to 2-inch fruit on vigorous plants.

'Stupice' (60 to 65 days): Bred in Czechoslovakia and very cold-tolerant, 'Stupice' bears sweet-tasting, 2-inch fruit all summer.

planting trench. Leave the top three leaves exposed. Form a small depression over the full area of stem and roots to catch and hold water. Install stakes when you plant.

Growing Tips. Keep the soil surface mulched to conserve water, both in the garden and in containers. Recent studies show that red plastic mulch can boost yields, so you may want to give it a try. (You can buy red plastic mulch from some mail-order companies and garden centers.) Check the soil moisture of container tomatoes every other day during hot and dry conditions, and never let the soil dry out.

Harvesting. If you're growing indeterminate tomatoes, keep picking fruits as they ripen to encourage additional bloom. With determinate types, expect fruits to ripen over a short period—you'll be picking a lot of fruit for about a week. Twist the fruits gently to remove them without damaging the vines, or cut them free with a pair of garden shears.

In the Kitchen. During tomato season, my daughter Mickey is in the garden long before the café is open for business. She uses small tomato varieties in salads and for garnishes. Her fresh tomato sauce for angel hair pasta is so exquisite you could eat it every day—in fact, we do. In a small saucepan, heat ¼ cup of olive oil, 2 cloves of crushed garlic, ¼ cup of minced onion, 2 large torn basil leaves, and ¼ cup of minced Italian parsley. When the onion is soft, add 2 cups of halved cherry or grape tomatoes. Toss together until tomatoes are heated through. Divide between two large serving dishes (or four side dishes) of angel hair pasta. Serve with freshly grated Romano cheese. Exquisite!

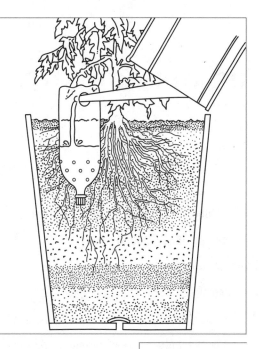

A 1-liter soda bottle can be a water reservoir for container tomatoes. Punch several small holes in the top half of the bottle, and cut one larger hole near the base. Set the bottle in place upside down as you fill the container. Add water twice a week.

149

CHAPTER 5

HERBS FOR SMALL SPACES

Gardening always lifts my spirits, but herb gardening is a special treat because it delights my senses, too. The freshness of chamomile, the spicy scent of basil, and the piney smell of rosemary are all aromas that I savor. Rubbing a leaf of nutmeg-scented geranium feels like touching velvet. The wonderful colors of variegated sages and nasturtium blossoms are a treat to look at. And last but far from least, fresh herbs bring exotic and satisfying flavor to everyday food.

Herbal Memories

The fragrances of lavender and rose always remind me of my grand-mother. She liked to tuck bags of lavender into closets and dresser drawers, and rose petals ended up in a homemade concoction of rose water. I still treasure one of her little crocheted hearts threaded with a pink ribbon and filled with rose petals. The thread is yellowed, the ribbon faded, and the rose fragrance only a memory, but it is one of my favorite things from my grandmother.

My grandmother also grew herbs just outside the back door for sea-soning her cooking. It was simple food: beans, greens, potatoes, toma-toes, and corn. For meats—pork, chicken, and wild game—the herbs of choice were sage, thyme, and lovage. And what would summer have been without frosty glasses of mint tea? These were among my grand-mother's favorite herbs, but there were many more.

Today, when I'm preparing a dish that includes celery (lovage is too large to grow in my small garden), onion, sage, and thyme, the aromas conjure up memories of my grandmother's cooking. I still love the taste of homemade sausage patties, herb-roasted chicken, and corn-bread stuffing. Mint tea in summer is still a must.

Memories of the savory dishes found in my family's recipe box helped guide me in growing and using a few basic herbs when I was a young cook. Over the years, my palate has become more refined, and I've gone from basic to advanced herb seasonings. I'll share many of my secrets of herbal seasoning when I discuss individual herbs later in this chapter.

Herbs for Today's Busy Gardeners

Herbs are easy to plant and care for. By using the lasagna method of creating quick, easy gardens, you can install and plant an herb garden in 3 hours or less. And a small herb garden plus a few con-tainers is plenty of space to produce a satisfying variety of herbs. Once you begin to grow herbs, it could open up a new world for you, just as it did for me.

During my days running Shandelee Herb and Perennial Gardens, I grew more than 100 different herbs. Can you believe it? I grew many herbs to sell, but some for no other reason than that I loved to see them in my gardens. I chose perennial herbs that would withstand the severe winters and to add texture and beauty to the display gardens. People bought these herbs because they looked so

HERB GARDENING FOR STRESS RELIEF

Unless you become an herb collector, like I have, chances are good that a small herb garden will be right for your lifestyle. A small herb bed will supply plenty of herbs for kitchen use and for some dried arrangements and will leave you some left over for gift items besides. I think gardeners today use their gardens, especially herb gardens, to release stress and bring a sense of order to their lives. This has to be as beneficial to one's health as the ingestion or application of the actual herb.

beautiful in the gardens and only secondarily because they were useful plants.

The gardens at Shandelee were a collection of small gardens, each with a different theme. The enclosed entrance garden featured a walkway made of randomly sized and shaped fieldstone. The path housed a collection of thymes in spaces between the stepping stones. A small rubble wall near the driveway contained plants that would grow in very little soil, such as alpine lady's mantle, winter savory, and more varieties of thyme. There were 30 gardens in all. I introduced new gardeners to delightful herbs like anise hyssop, borage, chervil, lemon grass, lovage, salad burnet, French sorrel, and winter savory. Familiar herbs—basil, chives, parsley, and sage—were then, and still are, the most popular.

Most home herb gardens I see today are quite small, especially in cities and suburban areas. Even in rural gardens where there's lots of space, gardeners often plant groupings of small herb gardens that are connected and enclosed. Herbs grow best in sheltered areas where they are protected from harsh winds. It's these small, enclosed spaces where you can appreciate their subtle and aromatic scents most.

Today's herb gardener usually grows herbs for cooking and for the beauty and fragrance herbs bring to the garden. Simple combinations of herbs give stunning effects. One of my favorites is the gray leaves of 'Pretty Carol' santolina paired with deep green curly parsley. Herbs grow very well in containers, too, so no matter how limited your gardening space, you can find room for herbs by tucking pots of them in and around your gardens.

Design a portable, multilayer herb garden by planting herbs in an old pedestal birdbath and surrounding it with several containers full of herbs.

Making Herbs Work in Small Spaces

The herb gardens that I tend at The Potager are similar to the ones at Shandelee Herb Farm, but they're much, much smaller. It's a challenge to grow all the herbs, vegetables, and perennials that I love in a very small space, but I've learned plenty of tricks to make the most of the space I have available.

One of the reasons my gardens are successful is that I choose plants that are naturally compact. When an herb does outgrow its space, I cut it back. When a plant starts to crowd out other plants, I dig it up and divide it, root-prune it, or both. If it outgrows the space again, I dig it up, plant it in a pot, and relegate it to the perennial border surrounding the parking lot.

Vertical supports are key to getting the most from my small herb gardens, too. For example, there's a ramp up to the entrance of The Potager, and I've attached lath to the sides, both to block the view of the unattractive dark space under the ramp and to support the plants that tend to sprawl. I attached window boxes to the ramp railing and planted them with fragrant herbs so customers will get a whiff on their way to the gift shop. (I think it puts them in a buying mood.)

I've acquired a collection of vertical supports and planting schemes from yard sales and auctions. I prop my collection of recycled wrought iron gates, wheels, and fence sections near or in the garden to support vines and climbers. This leaves growing room for tall plants with sturdy stems in the next plant tier. In front of these I can plant medium-size herbs and flowers, leaving room for short varieties in front.

Where and How to Plant

Where do you start when making an herb garden? You may have heard that herbs like poor soil, but it's my experience that they grow better in improved soil. Setting up a lasagna garden to grow herbs is just like any other lasagna bed-making routine. Once you've chosen the site and the design, mark off your space and begin the lasagna process: Place wet paper over the site, and layer organic materials on top.

There are no hard rules about where an herb garden should be planted. Most herbs need full sun, and my definition of full sun is 6 hours or more of direct sunlight every day. However, some herbs will grow quite well in partial shade. Experiment with herb placement. Remember, it's easy to transplant an herb if it doesn't like the spot where you first plant it.

In my front yard, I planted a lasagna bed with catmint, germander, lambs' ears, pansies, and parsley in full sun. Around the corner I planted the same herbs in partial shade.

The plants in full sun set more blossoms and flowered for a longer period of time. The plants in shade had fewer blooms, but the aroma of the foliage was just as intense, and the foliage looked more lush and green than it did on the plants in full sun. Over time, the lambs'-ears languished in the partially shady bed, so I dug it out and replaced it with 'Clear Gold' thyme (*Thymus camphoratus* 'Clear Gold'). I've also recently decided to replace the catmint with something else because it sprawls too much in shade.

I don't recommend planting an edible herb or flower garden next to the street, where exhaust from cars would contaminate the foliage and flowers. I do recommend planting herbs near your front or back door and alongside walkways. You're more likely to stop frequently to rub a leaf and enjoy the aroma or to harvest fresh herbs for cooking or garnishes if your herbs are easy to get at.

Seeds or Plants?

For the most part, I recommend that you start containers and small gardens with potted herbs rather than from seed. Many popular herbs are perennials, and they're slow to start from seed. Plus, chances are you only need one or two of each type of plant, so it makes sense to buy plants rather than a whole packet of seed. There are a few annual herbs, such as dill, that start quickly and easily from seed. Look for catalogs that offer minipacks of those seeds, or share your extra seeds with friends.

You can plant potted herbs directly in a newly made lasagna bed or in a mature lasagna bed. If you're planting seeds, create a seedbed of fine compost on top of the bed.

Many herbs are easy to start from cuttings, so another resourceful way to procure herbs is to ask friends if you can take a few cuttings from their plants. I carry a small pocketknife with me so I'm always ready. To take a cutting, cut 3- to 4-inch pieces from new tip growth, severing the stem just below a node. Wrap the cuttings in damp paper towels until you can pot them up in sterile potting soil or perlite. Cuttings will root best in high humidity; keep the rooting medium evenly moist. After 2 or 3 weeks, check for root formation by tugging gently on a cutting. If you feel resistance, success! Once roots form, you can pot up each cutting in a separate container or plant a few in one large container. Herbs that root well from cuttings include basil, lavender, rosemary, santolina, scented geraniums, and tarragon.

SMALL SECRETS FOR BIG SUCCESS

Welcoming Friends to the Garden

One of the things I learned from the first herb garden I planted was that everyone is eager to explore a garden. I always welcome visitors to my gardens, large or small. Because of this, I've also learned how to protect my delicate plants from nongardening folks who don't understand that many plants don't like being walked on or manhandled! Small, decorative barriers send a message not to go further or step into the beds. Here are some possibilities for protecting your plants while welcoming your friends to enjoy your garden:

- Set out a cute sign to remind visitors that it's fine to rub leaves to release fragrance, but it's not fine to pick leaves or stems.

- Cut sections of willow stems about 18 inches long. Bend the stems into arches and push both ends into the soil along the edge of the bed. Overlap the arches to create a lovely, romantic edging.
- Outline a bed with bricks laid on their sides on an angle, creating a zigzag edging about 2 inches high.
- Fence a bed with short wire fencing, which is easy to find at any garden center.
- Set up a pretty bamboo fence between your path and garden bed by pushing slender, 3-foot bamboo stakes into the ground along the edge of the path at about a 60-degree angle, 2 feet apart. The tips of each pair of stakes should cross. Add another stake as a fence rail parallel to the ground and in line with the crossed tips of the other stakes. Use a piece of stout twine to tie the bamboo rail to the other stakes where they cross. Repeat this all along the path.

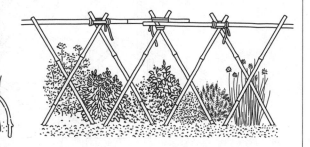

Please touch me, but don't pick me!

Designing Small Herb Gardens

Designing a small herb garden can be a process of discovery. Even though you're familiar with your yard, on any day, you may suddenly come upon a small space that will work perfectly for herbs. Your eye is your best tool. Each space is unique, and only you can be the best judge of where to put your garden. You will be surprised by how little space you need to plant.

My own small herb gardens are inspired by designs based on ancient wood-block prints, gardens at Colonial Williamsburg, and

shapes inspired by bees, birds, and butterflies. I've made gardens in places where it seemed impossible for plants to grow, but somehow those plants took root and thrived.

Most colonial kitchen gardens were small, located by the back door of the house, and fenced in. You can even design a formal herb garden with geometric beds and miniature hedging in a few feet of space. I look to examples like gardens in Williamsburg, Virginia.

I created this formal herb bed that's just 5 feet in diameter. I surrounded it with a path, benches, garden seats, and a picket fence to create a lovely herbal retreat.

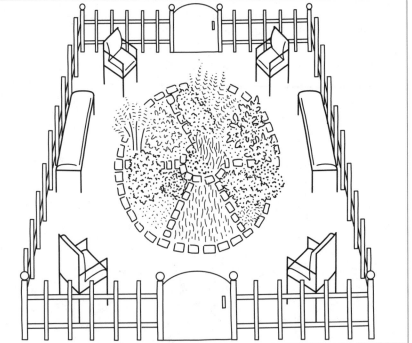

All of the general rules for garden design that I explained in Chapter 2 can also apply to herb gardens. Plus, keep in mind that there's no rule against combining herbs with annuals, perennials, vegetables, or any other plants you want to grow. You may discover that planting all of your small gardens with a mix of different types of plants uses space most efficiently.

An Alley of Herbs

I have a wonderful small-space herb garden at The Potager that I call "Herb Alley." It's tucked into a long, narrow space between a hoop greenhouse and an 8-foot-tall stockade fence. The fence provides privacy for my neighbor, a background for my garden, and support for climbing plants. The distance between the fence and greenhouse is only 8 feet.

To create the garden bed, first I built a low (about 2 feet tall) retaining wall 2 feet away from and parallel to the fence. I used flat fieldstone from an old stone wall near our home. Fieldstone isn't easy to move, but if you tote just a few at a time, you don't notice how hard it is. (If you have the money, you can have pallets of fieldstone delivered to your home and you'll only have to move it once or twice to build your wall. Or you could hire a stonemason to build your wall and you wouldn't have to move any stone at all!)

Once my little wall was finished, it was a cinch to build the lasagna bed. First I covered the grass behind the wall with cardboard. (As I noted in Chapter 1, I rarely use cardboard for building beds anymore because I think wet newspaper works best.) Once the cardboard was down, the area was ready to begin filling with a garden lasagna to grow herbs in. I covered the cardboard with a 12-inch layer of chopped leaves, a 2-inch layer of peat moss, 6 inches of grass clippings, and another thin layer of peat moss. As I cleaned up containers around The Potager, I emptied pots of soil from dead plants as a layer and topped that with 1 inch of composted cow manure. The soil reached to top of the stone wall, and I was ready to plant.

Garden Bullies: A Recipe for Disaster

I did many things right with that herb garden. I chose a protected, south-facing site that warmed up beautifully in spring and provided plenty of summer heat for herbs like rosemary and lavender. The stone wall along the front allowed excellent drainage and added some extra reflected heat for creeping herbs at the front.

"Herb Alley" was one of my first small-garden projects. I experimented with vertical gardening by using a tepee-style tower and two old rakes propped against the wall as supports for climbing plants.

The first year, the garden was wonderful. I planted creeping thyme in front to cascade over the wall. In the middle of the bed, I set out a variety of green- and gray-leaved herbs, and for bright color, I tucked nasturtiums and pansies in among the herbs. Along the back, next to the wall, I planted larger herb plants like artemisia, fern leaf tansy, mint, and oregano.

Now, if you know anything about herbs, you know that I also made one huge mistake with this garden. The big herbs I planted in the back of the garden are some of the worst bullies in the herb world. The second year, only the bullies remained, with some self-sown chives sticking up among them.

I decided to let the plants duke it out in a fight that only the strongest would win. Long before a winner was declared, though, I weeded out baskets of artemisia for wreaths. I dug fern leaf tansy and potted it in containers to sell. Mint was carried off to the kitchen to accent ice tea, decorate desserts, and make mint pesto. (It's a great topping for vegetable dishes and cold pasta.) I picked oregano blossoms, and I dried and harvested leaves and stems to use in the kitchen. This helped tame the bullies, and it kept my garden center full of things to sell.

So what's the lesson here? Unless you plan to go into an herb-related business like I have, beware of bullies in small gardens! If you want to plant mint or another herb with aggressively spreading stems or roots, plant it in a container or inside a root barrier, such as a flue tile or a 5-gallon plastic bucket (with holes cut in the bottom for drainage) sunk into the soil. You can buy flue tiles at building supply stores; 5-gallon buckets are available free from many food establishments.

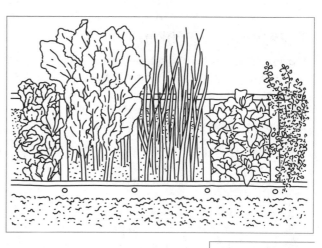

To set up a root barrier in a lasagna bed, you *will* need to dig. But as long as the bed is mature, even the soil below your lasagna layers should be loose and the job won't take much effort. See the illustration on page 179 for details on how to plant a perennial herb inside a barrier. Also, trim the plant back regularly, so that spreading stems don't take root outside the barrier.

Herbs in Containers

Growing herbs in containers is almost as easy as growing them in the garden. Even if you have space to grow herbs in a garden bed, plant some in containers, too, for your porch or patio. It's a pleasure to see, touch, and smell herbs close by when you're sitting outdoors! Mix some herbs into your containers of flowering annuals and perennials.

You'll need to pay a little more attention to container herbs, to make sure they don't dry out or become overcrowded. Other than that, most herbs grow well in containers filled lasagna-style, with plenty of nutrients in the layers of organic matter. Be sure to position your container herbs so they'll get enough sun, and don't forget to rotate large containers so all sides receive equal amounts of light.

In fall, you may want to try bringing some of your container herbs indoors, but keep in mind that many herbs will suffer indoors unless they receive supplemental light. Aloe, lavender, rosemary, scented geraniums, and tarragon are some of the herbs that should survive in a sunny window without supplemental light. Harvest lightly in winter, though, because the plants will grow slowly.

Block planting is a space-efficient way to grow herbs and salad greens. I use an old ladder as an instant planting grid that looks good in the garden all season long.

THERAPY FOR INDOOR HERBS

I bring several herbs indoors once the weather turns cold. Before I move them in, though, I administer plant therapy to help the herbs prepare for a change of light, temperature, and humidity. Here's what to do:

1. Remove the plant from the pot.
2. Brush away the soil and use sharp scissors or pruners to trim the roots by one-third.
3. Scrub the pot in soapy water.
4. Add a pot shard or sheet of newspaper to the bottom of the pot and a couple of inches of new potting mix.
5. Return the plant to the pot, setting it at the same level as it was growing previously. Add more soil as needed and firm the soil in place around the roots.
6. Trim the plant foliage and stems back by one-third.
7. Water the plant and let it rest for a week or so in a shady spot.

Once inside, keep the plant away from drafts, heaters, or hot sunlight (sunlight is good, but high temperatures aren't). Happiness is a windowsill filled with fresh, fragrant herbs basking in the winter sun.

My Herbal Basket

I love to create live arrangements of herbs in wooden fruit baskets. But I don't just stick potted herbs into the basket, I plant the herbs directly in the basket. This gives the roots more space, nutrients, and moisture. I don't bother to line the basket with plastic, either. If the basket has a tight weave, I fill it directly with soil mix. If it has a loose weave, I line the interior with two or three sheets of wet newspaper. (Once the herbs take hold and get growing, their roots will hold the soil mass together even after the newspaper degrades.)

Here's one case where I don't bother with lasagna layers. Instead, I combine a complete mix of compost, peat, and perlite. Let the filled container sit a few days so the soil mix can settle.

A basketful of fragrant herbs is a wonderful centerpiece for a patio table or a great gift for an herb-loving friend. Plant the herbs directly in a rich soil mix in the basket.

I plant the basket with small potted herbs, such as prostrate rosemary, scented geraniums, thyme, and variegated sage. I remove the herbs from their pots, tease out some of the mix, cut through any circling or potbound roots, and set the herbs close together. In addition to herbs, I sometime use small ivy plants as filler.

Once the basket is planted, I water it thoroughly and place pretty moss over the soil to keep the soil from drying out. I set the basket on an old platter or plastic tray (flea market finds!) so any soil or water that leaks out won't spoil the counter or table beneath.

Give the Gift of Herbs

At The Potager, I use herbs to add atmosphere to the surroundings and to create a special touch for my customers. Many of my customers are shopping for gifts for a friend or family member. Any time a customer tells me that their purchase is a gift, I "dress up" the bag with a few sprigs of herbs, a few flowers, and a raffia bow tied to the flowered bag. As long as you have a backyard or balcony herb garden—even a tiny one—you can use this same trick to turn an ordinary gift bag into something unique!

Herbs also make wonderful hostess gifts. Friends invite you to dinner? Instead of bringing wine, bring a bouquet of fresh herbs and flowers. Your friends will be delighted. Have friends who love pets? Grow a hanging basket of pennyroyal (*Mentha pulegium*), a creeping type of mint. Twist stem cuttings into a collar for a cat or dog; it's thought to help as a natural flea repellant. And of course friends with cats will always welcome a gift of catnip for their kitty.

Herbs are terrific for easy, informal decorating, too. Here are a few of the herbal decorations we use at The Potager:

- Simple bunches of herbs tied with raffia bows adorn the tables in my shop; I simply scatter them among the gift items I offer for sale.
- Bunches of dried and fresh herbs hang from a length of twine tacked to the wall.
- Bundles of herbs fill a wooden dough bowl and several small baskets around the dining room.
- Small herbal wreaths adorn the walls. (See page 162 for step-by-step instructions for making herbal wreaths.)

I used to sell these herbal crafts, but one day I made some calculations and figured out that I was earning only 25 cents per hour for my labor. Did I stop making them? No, I just stopped selling them! My philosophy is to do what I love to do and not spend all my time working to make money.

I enjoy dabbling in herbal decorations whenever I find the time. My favorite thing is to make them right out in the garden, but I also work on them between serving customers at The Potager cash register. It's great to be surrounded by the scents of the herbs I've grown and harvested. Try it around your own home, and you'll see what a lift herbal fragrances can give your spirits.

PROJECT

An Herbal Wreath

One of my favorite ways to use herbs when they're in bloom is to cut sprigs for an herbal wreath. I start with either a purchased wire wreath base or a grapevine wreath base made from the wild grapevines that grow right along the road by The Potager.

If you have grapevine available for a wreath base, start with a length of green, supple vine. At one end of the vine, make a loop about 24 inches in diameter. Hold that loop in place with one hand, and continue winding the vine around itself with the other hand, tucking the vine in and through the loops as you work. When you've finished winding, stick the loose end into a cranny of the wreath to secure it. If it seems like the vine may unravel, you can tie twine around it in a couple of spots to secure it.

To make a wire wreath base, use wire cutters to snip the hook off a wire coat hanger. Bend the wire into a circle and twist the ends around themselves to secure. (If the cut ends are sharp, you may want to wrap them with electrical tape or floral tape first.)

Here's how to decorate the wreath base with fresh-cut herbs:

Materials

6-inch-diameter wire wreath base or 24-inch-diameter grapevine wreath base

Clippings of fresh herbs, trimmed to 6 to 8 inches

Spool of floral wire

Raffia bow (optional)

1. As soon as your garden has plenty of herbs in bloom, head outdoors with your wreath base, flower clippers, and some floral wire.

2. Cut a supply of fresh herbs, such as chive blossoms, santolina stems, oregano blossoms, mint sprigs, and whatever else your garden has to offer. For a small wreath, two or three generous handfuls of cuttings will supply enough material. For a large wreath, you'll want a large basketful of materials to work with.

3. Make a bundle of herbs by selecting from one to three stems of the different types of herbs you've collected. Add or subtract stems until the bundle has an appearance that pleases you, with

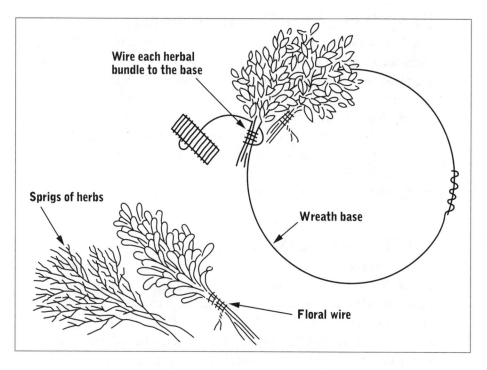

Wire each herbal bundle to the base

Sprigs of herbs

Wreath base

Floral wire

an attractive mix of colors and textures. Cut a length of floral wire and wrap it around the base of the bundle.

4. Once you're satisfied with your combination, make about 15 (more or less) bundles of herbs to cover a small wire frame or about 65 bundles for a 24-inch grapevine base.

5. Lay one bundle of herbs across the wreath base. Attach it to the base by wrapping wire around the bundle and base several times. (Work with the wire on the spool as you do this, waiting to cut the wire until the last bundle of herbs is attached.)

6. Continue with each bundle of herbs. Position all the bundles on the same angle, or alternately to the left, center, and right for a fuller look.

7. If desired, tie a raffia bow onto the wreath as a finishing touch.

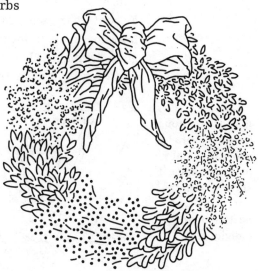

Easy Herbs for Small Gardens

Here's a rundown of 25 of my favorite herbs for small gardens. (I've included a few of my favorite edible flowers in this section, too.) There are plenty of other herbs that are great choices for small gardens also, so don't be afraid to experiment. Do some research before you plant to help you choose a site with enough light and to know in advance whether the herbs you want to grow have the potential to become "bullies." It's much easier to plan ahead and plant aggressive herbs in containers or behind root barriers than it is to extricate herbs from a garden overrun by a dominant spreading plant.

ALOE, MEDICINAL

Aloe is a standard ingredient in everything from hand cream to facial tissues these days. Aloe juice is extracted from the leaves of medicinal aloe (*Aloe vera*), a succulent perennial with prickly leaves. The gel is an effective healing salve for skin irritations. If you garden in Arizona, California, Florida, Texas, or another warm-winter area (Zones 9 and 10), you can plant aloe vera right in your outdoor herb garden. If you live in a colder region, grow it as a container plant outdoors in summer and as a houseplant in winter.

How to Grow. In the garden, plant aloe in a lasagna bed in full sun; it will tolerate partial shade. If you're planting aloe vera in a container, use sand as your bottom lasagna layer to provide good drainage. Place the container in strong light away from drafts.

It's easy to propagate aloe vera by separating baby plants, called offshoots, from the parent plant and potting them up individually.

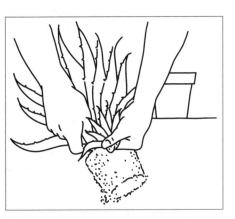

SMALL SPACE TIPS

Aloe Vera

At those times when you touch a hot pan by mistake, aloe will soothe the pain. Also, you can get quick results by pinching a leaf and applying the juice to your hands when they're chapped. This works best if you apply the juice to your hands after you've done the dishes, while your hands are warm, and if you wear a pair of clean cotton gloves to bed.

How to Harvest. Cut or pinch individual leaves. Squeeze the juice onto the cut or burn, or slice open the leaf lengthwise and lay the leaf on the irritated area.

Pat's Favorite Uses. I like to use aloe vera as a skin softener and to ease the sting of minor burns.

BASIL, SWEET

Sweet basil (*Ocimum basilicum*) is much loved by cooks for its warm, spicy taste and seductive aroma. There are oodles of choices when it comes to basil—I've seen more than nine varieties of basil listed in the seed catalogs I receive, from tiny-leaved 'Fino Verde' to 'Purple Ruffles'. Most types grow well in small spaces and containers.

The elusive flavor of basil changes when the leaves are dried. The best way to preserve basil flavor is to store the leaves in olive oil (pesto!) or to freeze them. Cooks pair basil most frequently with pasta, rice, tomatoes, and vegetables. Purple leaf basil adds color and flavor to herbal vinegars.

SMALL SPACE TIPS

Basil

Bush basil, cinnamon basil, lemon basil, and licorice basil are naturally small in size and good choices for small beds. However, it's easy to keep basil trimmed to fit a confined space, so even if your favorite variety grows large, don't be afraid to plant it. Pinch and prune it as needed to keep it small. Trimmings go into the saucepan or freezer.

If you grow a large basil plant in a container, position the container at the rear of a garden bed. At the base, plant lettuce or other plants that will benefit from the light shade of the basil plant.

I also like to grow 'Purple Ruffles' and bush basil as border plants in my small herb gardens just for their good looks.

How to Grow. Basil will grow well in a rich lasagna bed in full sun or partial shade. Lettuce leaf or sweet basil is the best-known variety. It grows about 2 feet tall, producing white flowers that signal the end of its annual cycle. Pinch flower stems as soon as they appear to keep plants bushy and to prolong the harvest. Basil will not survive frost; be sure to cover it on chilly fall nights.

How to Harvest. Harvest on warm days when the leaves are dry. Use or preserve the leaves quickly to retain their flavor; put the cut stems in a jar of water in a cool place until you are ready to use them.

Basil is the star of the herb-garden world. Smooth or ruffled, large or small, green or purple—every gardener is sure to find a favorite basil variety.

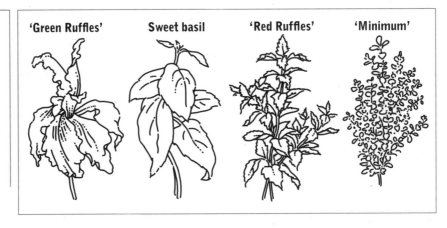

'Green Ruffles'   Sweet basil   'Red Ruffles'   'Minimum'

Pat's Favorite Uses. For a true taste treat, I sprinkle roughly torn fresh basil leaves over slices of homegrown tomatoes still warm from the sun. Add slices of fresh mozzarella cheese, then drizzle the dish with virgin olive oil and balsamic vinegar.

Of course, I also make pesto with my basil. Here's my recipe for "Pat's Perfect Pesto." In a blender, combine 2 cups of chopped basil leaves, ½ cup of broken walnuts, 4 ounces of grated Parmesan cheese, and 6 large cloves of garlic that have been finely chopped. Process these ingredients until you have a thick, aromatic paste. Add ¼ cup of olive oil, a little at a time, and continue blending until the ingredients are thoroughly combined. Add more olive oil if needed to make a smooth paste. I roll my pesto into 1-inch balls (equivalent to 1 tablespoon) and freeze them on a cookie sheet. Store the balls in the freezer in a tightly sealed container. Thaw them as needed to use in pasta dishes, soups, and stews.

CALENDULA

Sometimes known as pot marigold, calendulas (*Calendula officinalis*) bear flowers with bright orange and yellow petals on sturdy stems that grow from 1 to 2 feet tall. Calendula is an annual, but it self-seeds readily. Although calendula petals aren't flavorful, you can use the dried petals to imitate the rich color that saffron gives foods.

How to Grow. It's usually no problem to find a friend with some calendula seeds or plants to spare. Calendulas grow best in full sun in rich, improved soil, so they love a lasagna bed. In the South, they may appreciate a partially shady spot. If you want to move self-sown seedlings, just shove a trowel into the soil beneath them and lift them

SMALL SPACE TIPS

Calendula

Calendula grows well in pots, too. Try seeding a pot of calendulas in midsummer. The plants will be blooming beautifully at frost time, when you can bring them inside to add cheery color on a windowsill.

from the bed. Set the clump of soil and plants in the desired spot. If there are more seedlings than you can use, give some away or toss the excess onto the compost pile.

How to Harvest. Snap or cut the flower heads off. Pluck individual petals from flower heads. To dry calendula, spread individual petals between two pieces of brown paper in the shade. Once they're dry, store them in an airtight container.

Pat's Favorite Uses. It only takes about ¼ cup of calendula petals to make a pot of rice or paella look like it has been seasoned with saffron. A sprinkling of rich yellow calendula petals turns a ho-hum salad into something exciting. Try sprinkling some petals on cooked chicken or fish, too.

CATNIP

Catnip (*Nepeta cataria*) is a hardy perennial with gray-green leaves and a mass of purple flower spikes in midsummer. Cats go nutty over this herb. Catnip grows from 2 to 3 feet tall and just as wide. I love the catnip relative called garden catmint or Faassen's catmint (*N.* × *faassenii*), and I use it as a low-growing border for my miniature rose garden. I believe it helps repel insect pests, because my roses are amazingly pest free. Some cultivars of garden catmint grow only to 15 inches tall and bloom in shades of blue to purple.

How to Grow. Choose a site in sun or partial shade. Catnip loves the rich soil of a lasagna bed. In fact, it will love it so much that it may spread farther and faster than you'd like. To keep catnip in its place, grow it in an aboveground or sunken container.

How to Harvest. Use sharp scissors to cut handfuls of foliage and blossoms free. Lay the stems on a wire screen or tie them into bunches, and hang them to dry in a dark, airy place. Keep the plants

Garden catmint is my favorite catnip relative. Growing it in a container means no worries about keeping the plant from spreading. To dry the flowering stems, fasten bunches with twine or rubber bands and hang them in a dark, airy spot.

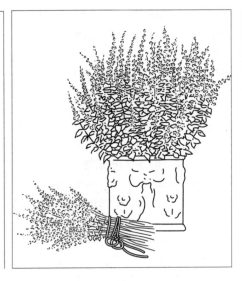

Catnip

For a fun gift, when you divide your catnip, pot up the divisions in small pots with cat faces or silhouettes painted on them. Your cat-loving friends will be delighted!

well watered and they will re-bloom after cutting.

Pat's Favorite Uses. I stuff dried catnip into small cloth bags to give to my friends who like to spoil their feline friends. I also like to plant sturdy little garden catmint plants as a border for a lasagna bed. I keep the border closely trimmed.

CHAMOMILE

You have two choices when growing chamomile: Roman chamomile (*Chamaemelum nobile*), a perennial, or German chamomile (*Chamomilla recutita*), an annual. All chamomiles sport finely divided leaves and daisylike flowers that grow on straight stems above the foliage. German chamomile has a sweet apple scent and is purported to have a calming effect. Roman chamomile is low-growing and can be planted as a lawn substitute. Both types can be used for making tea.

How to Grow. You can grow chamomile from seed, but when you have a small-space garden, it's just as convenient to buy started plants. One good-size plant can go a long way—see the illustration at left to dis-

One 1-quart size pot of chamomile can be pulled apart into several small plants. If you can't plant the divisions right away, protect the roots by "heeling" them into a box of moist potting soil.

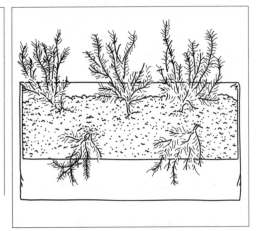

SMALL SPACE TIPS

Chamomile

'Treneague' is a variety of non-flowering Roman chamomile that's been developed especially for planting as a lawn substitute. It's a creative, aromatic alternative to lawn grass for a small, open area that won't get a lot of heavy foot traffic but where you want the effect of a green lawn. To create a chamomile "lawn," start by making a lasagna bed, using wet newspaper as the bottom layer. As you layer organic materials, add some sharp sand to each layer for good drainage. Build the bed about 8 inches high. Set out plants equidistant, and mulch the area between plants well to repress weeds while the chamomile spreads. Once the bed has settled and the lawn is established, you can mow it just as you would grass.

cover how to turn one chamomile plant into many. They'll grow best in full sun, but a partially shady site is acceptable. German chamomile likes well-drained, moderately fertile conditions, and it should do fine in a mature lasagna bed. Roman chamomile prefers rich, moist conditions, so you may want to add extra compost to its planting area. Plant German chamomile about 6 inches from neighboring plants; give Roman chamomile an 18-inch buffer so it can spread. German chamomile self-sows, so if you're concerned about keeping it controlled, trim off the flowers before they set seed.

How to Harvest. When harvesting German chamomile for tea, cut whole stems. For Roman chamomile, pinch off individual flowers. Dry the stems or flowers on a screen in a dark, airy place.

Pat's Favorite Uses. In my small tea garden, I grow a mat of Roman chamomile on the seat of an old rattan chair.

CHIVES

For an oniony accent in salads and other dishes, grow chives (*Allium schoenoprasum*). This perennial herb forms clumps of bright green, slim leaves that are like drinking straws: tube-shaped and hollow. The pink to purple blossoms form in early summer atop hollow flower stems. The blossoms also have an oniony flavor, and they look beautiful in salads.

How to Grow. Start chives from seed, buy a plant, or find a friend with divisions or volunteers to give away. (Chives self-sow readily, so

I like to border a small garden with clumps of chives. Trim off blossoms before they go to seed, and the plants will rebloom several times.

it's not hard to find plants for free from friends.) Chives are so easy to grow that there's no excuse not to include a clump in a pot or in your garden. They like full sun but will tolerate partial shade. Keep the blossoms pinched before they set seed to prevent self-sowing. Divide clumps every 3 years.

How to Harvest. Harvest blossoms just before they open fully. Pluck or cut them off of the stem (discard the flower stem). Harvest leaves by using sharp scissors to cut through a clump about 1 inch above ground level.

Pat's Favorite Uses. We use fresh, finely chopped chives as one of the main flavorings in our vegetable cream cheese at The Potager. Chive blossom vinegar is so pretty and delicate that it's my favorite herbal concoction. Pull petals from blossom heads and sprinkle them on salads and on top of herb omelettes. Dry whole flowers to include in dried herb arrangements.

SMALL SPACE TIPS

Chives

Chives are easy to grow in a pot if you want to save space in the garden. I plant two or more pots, harvesting leaves from one and letting the plants in the other keep growing to produce blossoms for picking.

Note: **Never let potted chives go to seed. Even seed from a potted chive plant can spread to a garden bed and create a weed problem!**

CILANTRO/CORIANDER

Coriander (*Coriandrum sativum*) and cilantro are two names for the same herb. This pungent annual bears two types of leaves: lower leaves that look like those of Italian parsley and upper, finely cut leaves. These cilantro leaves are used to flavor salsa and other dishes. The plants produce tiny white flowers; seeds from those flowers can be dried and crushed to make a sweet powder. In China, Mexico, and the Middle East, coriander seed is a popular flavoring for many foods. Coriander is one ingredient in curry powder. Whole seeds are baked into breads and cakes.

How to Grow. Cilantro is easy to grow from seed in full sun in a well-drained lasagna bed. Don't add any extra boost of nitrogen, or your plants may grow too lushly and topple over. Sow seeds after your last spring frost, or set out started plants. After you buy and plant cilantro once, you should never have to buy it again because it self-sows readily when you allow a few flowering stems to go to seed in the garden.

SMALL SPACE TIPS

Cilantro/ Coriander

If you want to collect coriander seeds efficiently, cover the ripening seedheads with a brown paper bag and tie the bag shut around the stem. Cut the stem off the plant below the bag, and hang the stem and bag in a dark, airy place so the seeds can finish maturing.

If you're just growing cilantro for its leaves, snip off the plant tops before the seeds have a chance to mature. Sideshoots will continue to put out leaves, but you won't be overwhelmed with self-spreading plants.

How to Harvest. Use sharp scissors to cut leafy stems from the outside of the clump.

Pat's Favorite Uses. I like to use cilantro leaves in salsa and ground coriander in shrimp, chicken, or lamb curry. To make a curry sauce, melt 3 tablespoons of butter over low heat in a heavy saucepan. Sauté 3 tablespoons of minced onion

Snip outer leaves from cilantro plants. New leaves will continue to sprout at the center of the plant, so you can harvest repeatedly.

and 1½ tablespoons of curry powder in the butter. Blend in 3 tablespoons of flour, ¾ tablespoon of sugar, ⅛ teaspoon of ground ginger, and ⅛ teaspoon of ground coriander. Cook over low heat until the mixture is smooth and bubbly. Remove from heat, and stir in 1 cup of milk and 1 cup of chicken broth. Bring to a boil over medium heat, stirring constantly. Boil for 1 minute, and then add 2 cups of cooked and cleaned shrimp or 2 cups of cooked and cubed chicken or lamb. Add ½ teaspoon of lemon juice. Reduce heat to low and heat the mixture. Serve over rice, and garnish with chopped cilantro leaves.

DILL

A self-seeding annual, dill (*Anethum graveolens*) is a graceful addition to any herb garden. The stems send out feathery, bright-green foliage and are topped with flat, lacy heads of greenish-yellow flowers. Be prepared for stems that stretch up to 5 feet tall in ideal conditions. For a small garden or container, choose new compact varieties such as 'Fernleaf', which has bushy, short stems. Once the flowers mature, they turn into small, brown, aromatic seeds.

How to Grow. Plant in an average, well-drained lasagna bed in full sun with protection from strong winds. Sow seed after the last spring frost, or if you're impatient, buy started plants. Thin seedlings to 6 inches apart.

How to Harvest. When plants are 4 to 6 inches high, use sharp scissors to trim off the tops of a densely planted pot or bed. These leaves will be very fine and tender.

Dill

For a summer-long supply, sow several pots of dill—one pot every 2 weeks. We need lots of dill for the kitchen at The Potager, so I keep sowing for 8 weeks! I harvest in succession, so I always have a pot of dill ready to harvest while other pots are growing. Your dill supply will be steady even if you only have room or time to sow two pots' worth. Before summer's end, be sure to let one pot send up flower heads and gather the seeds for sowing next year.

Pat's Favorite Uses. Fresh dill is another herb we use in The Potager's vegetable cream cheese, but my favorite dilly dish is fresh salmon with dill. To prepare this, put the salmon filet skin side down in a shallow baking dish. Coat the top and sides of the filet with about 1 tablespoon of brown mustard (use your personal favorite). Add a sprinkling of fresh chopped dill leaves (a generous teaspoon is about right). Add 2 to 3 tablespoons of white wine to the dish. Bake at 400°F for about 30 minutes or until the salmon is flaky. Serve with wild rice or small oven-roasted potatoes.

GERANIUMS, SCENTED

These relatives of flashy zonal geraniums (*Pelargonium* spp.) are tender perennials that have barely noticeable flowers but delightfully scented leaves—lemon, lime, nutmeg, rose, and spicy ginger, just to name a few. The list is seemingly endless. The leaves also have wonderful crinkly or curled textures and may be scalloped, curly, or lacy in appearance.

How to Grow. Starting scented geraniums from seed is challenging,

SMALL SPACE TIPS

Scented Geraniums

Once you start growing scented geraniums, be prepared to fall in love and want more. These plants are very slow to start from seed, but cuttings are easy to root, so start a geranium network with your friends. Offer them cuttings of your favorite varieties of scented geraniums in exchange for cuttings of theirs. Grow a wide sampling in pots (use a pair of cuticle scissors for regular pruning, so they'll stay small) and set them around your house and garden. That way, you'll find plenty of opportunities to rub a leaf and enjoy the wonderful scents as you go about your day.

Take cuttings of scented geraniums just below a leaf node. Stick the stems in moist perlite, and cover them to keep humidity high. The cuttings should sprout roots in 4 to 6 weeks.

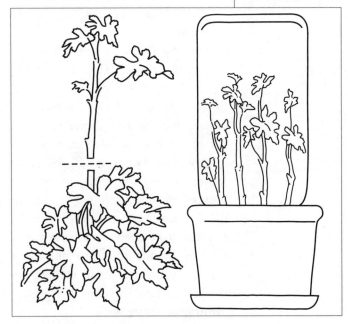

so I suggest you start with purchased plants. Grow them in containers that have compost-rich layers. Don't set the containers outside until all danger of frost is past—these fragrant plants are only hardy in Zone 10. They like a site with full sun. Indoors, be sure to put them on a south-facing windowsill or they'll languish. Keep them moist.

How to Harvest. Cut or pinch leaves once the plants are about 6 inches tall. Spread the leaves on a screen to dry for potpourri.

Pat's Favorite Uses. Nutmeg is my favorite scented geranium. I grow it for the scent, the feel of the velvety leaves, and the tiny, orchidlike flowers. Citrus-scented geranium runs a close second. I love its smell, but it gives me lots of pleasure when I train it over a frame or to a standard. Fresh-scented geranium leaves add flavor to iced tea, jams, and baked goods.

HYSSOP

Hyssop (*Hyssopus officinalis*) is pretty enough to grow for beauty's sake alone, but you can also harvest the slightly bitter leaves and flowers to use in salads or with fish or meat. Hyssop is a bushy perennial with narrow, dark green leaves and blue flower spikes. It grows to 2 feet tall.

How to Grow. Plant in full sun and well-drained soil. Sow seeds about 1 week before your last expected spring frost, or set out purchased plants. Don't overwater, or the plants may develop root rot.

How to Harvest. If you want leaves for seasoning, clip individual stems before they flower, and strip off the leaves. Discard the stem. To harvest flowers, choose flower stems with blossoms that are not quite fully open, and cut whole stems from the plant. Hang bunches of stems to air-dry for arrangements.

SMALL SPACE TIPS

Hyssop

If you don't choose to clip hyssop as a hedge, like I do, just plant one or two plants and let them flower. The flower spikes will attract bees, butterflies, and perhaps even hummingbirds to your garden.

Pat's Favorite Uses. I like to use hyssop as a substitute for boxwood in a miniature hedge to border a bed of herbs and flowers. I set plants about 4 inches apart in a border at the front of the bed and keep the top clipped to encourage side growth. It's also nice to brew a tea from a mix of equal amounts of dried hyssop leaves and lemon balm leaves. Use ½ teaspoon of the dried mix per cup of hot water.

SMALL SPACE TIPS

Lavender

Lavender will grow well in a container. Be sure your layers include some sand or perlite, to promote good drainage. Also be sure to keep the container in a sunny spot. If you're planning an outdoor event on your shady patio, you can always move the container to the patio for the party (people love to touch and smell lavender). You can even bring your lavender plant indoors for the winter. To thrive, the plant will need sunny but cool conditions.

LAVENDER

Be sure to save a space for lavender (*Lavandula angustifolia*) in your small-space herb garden. These wonderfully aromatic, shrubby plants have spiky silvery or gray-green leaves and delicate, lavender-blue flowers borne on long stems above the foliage. Lavender blossoms are essential for potpourri and wreaths, and lavender oil is used in lotions and soaps. Lavender lends a distinctive flavor to vinegar, desserts, and breads. Plants are hardy in Zones 5 to 8, but they'll need protection from winter winds.

How to Grow. Lavender needs good drainage and full sun. It may rot if overwatered, but it will die in prolonged drought. It likes alkaline conditions, so mix in some lime where you plan to plant it. Lavender is slow to start from seed, so it's best to buy plants from a nursery.

How to Harvest. Cut flower stems just before the flowers open. Bind five or six stems together with a rubber band and hang in a dark, well-ventilated area to dry.

Pat's Favorite Uses. Lavender is one of the most popular herbs for arrangements and crafts, but I like to keep things simple. I use my dried lavender blossoms to fill pretty cloth sachets and as part of my potpourri mixture.

The scent of lavender is said to relieve stress and promote restful sleep, so it's perfect for filling a sachet to tuck under your pillow.

LEMON BALM

The lemony scent of its bright green, heart-shaped leaves gives lemon balm (*Melissa officinalis*) its name. You can dry the leaves for potpourri or herbal tea, or you can use them fresh in cakes and cookies. Lemon balm is a perennial that's hardy in Zones 4 to 9.

How to Grow. Grow lemon balm in a sunny or partially shady site with well-drained soil. Lemon balm grows quickly from seeds, rooted cuttings, or divisions. You won't need more than one or two plants. If you buy seeds, share the excess with friends; or perhaps you have a friend who will give you cuttings or a division from her garden.

Lemon balm self-sows; don't let the plants flower and set seed. Plants will produce flowers from late spring through midsummer, so keep watching for new blooms and pinching them as they mature and fade. A mature plant can be tough to divide, so if your lemon balm is outgrowing its space, take cuttings in spring and root them. Then give away the overgrown plant or toss it on the compost pile, and plant the rooted cuttings in its place.

SMALL SPACE TIPS

Lemon Balm

The fragrance of lemon balm leaves is a delight, so try growing a lemon balm plant in a large container near an outdoor sitting area. Brush your hand lightly over the leaves, and you'll enjoy a wonderful lemony scent whenever you spend some time in your outdoor retreat.

How to Harvest. Clip stems before flowers form, cutting the plant back to about 3 inches tall. Plants will send out new shoots, providing more leaves for harvest at the end of the season.

Pat's Favorite Uses. Brew delightful lemon tea by steeping fresh lemon balm leaves. Add dried leaves to potpourri. The leaves lose their lemony flavor when dried, but they'll still give the potpourri bulk and a lemon fragrance.

For decorative ice cubes that will add a lemony touch to iced tea, drop individual lemon balm leaves into ice cube trays filled with water, and freeze them.

LEMON VERBENA

Lemon verbena (*Aloysia triphylla*) is well suited to container growing because it's a very tender perennial that won't survive the winter outdoors. This graceful shrub has light green pointed leaves and a delightful lemon flavor. Delicious in teas and desserts, the fragrance also is useful in potpourris and soaps.

Help lemon verbena thrive by positioning it near a south-facing fence or wall protected from drafts. Set the container in a saucer or on a hard surface so the roots can't grow out of the drainage holes and into the soil beneath.

How to Grow. Buy a lemon verbena plant from a local nursery, or ask an herb-growing friend to let you take a stem cutting from her plant in summer. Lemon verbena is undemanding and will grow well in a container with an average mix of lasagna layers, or even in ordinary potting soil. If you live in Zones 8 through 11, you can try planting lemon verbena directly in your garden. Choose a sunny, sheltered spot.

In fall, cut off the old branches before bringing the plant indoors. Lemon verbena needs cool conditions over winter (about 55°F). The best location for this plant might be in your basement. Don't worry—it's natural for this deciduous plant to drop its leaves during winter. Water the plant about once a month in winter and set it out after your last frost in spring.

SMALL SPACE TIPS

Lemon Verbena

For a fun gardening project, try training a lemon verbena plant as a standard (a miniature tree form, like the illustration shown in "Small Space Tips" on page 183). Trimming and shaping the plant will give you a lemony lift!

How to Harvest. Snip stems from the top of the plant as you need them, and pick off the individual leaves. Use them fresh or dry them on a screen in a dark, airy place. Frequent cutting encourages plants to produce more sideshoots, which will make the plants fuller and less leggy.

Pat's Favorite Uses. Lemon verbena is the only lemon-scented herb that retains its flavor after drying. It's fabulous in tea and potpourri.

MARJORAM, SWEET

Cooks rely on the sweet flavor of sweet marjoram (*Origanum marjorana*) to flavor Italian dishes. Sweet marjoram is a tender perennial herb grown as an annual. The bushy plants have small, green, oval leaves and clusters of pink flowers. Plants rarely reach more than 12 to 18 inches tall and wide—it's a perfect herb for small gardens.

How to Grow. Plant in full sun in an average lasagna bed with excellent drainage, or in a container. Marjoram's not easy to start from seed directly in the garden, so I recommend buying transplants. The flowers are pretty, but for the best harvest of leaves, cut back the plants before the flowers open. Keep the plants evenly moist. Sweet marjoram is hardy in Zones 7 to 9. In other areas, bring containers of marjoram inside to a cool location to overwinter.

How to Harvest. Cut stems and remove leaves immediately for fresh use. For a supply of dried marjoram, cut stems and bind them with a rubber band to hang and dry in a dark, airy location.

Pat's Favorite Uses. I use marjoram in Italian dishes and in soups and fresh vegetable dishes. I let one marjoram plant go to flower so I can use the small pink flowers as a garnish. (They taste good, too.)

At The Potager, we pick fresh marjoram stems each morning and keep them in a jar of water near the salad station.

>
> **SMALL SPACE TIPS**
>
> ## Sweet Marjoram
> Sweet marjoram is a great substitute for oregano in cooking, so it's a boon to small-space gardeners who are worried about keeping aggressive oregano plants in-bounds. You can substitute sweet marjoram one-for-one for oregano in a recipe. Remember, like most herbs, fresh sweet marjoram is about four times as potent as dried!

To prepare sweet marjoram for air-drying, loop a rubber band around a bunch of stems. Wrap the free end of the rubber band over the bottom length of a clothes hanger, and then loop it around the stems again.

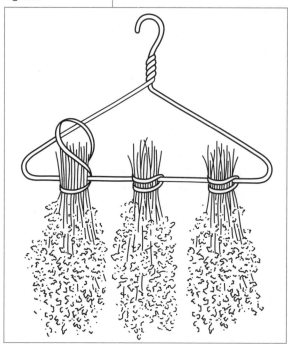

MINT

Mint (*Mentha* spp.) has quite a reputation as a bully in the herb garden, but I keep it on my "great herbs for small gardens" list because I wouldn't be without it in the kitchen. As long as you're careful right from the start, you can keep mints under control. There are so many appealing varieties of mint—chocolate mint, orange mint, peppermint, pineapple mint, and many more. Mint is a perennial that's hardy in Zones 5 to 9.

How to Grow. Even if you have a large garden, grow mint in a container or inside a root barrier, or your garden will be overwhelmed by this space hog. In the garden, I like to plant it in a flue title, as shown at right. Cut the stems back frequently to keep them from becoming woody. If you want to start new plants, stick stem cuttings in water to root. Mints are very hardy and grow best in partial shade and moist, moderately fertile soil.

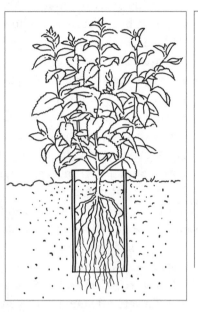

Flue tiles are effective barriers to the roots of mints and other aggressive herbs. Dig a hole 1 foot deep and set the tile in place, leaving the top few inches exposed. Fill the tile with organic materials and set the plant in place inside it.

How to Harvest. Cut sprigs about 3 inches long to use as garnishes for iced tea and other drinks. Just before the plants bloom, cut the stems back close to ground level and hang them in bunches to air dry. Peppermint is one of the best choices for drying.

SMALL SPACE TIPS

Mint

Old cooking pots that I would have discarded now serve as funky containers for my collection of mints. I used a hammer to pound a large nail through the bottom of each pot to make drainage holes. (Make several holes in each pot.)

Pat's Favorite Uses. As an alternative to green-dyed mint jelly, I make a mint vinegar sauce to serve with lamb. I chop a few handfuls of fresh leaves into small pieces and place them in a jar. Then I add just enough vinegar to cover the leaves. I serve the vinegar in a little bottle on the side so each person can apply the amount they like.

NASTURTIUM

A window box of nasturtiums (*Tropaeolum majus*) is such a cheerful sight, with round, bright green leaves and open-faced flowers in yellow, red, orange, and creamy white. Nasturtium is an annual that will bloom all summer. Both flowers and leaves have a peppery taste that adds a lift to salads. You can chop the flowers and blend them into soft butter for a spicy addition to fish or chicken. Pickle the seedpods as a substitute for capers.

How to Grow. Here's one plant that you may *not* want to plant in a lasagna bed. In rich soil, nasturtiums tend to produce all leaves and no flowers. I plant nasturtiums in pots in a lean soil mix. You can sow seeds directly in the containers or start seeds early in peat pots or newspaper pots for transplanting into the containers. Don't sow seeds outdoors or set transplants outside until danger of frost is past. Give them a spot in full sun for best flower production.

How to Harvest. Pick leaves and flowers all summer, as you need them. Picking flowers daily will help stimulate new flowers to form.

Pat's Favorite Uses. I buy a bottle of cheap vodka, add 2 cups of nasturtium flowers, and leave the bottle sitting for 2 weeks in the closet. The result is cheap vodka with the flavor of expensive Russian pepper vodka. Serve this treat ice cold in tiny glasses. I also like to make and freeze nasturtium butter so I can enjoy the taste of this peppery butter on homemade bread all winter. To make nasturtium butter, chop 1 cup of nasturtium flowers and blend them into 1 pound of softened butter. Freeze in ¼-pound logs.

SMALL SPACE TIPS

Nasturtium

I grow trailing nasturtiums in window boxes along the ramp to The Potager. The flowering stems trail down the side of the ramp, providing a marvelous display of color but taking up no garden space. You can achieve the same effect by growing trailing nasturtiums in boxes on a deck railing or in hanging baskets on your porch, balcony, or patio. You have to see it to believe it, but 'Tall Climbing Single Mix' from Renee's Garden (see "Resources for Lasagna Gardeners" on page 271) grows 4 feet in one season and flowers in red, gold, yellow, mahogany, and orange.

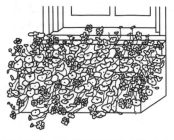

OREGANO

In a small garden, you may find yourself facing a choice when it comes to oregano: Do you want to grow it for seasoning pizza and spaghetti sauce, or do you want to grow it for flower arrangements? You see, there are different types of oregano, and only Greek oregano (*Origanum vulgare* subsp. *hirutm)* is reliable for flavor. Unfortunately, Greek oregano doesn't produce the showy pink flowers of common oregano (*O. vulgare*). In general, though, oregano is a vigorous grower with spreading stems, so one is probably enough in a small space! Here's my hint—grow sweet marjoram as a culinary substitute for Greek oregano, and enjoy growing common oregano as an ornamental herb.

How to Grow. Oregano likes full sun and well-drained, improved soil. Keep it cut back so it doesn't overrun neighboring plants. Oregano is reliably hardy to Zone 5, but it may or may not survive winter in colder areas.

Common oregano (*Origanum vulgare*) doesn't have highly flavorful leaves, but it does produce charming stems studded with small, pink flowers. Try air-drying some flower stems for flower arrangements.

SMALL SPACE TIPS

Oregano

Oregano is another herb that can become a bully. To protect your small garden from an oregano invasion, dig and divide your oregano plant every year in either early spring or fall. Replant one small division, and give the rest away or bury it deep in a compost pile. Diligently cut off *all* flower stems before they go to seed to prevent self-sowing.

How to Harvest. Once flowers open, cut long stems and hang to dry.

Pat's Favorite Uses. I use dried flowering stems in arrangements. They pair especially well with artemisia, boxwood stems, lavender chive blossoms, gray-leaved sage, and pale yellow yarrow blossoms. I also make fresh arrangements of ferns, oregano blossoms, and Queen-Anne's-lace. For the tables in the café at The Potager, I arrange mint, oregano, curly parsley and 'Nearly Wild' roses in crystal vases, and I encourage the diners to touch and taste!

181

PARSLEY

I probably use more parsley than any other herb in my gardens because it enhances the flavor of many other herbs and foods, and it's also a great garnish. Parsley (*Petroselinum crispum*) is a biennial that goes to seed the second year. The fresh-tasting ruffled leaves of curly parsley grow in clumps 8 to 12 inches tall that continue putting out new leaves all season. Italian parsley has flat leaves and a stronger flavor and grows to 20 inches tall.

How to Grow. Plant in rich, well-drained soil in full sun or partial shade. Propagation from seed takes too long for most gardeners, so it's best to buy started plants in early spring. Curly parsley is an excellent choice for a border planting. It's best to buy new plants each year because in its second year, parsley will go to seed by midsummer and there will be nothing to harvest after that. If you plant parsley in containers, use lots of compost in the layers to supply nutrients, or mix some alfalfa meal into one layer.

How to Harvest. Cut stems from the outside of the plant as needed. During peak season, cut and chop leaves in quantity, then fill storage containers and freeze.

Pat's Favorite Uses. Parsley has a wonderful flavor, and it enhances the flavor of otherwise bland food. We always keep bowls of parsley in ice water on hand for garnishing dishes served in The Potager café. I also keep small jars of chopped parsley in olive oil in the salad fridge to use on pasta and potatoes, in vegetable dishes, and in sauces. It's our "secret ingredient." If I still have parsley left over after that, I chop it and freeze it.

When my lettuce baskets are producing more than we need for salads, I whip up my "cream of green" soup. The amounts aren't exact because I tend to use whatever

SMALL SPACE TIPS	Parsley

Parsley

A pot of parsley is a pretty accent in a small herb garden, but once you harvest it, the plant looks forlorn until it regrows. So buy a four-pack of parsley and pot up each transplant individually in its own 6-inch pot. After you harvest, rotate a fresh plant into your garden and put the shorn plant in an out-of-sight spot until it recovers.

I have on hand, but I start with vegetable broth and add a roux to thicken it. As soon as the broth thickens, I add a large colander of mixed lettuce, parsley, chives, and sometimes cilantro. I cook the greens for about 3 minutes. Then I remove the pot from the heat and add a little light cream. When it has cooled, I put it through the blender. I reheat the soup in bowls in the microwave and serve it warm with a dollop of sour cream, chopped chives, and minced red peppers on top.

ROSEMARY

Rosemary (*Rosmarinus officinalis*) is one of the "big four" kitchen herbs, but it's also valuable in the craft room for potpourri and dried arrangements. The narrow, spiky leaves have a piney taste that gives lamb, chicken, and pork a delicious flavor.

How to Grow. Buy plants from a nursery and plant them in full sun in light, fast-draining soil. You can try planting rosemary in partial shade, but the plants may be leggy, with few flowers. Hardiness varies by cultivar, with most types hardy only in Zones 8 to 10. Your best choice may be to grow rosemary in a container, so it's ready to bring indoors for winter.

Prostrate rosemary (*R. officinalis* 'Prostratus') looks beautiful in a hanging basket. It usually grows about 2 feet long, but in areas with warm winters, stems may trail up to 6 feet long.

How to Harvest. Cut long individual branches to weave into small herbal wreaths or to hang and dry. Cut small sprigs to use fresh in cooking.

Pat's Favorite Uses. One of my standards is rosemary with chicken breast and sweet potatoes. Add a sprig of fresh rosemary to ¼ cup of olive oil in a frying pan. Bring the

---

SMALL SPACE TIPS

Rosemary

Rosemary is a true shrub, and you can train a potted rosemary plant to a standard (miniature tree) form. Add prostrate rosemary to cover the soil and spill over the sides of the pot, and voilà—a truly elegant container planting.

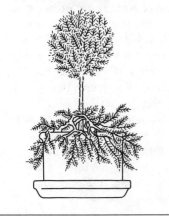

heat up to medium, remove the rosemary, and add slices of sweet potato. Cook until tender and remove to a warm plate. Dredge a chicken breast in flour and add it to the cooking oil. Cook until the chicken is cooked through. Serve garnished with a sprig of fresh rosemary.

You can also use rosemary-flavored olive oil (prepared as above) to sauté lamb, pork, or veal. I especially like pork cutlets with a dusting of seasoned breadcrumbs sautéed in rosemary oil and served with tomato sauce and grated cheese, or plain with lemon wedges to squeeze over the top.

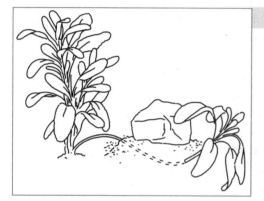

To propagate sage by layering, choose a sage stem and pinch off some leaves. Heap soil over the bare section of stem, leaving the tip exposed. After several weeks, check to see if roots have formed. Cut the layered stem to separate the new plant from the parent plant.

SAGE

The strongly scented, gray-green leaves of common sage (*Salvia officinalis*) are good with cheese, pasta, pork, poultry, and rice. Dried sage branches are useful in wreaths and floral arrangements. Let sage go to flower and the purple flower spikes will attract bees, butterflies, and hummingbirds.

How to Grow. Grow in full sun in an average lasagna bed. I suggest you buy plants that have substantial growth so you can take some cuttings right from the first season for cooking or to use in arrangements. Sage grows well in a container, too. If you'd like to start a new sage plant or two to give to a friend, try the technique called layering, shown in the illustration above.

How to Harvest. Cut tips of stems to encourage side growth. Pinch individual leaves for fresh use. To harvest sage for drying, cut stems back to the point where the stem becomes woody. Hang bundles of stems upside down to dry in a dark, airy place.

Pat's Favorite Uses. I mix a crusty coating for roast loin of pork

SMALL SPACE TIPS

Sage

Common sage is a must for the kitchen, but you may want to try growing some other types of sage just for fun. At the front of a bed, tuck in a low-growing variegated sage such as 'Tricolor', which has green, white, and purple leaves, or golden sage (*S. officinalis* 'Aurea') with gold-edged, light green leaves. I also love 'Berggarten', which has large, rounded, gray-green leaves.

by combining equal amounts of fresh chopped sage, rosemary, and parsley with salt, coarsely ground black pepper, and olive oil. Spread the mixture on top of the pork loin and bake at 375°F for 1 hour.

I also like to use sage in my cornbread stuffing for chicken, pork, or turkey. And I make a small sage wreath every year as a decoration to hang in my kitchen.

SANTOLINA

Santolina (*Santolina chamaecyparissus*) is also called lavender cotton, and the scent of the foliage is similar to lavender. This perennial herb is actually part of the daisy family, and the flowers are yellow and buttonlike, while the lacy leaves are silver-gray.

How to Grow. I suggest buying santolina plants from a nursery rather than fussing with seeds, because one or two plants is all you'll need unless you're a professional herb crafter. Plant santolina in full sun in average, very well-

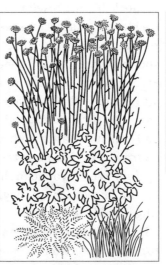

Plant santolina in the background of an herb garden, and give it some space because it will reach 2 feet tall and wide when it flowers.

drained soil. Plants will grow 2 feet tall and wide unless you prune them to control their size. Each spring, cut back old growth to promote healthy new stems to sprout. It's hardy in Zones 5 to 8.

How to Harvest. Cut bunches of stems 8 to 10 inches long in summer and hang them in a dark, airy spot to dry. Cut long, flowering stems when the flowers are in full bloom, but be sure to wait until the dew has evaporated from flowers before harvesting.

Pat's Favorite Uses. I love my santolina hedge in the rose garden. I'm sure the fragrance helps to repel some insect pests from my roses. I also like to plant santolina with other herbs with gray foliage, such as catmint and silver thyme.

SMALL SPACE TIPS

Santolina

A low hedge of santolina is a charming border for a small herb garden. Plant small plants 10 inches apart, and keep the tops pruned to prevent flowering and to encourage side growth. Use the trimmings to fill small cloth bags and use them as a moth repellant in a linen chest.

SORREL, FRENCH

For a touch of lemon flavor in a soup, salad, or sauce, try French sorrel (*Rumex scutatus*). The bright green leaves are high in vitamin C.

How to Grow. Don't confuse this wonderful plant with red sorrel or dock (*R. acetosella*), a common weed. Buy plants or seeds from a reputable source to make sure you're getting true French sorrel. French sorrel is perennial in Zones 4 to 9 and will come back for many years. It thrives in good, rich soil and can stand a little shade.

How to Harvest. In early spring, when you can harvest at least a cup of leaves, begin by cutting outside leaves.

Pat's Favorite Uses. I like to top fish or chicken with sorrel sauce. To make the sauce, clean and chop 1 cup each of sorrel, lettuce, and watercress. In a medium-size saucepan, cook the chopped greens in 1 cup of water with 1 whole peeled onion. When the greens are mushy, remove the onion and discard it. Allow the greens to cool, and add 1 tablespoon of olive oil, 1 teaspoon of white vinegar, and salt and pepper to taste. Stir all ingredients together until creamy. Stores well in a covered container.

 French Sorrel

I always find room for a few sorrel plants. You can grow up to three French sorrel plants in a 10-inch pot. Harvest leaves before they get too large to keep the plants producing tender new leaves. You can blanch and freeze excess leaves to use later.

TARRAGON

A single clump of French tarragon (*Artemisia dracunculus* var. *sativa*) is all that's needed in a small herb garden. This perennial herb has a strong, aniselike taste and is hardy in Zones 4 to 8.

How to Grow. Start with purchased plants because you cannot grow tarragon successfully from seed. Grow in full sun in a well-drained lasagna bed. After harvesting, top-dress the plant with compost. You probably won't need to propagate your tarragon for your own garden, but if you want to share it with a friend,

SMALL SPACE TIPS

Tarragon

You can bring a container of tarragon indoors for the winter, but not until it's had a dormant period. Leave the container outdoors until January. Then bring it into your garage or basement (if it's cool) for a week. After that, you can set it up in your house under grow lights or in a sunny window. The leaves should resprout, providing fresh tarragon to season savory roast chicken and other dishes.

take stem cuttings in spring or early summer.

How to Harvest. Cut sprigs of fresh, green, 1-inch-long leaves. I wait until midsummer to harvest leaves for freezing. Put the leaves in resealable plastic bags, and label them before sticking them in the freezer.

Pat's Favorite Uses. I collect tarragon sprigs in early spring for tarragon and shallot vinegar. Tarragon complements the favor of hearty fishes like monk fish, salmon, and tuna. Lay a sprig across each filet and prepare it your favorite way: baked, poached, or grilled.

Here's how I fix a quick tarragon chicken salad: Cook and cube 12 ounces of chicken breast. Toss with 3 ounces of mayonnaise; 1 ounce of heavy cream; 1 teaspoon of chopped tarragon leaves; 1 large spring onion, chopped; and salt and pepper to taste. Serve the salad on a bed of spring mix and garnish with green grapes.

THYME

There are as many as 300 different species of thyme (*Thymus* spp.)—some have culinary uses, while others are great landscape plants for borders and rock gardens. This hardy perennial herb is available in ground-hugging creeping forms or spreading, upright forms up to 15 inches tall. The leaves have a pungently delicious scent and flavor. Flowers range from white to magenta. Lemon-scented thyme (*T. × citriodorus*) is one of my favorites. Most species are hardy in Zones 4 to 9.

How to Grow. Thyme will grow in any average garden bed in full sun, but it requires warm summers to flower and flourish. Some varieties of thyme will grow in partial shade, but they may not produce flowers. I suggest planting purchased plants rather than starting from seed.

How to Harvest. Grab a handful of foliage and flowers, and use sharp scissors to cut it free near ground level. Tie into bundles and hang to dry.

Pat's Favorite Uses. Fresh lemon thyme is a favorite with chicken or fish. Mother-of-thyme (*T. pulegioides*) is the type I cut and dry in quantity. Tie sprigs of thyme and parsley along with a bay leaf in cheesecloth to make a bouquet garni for use in soups and stews.

When thyme is in bloom, take cuttings to add to herbal wreaths. The flowering sprigs work just as well as baby's-breath does as a filler, and they smell twice as nice!

SMALL SPACE TIPS

Thyme

Most varieties of thyme are compact enough to fit in a small garden. Thyme can even grow in a small pot if you choose a slow-growing type. Lemon thyme is my favorite for a small space because it grows slowly and stays small as long as you harvest a bit now and then for cooking or arrangements. Caraway thyme (*T. herbabarona*), with its rye-bread aroma, is wonderful to plant in a container on a patio where you can run your fingers over the top to release the fragrance. Woolly thyme (*T. pseudolanuginosus*) has gray leaves and rose-pink flowers, and it looks gorgeous tumbling over a rock wall.

If you like to use lots of thyme in the kitchen, try planting common thyme (*T. vulgaris*) as a short hedge to edge a garden bed. Trim the hedge frequently, and you'll have plenty of thyme for cooking.

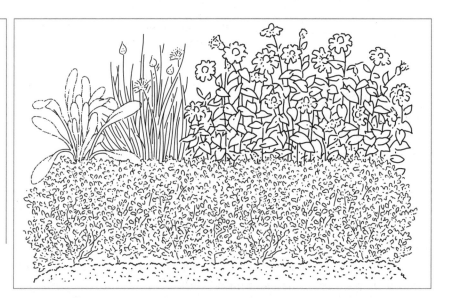

SMALL SPACE TIPS

Sweet Violets

I love the look of violets as a living mulch for a shrub planted in a large container. Very early in spring, buy six-packs of violets and plant them on 3-inch centers under the base of the shrub. They will form a beautiful living carpet of sweet-smelling flowers. If they die back in summer heat, stick in petunias or alyssum for the rest of the season. The violets may reseed themselves and come back the following spring.

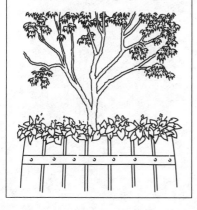

VIOLETS, SWEET

Sweet violets (*Viola odorata*) are a hardy perennial that grows in thick clumps of foliage with fragrant white, deep purple, or blue flowers on single stems. The old-fashioned fragrance of violet toilet waters was popular during my grandmother's time. Sweet violets will grow to 12 inches tall and are hardy from Zones 5 through 9.

How to Grow. Plant sweet violets in a rich lasagna bed in dappled shade. It's easiest to buy plants from the garden center. After the first year, they'll reseed themselves. In hot areas, plants may die out during the summer. Protect the plants from hot sun, and mulch with leaf mold to keep the roots cool and moist.

How to Harvest. Cut young leaves, wash them in cold water, and add them to salads. Pick individual flowers for use in salads or for pressing.

Pat's Favorite Uses. Candied violets are an old-fashioned treat. At midday or in the early afternoon, pick a few flowers—don't overdo it, or the flowers wilt before you're ready to candy them. Set them on a paper towel on your kitchen counter for about 30 minutes, until they don't feel dewy. Cover a drying rack with parchment paper. Separate 1 egg, and beat the egg white to a light froth. (Or, if you are concerned about using raw eggs, use a powdered egg-white product, instead.) Add 2 or 3 drops of vodka to speed drying. Hold a flower by its stem and use a small paintbrush to gently brush the egg-and-vodka mixture on all sides of the petals. Then dust all surfaces with super-fine sugar. Set the flower face-up on the drying rack. After you've brushed and dusted all the blossoms, move the rack to a cool, dark place. When the violets are dry, they will be stiff and brittle.

CHAPTER 6

FRUITS & BERRIES FOR SMALL SPACES

As one of the world's most enthusiastic berry pickers and fruit lovers, I promise you that there are few pleasures to equal the taste of homegrown fruit. You may not think you have enough space to grow fruit, and if you're picturing 25-foot apple trees, you're right. However, there's a big world of dwarf fruit trees and other small fruit crops to discover. Even if you're a balcony gardener, you can grow a berry bush in a container or a few strawberry plants in a window box.

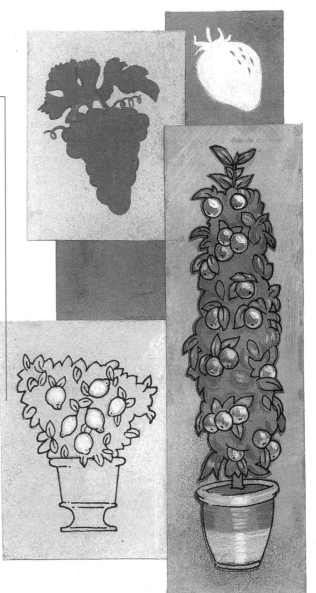

Fitting Fruit in Small Spaces

I started picking wild fruits and berries as a child. We picked apples, blackberries, grapes, peaches, pears, plums, and raspberries. Grandmother depended on a good harvest to make jam, jelly, canned juice, cobblers, and pies. How bland winter meals would have been without the fruit we had picked all summer!

Once my own children were old enough to help pick fruit, I took them along to berry patches and fruit orchards. We would come home with boxes full of strawberries and bushels of apples. We picked sacks of plums and pecks of peaches. We harvested blackberries and raspberries from the wild, sometimes traveling miles to find fruit.

On the farm in Shandelee, I picked from my own patches of red currants and gooseberries growing out by the barn. Strawberries grew in 4 × 8-foot lasagna beds and 'Concord' grapes clambered along the side of the garage.

At The Potager, I now grow blueberries, gooseberries, grapes, plums, raspberries, and strawberries in beds that measure in inches rather than acres. Many of my fruit and berry plants are trained to grow up: grapes on arbors, strawberries in tiered pots, and gooseberries snuggled up to a plum tree that is espaliered on the side of the building. I've learned from years of experience that I can grow fruit and berries in very little space. It's also possible for you to grow

A dwarf fruit tree can be a perfect focal point for an informal garden of edibles. Surround a dwarf apple tree with herbs, edible flowers, lettuce, and berry bushes for a garden that will delight you with its good looks and great flavors all season.

fruit and berries in your backyard by finding the right compact varieties to match your site and climate.

There are dwarf fruit trees that will fit into a flower border and single-stemmed "columnar" apple trees that will thrive in a large pot. You can interplant berries in flower gardens and grow them in containers, too. Planting your own miniorchard may seem like a luxury, but you *can* do it. Even if you're just renting your home or apartment, plant some fruit trees and bushes in containers. They will give you a sense of permanence that other plants won't. In a world of quick and sudden change, a little permanence is a good thing.

Fruit trees, including apples, pears, and some plums, can be grown in most climates in small spaces or in large containers. I think all these trees are best suited to small gardens where they can be trained into freestanding standards or espaliered or fanned against a wall.

Espaliered or fanned, a fruit tree can be tucked in the smallest place, where it will provide garden interest from the time the first buds appear through harvest season and even in winter, when the bare limbs have a stark beauty. Inch for inch, space given to a fruit tree is the best investment you can make.

A Mixed Berry Bed

One of my new fruit crop projects at The Potager is a mixed bed of raspberries and blueberries. Despite my best intentions, it took years for this bed to come to fruition. My daughter Mickey and I had picked out a site for berry bushes near the parking area. Dreaming of the wonderful berries we would harvest, we built up wonderful lasagna layers. Each spring we ordered small fruit bushes from our supplier to sell to our garden-center customers. We always ordered extra for our own berry bed, but each year, we sold all the bushes before we had a chance to plant any ourselves! Meanwhile, that lasagna bed kept getting richer as we added more layers.

After 4 years' worth of berry bushes had slipped through our fingers, I was determined not to be sidetracked again. I planted our bushes the day they arrived from our supplier! In the 2 × 8-foot bed, I planted four 5-gallon pots of red raspberries and four dwarf blueberry bushes in a zigzag row, alternating the raspberries and blueberries. This is much closer than conventional spacing, but in the rich conditions of a lasagna bed, intensive planting schemes usually work quite well. (As the bed matures, if I observe that conditions are too crowded, I'll have to build yet another bed in the parking area and transplant the raspberries.)

The following spring, I added metal corner posts and ran wire along each side of the bed to support the raspberry canes. I harvested raspberries in June and blueberries in late July. I was in berry heaven!

My Bountiful Grape Arbor

Nothing in the gardens at The Potager gives me as much satisfaction as the grapevines that cover a cedar arbor in Mickey's kitchen

garden. They remind me of my Grandmother Webb's grapes, which were trained to wires supported by a long series of T-bar posts. Sometimes the vines would be so heavy with grapes that they weighted the wires down. Grandmother would use a small sapling to brace up the vine, similar to the way she hitched up her clothesline when it was heavy with wet laundry. Her grape jelly was divine, and grape juice was a rare treat in the dead of winter. Years later, as an adult, I learned that Grandmother also had a penchant for homemade grape wine—she'd always called it "medicine" for her cough.

I don't have the space to grow the grapes that my Grandmother did, but I'm a sucker for a good plant sale, so when I found 'Concord' grape vines at a local nursery for an unbelievably low price, I couldn't help myself. I bought three, even though I only had one arbor available to support them.

I had to plant the vines 9 inches apart at the base of that arbor (ridiculously close, when you consider that commercial growers plant vines 8 feet apart). But there's something to be said for my kind of blind faith. I rush in and plant while others stew over the "what ifs." The arbor filled very quickly with wonderful vines, and there are no signs of disease.

No garden space for fruit trees? Believe it or not, you can grow delicious apples in large pots. Columnar apple trees produce fruit along a single upright trunk. Try planting a pair in matching decorative pots to highlight a sunny front entry.

Citrus by the Canal

Northern gardeners can only dream of picking oranges or grapefruit from a back-yard tree. But gardeners who live in Florida or parts of Texas or California can grow citrus trees, even in a small yard.

On a trip to Palm Coast, Florida, to the home of Eddie and Jenne Rossi, I measured the space they used to grow dwarf grapefruit and orange trees. Each tree took up a circular area less than 2 feet across. The trees were short, allowing for easy picking.

The Rossi home is on a canal, and they dock their boat right behind the house. The lawn slopes gently down toward the bulkhead, and just before you reach the landing slip, you pass the fruit trees. The trees bear over 50 grapefruit and 100 oranges each year.

The family next door to the Rossis has turned a strip 3 feet wide and 20 feet long down the side of their property into a minigrove of four trees. They hadn't picked their fruit at the time I visited, and I lost count of the individual oranges and grapefruit. It was a beautiful sight.

I prune them hard each year, being careful to preserve some of the new wood because the vines produce fruit on 1-year-old wood. Each fall I layer on grass clippings, leaves, and compost. I was worried 2 years ago when we had a drought and water was rationed, but the vines didn't appear to suffer and produced lots of sweet grapes.

Fruit-Growing Basics

Fruit crops are a mixed bag: Apples, citrus, plums, and pears grow on trees, grapes grow on woody vines, while raspberries and many other berries grow on woody canes. Blueberries grow on shrubby bushes, while strawberries are small, herbaceous perennials. Because of this, they need different kinds of care at various times of year, but you can grow all of them quite successfully in lasagna gardens in a sunny spot. The basics are the same. Start by spreading thick pads of wet newspaper on your planting site and add layers of organic materials: garden wastes, compost, shredded leaves, peat moss, grass clippings, and whatever else you can collect.

Planting Trees and Shrubs

If possible, it's best to prepare beds for fruit crops in advance, rather than planting immediately after building the bed. This gives the soil time to settle and mature so it provides a more stable base for trees and shrubs. Build beds in fall for spring planting or in spring for fall planting. However, in a pinch, I've planted fruit trees and berry canes successfully in new lasagna beds, using rocks to weight down the roots while the bed settled.

Spring is the best time to plant fruit trees and bushes. If you order bareroot plants from mail-order suppliers, they'll be shipped at the time of year that's appropriate for planting. When the plants arrive, I remove them from the wrapping that they were shipped in. If I'm prepared to plant them that day, I set the plants with their roots in a bucket of water in my garage while I gather my tools and get ready. Once the plants have had a good drink, I'm ready to plant. Sometimes, though, plants arrive at an inconvenient time. When this happens, I "heel them in" in a trench on the south side of my house, under the eaves. (It's the first area that thaws.)

Supporting Young Trees

Young dwarf fruit trees need support to keep them growing upright, especially in the loose soil conditions of a lasagna bed. I use sturdy wooden or metal stakes, one per tree, which I pound through the bed and into the soil below at planting time. Use soft ties to anchor the tree to the stake, allowing some slack in the ties.

For fruit trees in wooden containers (like a box-type planter or a whisky barrel), I sometimes support the trunk at container level. I screw two large eye hooks into the inside of the container above the soil level, opposite each other. I run wire through the eye hooks and pass it through protective rubber hose to encircle the tree trunk (bare wire could easily damage the bark), as shown in the illustration on this page.

Whenever you stake, don't imprison the tree in an iron grip. Your goal is to give the tree gentle support, but it should still be somewhat free to sway in the wind.

Support fruit trees planted in containers by anchoring them to the container itself. Check the anchors frequently to ensure that they're not too tight.

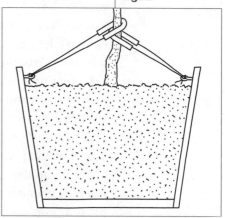

Pollination

If you want terrific crops of homegrown fruit, learn to think of bees as your friends. Fruit crops are insect-pollinated, and honeybees, bumblebees, and native bees are terrific pollinators.

It's also important to understand pollination requirements when you grow fruit. To explain this, I'll start with a quick review of how flowers are pollinated. Flowers have both female structures (pistils) and male structures (stamens). The stamens produce pollen. Insects pick up pollen on their bodies when they visit a flower, and they transfer the pollen to the pistils of other flowers they visit.

Some fruit crops aren't receptive to their own pollen for fertilization. They need pollen from a different cultivar for the flowers to be fertilized and to produce fruit.

For success with pollination of these crops, you need pollinators and at least two different cultivars of the crop. Plus, those two cultivars must bloom at the same time! Don't get flustered, though: Your supplier will be able to suggest compatible cultivars that bloom simultaneously. In the descriptions of individual fruit crops later in this chapter, I've noted which crops require a second variety for pollination.

Pruning

Pruning trees, bramble canes, and shrubs controls plant size, encourages good fruiting, and keeps the plants open to light and air. The specifics of pruning vary from crop to crop, and you'll find specifics in the crop-care descriptions later in this chapter.

Basic pruning cuts are the same for all crops, though. When you prune, you make two types of cuts: heading cuts and thinning cuts. When you make a heading cut, you remove a portion of a branch or cane. Make heading cuts on an angle, just above a bud. Heading cuts will stimulate the growth of sideshoots on the part of the branch or cane that remains.

To thin a branch or cane, you'll cut it back completely. For branches, you'll cut back to the main branch or trunk. Make a clean cut, and don't leave a stub. With canes, you'll thin by cutting right to the crown of the plant, again not leaving a stub.

When you use good tools, pruning is a pleasure. Felco has simply the best pruning tools I have ever used. I own a short-handled pair of pruning shears that are a great fit for my small hands. They are smaller and lighter than heavier pruners, and they're perfect for light pruning of berry canes, small branches on fruit trees, boxwoods, and roses. I also have long-handled pruners with a spring action that I use for removing branches that are out of reach over my head.

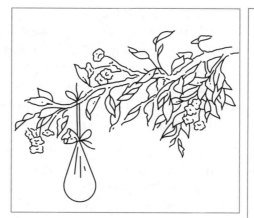

Hang small, weighted bags of sand on fruit tree branches to encourage them to spread. An angle of 45 to 60 degrees between trunk and branch is ideal. Horizontal branches produce more fruit than vertical branches do.

When it comes to pruning, I go by the farmer's motto: Prune when you have time. I keep my pruning tools handy so I can grab them on a whim and run out to make a few cuts at odd moments. This is one of my secrets for getting so much done in my busy life!

Creating an Espalier

Many of my gardening projects are inspired by some plant that's left over in the garden center at The Potager. One year, when a nice plum tree didn't sell, I decided to espalier it in the little sheltered side garden against the wall next to the entrance to the café. My experience is a good guideline to follow in planning your own espalier. Here's how the process works.

1. Choose your site and design your branching pattern. After observing the sun and shade patterns in the side garden, I decided that I needed to plant my plum tree to the right of the grape arbor to avoid being in shade. I sketched a pattern for the branches that appealed to me and that wouldn't block the view from the café windows.

2. Prepare your trellis or support. If you're planning a freestanding espalier, you'll need to install a fence or sturdy end posts with wires strung between them. (Typically, the wires are strung 18 to 24 inches apart.) In my case, I decided to attach 1 × 2-inch strips of wood to the wall as spacers so there would be more distance between the branches and the wall. This was important for air circulation and so that the rootball wouldn't be too close to the building foundation. I nailed large wire staples into the wood strips and strung my wires along the wire staples.

3. Plant the tree. With the lasagna gardening method, this is the easiest step! I'd been layering materials on this bed for 5 years, so it was well matured. I just scooped out the loose soil to the proper depth and set the tree in place. I also set a large piece of broken terra cotta flue tile between the building and the tree roots to prevent the roots from growing into the foundation. After planting, mulch and water well.

4. Begin training the first growing season. If your tree doesn't have good form for training, cut the main stem back to a few inches above the first wire. I was lucky; my little plum tree had sideshoots at the proper heights to train onto the wires. I cut away all the side branches that I didn't want to train and tied the remaining sideshoots to the wires with soft garden twine.

5. Follow-up through the summer as the tree produces new growth. If you cut your tree back to the first wire, your goal during the first summer will be to choose and train a main upright shoot and two sideshoots (at the level of your lowest wires). Remove buds that point in the "wrong" direction for your pattern. If your tree already has a main shoot with side branches, continue to tie the branches to the wires as they elongate.

6. Guide the shape each year. Late winter is the best time to prune espaliers. In winter, continue to encourage good structure by cutting the main shoot back a few inches above the next tier of wires. Once your espalier has reached full size, the only winter pruning needed is to thin out congested branches and fruiting spurs (on apples) to prevent crowding. Your summer pruning will concentrate on the top tier because that's where the tree naturally wants to produce the most new growth. Thin out some

Training fruit trees as an espalier will give you great yields from a small space.

of the side branches that sprout from the laterals to keep growth in balance on all tiers.

Espalier is an art form with many variations. If you'd like more detailed information on espalier, check some of the books on pruning and training in "Pat's Picks (Recommended Reading)" on page 274.

I love the interesting geometric form of my espaliered plum tree. Plus, it bears lovely flowers in spring and fruit in fall, and it provides structure for the small garden during the winter. An added bonus is that lots of my customers want to buy little plum trees now!

Care During the Season

Fruit crops need a little more care than some other crops, but they're well worth it!

PAT'S SMALL SPACE STORIES
A Poolside Berry Garden
One of the most delightful container gardens I've ever seen is the small fruit garden growing poolside at the home of my friend Walter Chandoha, a terrific gardener, professional garden writer, and photographer. Over the years, Walter has collected antique cast-iron urns and displayed them around his property. In the past, he has filled them with annuals, perennials, and ornamental grasses.
Today, Walter's containers are filled with black currants, gooseberries, and red raspberries. They surround one end of the swimming pool, in full sun, creating a miniature fruit garden. Even when they're not in leaf or flower, the berry canes offer a delightful display. Wow! What a great idea.

In the first year after planting, water fruit trees and bushes regularly, soaking the soil well. After the plants are established, your watering schedule will depend on your climate. During dry spells, check soil moisture regularly, and water if the soil is dry more than an inch or so deep. (This is true even during cold weather.) Keep the areas around the plants mulched to conserve moisture.

If you fertilize your fruit crops, do so in spring. Spread the compost or other organic fertilizer in a broad circle around the plants, not just at the base of the trunk, and don't use high-nitrogen fertilizers.

There are plenty of insect and animal pests that would like to share your harvest because fruit is so tasty! For advice on controlling insect pests, see Chapter 8.

Birds can be the most troublesome animal pests of fruit, whether you live in the city, suburbs, or country. There's a great product for keeping birds away from fruit, though: plastic bird netting. This is available at garden centers or from mail-order suppliers. And it's easy to protect dwarf plants with bird netting because you can swath the entire plant in netting. (This is not so easy to do with full-size fruit trees.)

A Few of My Favorite Fruits

From apples to strawberries, I love to grow fruit. I can grow a wonderful variety of fruit in my garden, although I'm limited to growing citrus in containers. I don't try to grow peaches because they won't set fruit reliably in my area and because they are prone to several serious insect and disease problems. If you're bold enough to try peaches, their care is similar to plums.

APPLES

Apples (and apple pie) are up there with America and mothers on our "best-loved" list. Lucky for the gardener with limited space, plant breeders have developed dwarf trees that are just right for small gardens. Dwarf apple trees grow only 8 to 14 feet tall, compared to 25 to 30 feet for standard-size apple trees. Some companies offer "minidwarf" apples that grow only 4 to 8 feet tall. Special columnar varieties grow as a single tall "stem" about 8 feet tall. I like to train dwarf apple trees as an espalier against a warm, sunny wall.

There are hundreds of apple varieties to choose to grow—from early midsummer varieties to late-autumn favorites. Whenever possible, choose varieties that have the most resistance to major diseases, such as apple scab, fire blight, powdery mildew, and cedar-apple rust. You'll have a fairly wide choice of varieties in dwarf form, more limited choices for minidwarfs, and very limited choices for columnar trees. In general, apples are hardy in Zones 3 through 9.

Site and Soil. Soil preparation is very important because apple trees live for 20 years or more. Prepare the lasagna bed in advance and allow it to settle for several months or a year before you plant.

If your apple trees are delivered at an inconvenient time, protect the trees by "heeling in" the roots. Dig a shallow trench with one straight side and one slanted side. Lay the roots in the trench on an angle and cover them with soil.

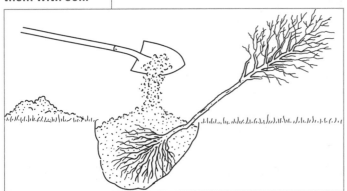

Planting. Buy bareroot trees from a reputable mail-order supplier. Plant in early spring or in fall. Keep roots cool and moist by heeling in until you can plant. Dig a wide planting hole so that you can spread the roots out fully. Set the tree in place and check to be sure the graft union (the crooked part of the trunk) is about 2 inches above ground level; adjust the hole depth until it's right. Refill the hole and tamp the soil in place. Water deeply and slowly immediately after planting, to soak the soil. Plant more than one variety to ensure cross-pollination, and space the trees at least 12 feet apart. Choose varieties that bloom at the same time. Read the catalog you plan to order from—it should have all the information about what varieties to plant together for successful pollination. If your neighbor has a crabapple tree, that helps with cross-pollination, too.

Plant a columnar apple tree in a large container, such as half of a whisky barrel, in layers that are rich in compost. Firm the soil well around the roots. Support freestanding trees in beds and containers by anchoring them loosely to a stake.

Growing Tips. Watering is the single most important part of caring for new fruit trees. Apply a 1½- to 2-inch layer of bark mulch around the tree, but leave a 2- to 4-inch-wide space unmulched all around the tree trunk. This prevents problems with diseases and discourages rodents from gnawing on the trunk. Keep this unmulched area free of grass and weeds by hand-weeding.

Even after mulching, you may need to water every week the first year. Adjust the supports as the trees grow to maintain a little slack.

PAT'S PICKS ~ APPLES

'Freedom': This large, red, juicy apple is resistant to all the major diseases. A cold-hardy, vigorous variety that is good for eating and cooking.

'Granny Smith': This is a solid green apple with great flavor that stays firm in a pie and is a favorite for fresh eating. Requires a long growing season (fruit is ready to harvest about 170 days after bloom) and is susceptible to apple scab.

'Gravenstein': This beautiful old apple has red color dripping down onto pale green. It's a great pie, sauce, and cider apple. You will need to plant at least two other apple varieties to ensure pollination.

'Jonagold': A classic red-and-yellow juicy apple that stores well and is good for cooking and fresh eating. Susceptible to scab and mildew.

'Liberty': Very disease resistant, similar to 'McIntosh'. Excellent for fresh eating, sauce, and baking. Does not store well.

'Newton Pippen': Sweet, yellowish green dessert apple. It's not particularly pretty but it has a wonderful rich, aromatic flavor and it stores well. Susceptible to apple scab.

'Pristine': Early-season yellow apple. Very disease resistant, with a mildly tart flavor that is excellent for fresh eating, baking, and sauce.

During the first few years, you will need to train your apple trees to have a central trunk with three or four well-spaced "scaffold" branches on each side of the tree. Spread the branches so they develop with 45 to 60 degree angles from the trunk. (One type of homemade branch spreader is shown on page 197.) Wide-angled branches will develop more fruit buds and be less likely to split under the weight of the fruit than narrow-angled branches. Columnar trees don't develop significant side branches, and the only pruning they need is to maintain the height you prefer.

If your trees develop too much fruit, it's a good idea to thin some out. A rule of thumb is to pick excess fruit so that branches bear one fruit every 6 to 8 inches. The tree will thin itself in midsummer, but you may need to thin more by hand. Remove any small or misshapen fruit.

Espaliers need to be pruned in summer to retain their shape. Cut off all suckers (straight upright growths that sprouted from the scaffold branches) and crossing branches.

Harvesting. You'll be able to start harvesting apples in the third year after you plant. Once the trees reach full production, you'll pick between 20 and 50 pounds of apples a year. When apples are ripe, their color will be fully developed. Read the catalog description to find out when the apples normally ripen. Around that time, for fresh eating, begin picking single apples and taste-testing. Pick storage apples when their color is fully developed; they may not develop full flavor until after harvest.

BLUEBERRIES

When I moved to the Catskill Mountains, I discovered wild blueberries growing in every field and swamp. Picking forays produced buckets of berries for pies, cobblers, and jams, plus bags of frozen fruit for winter pancakes. I don't forage for wild blueberries much anymore, but I enjoy growing them in containers. The modest-size bushes bear tassels of white flowers tinged with pink in late spring or early summer. In upstate New York, berries are ready for picking in August.

There's more than one type of blueberry, and the type you choose will depend on where you live. Highbush blueberries are native to the coastal areas of the East. They grow about 6 feet tall and are hardy in Zones 4 through 7. Lowbush blueberries are cold-hardy (Zones 3 through 7) and short; you have to squat down to pick the berries.

Southeast gardeners with large gardens grow rabbiteye blueberries. They will prosper as far north as Zone 7 and may reach an impressive 15 feet tall. There are hybrids of highbush and lowbush blueberries known as midhigh blueberries; they thrive in Zones 5 through 7 (and some varieties will grow well in hot-summer regions).

Site and Soil. Blueberries need acid soil conditions. A pH between about 4.0 and 5.5 will give the best results. Because of this, plan for a separate planting bed or area for blueberries, or plant them in a container. To amend soil for growing blueberries, add one or two buckets of peat moss or composted beech, chestnut, or oak leaves. Use oak leaves, pine needles, or wood chips for mulch.

Blueberries will grow in partial shade but need at least 6 hours of sun and good air circulation to produce a successful crop of berries. I can't help but wonder why anyone wouldn't include them in a foundation planting for the autumn color they would bring to fading borders.

Planting. Plant blueberries in spring in cool climates and fall in warm climates. Buy plants that are 2 or 3 years old. (If you buy plants that are locally grown, you may be able to buy 3- to 5-year-old plants. They may produce a harvest sooner than young plants will.) For best pollination results—bigger berries, longer harvest— plant more than one variety.

Make a shallow hole in the bed, and set the roots in the hole. Push the soil back over the roots and up to the level where the roots join the stem. Water thoroughly and apply 2 to 3 inches of mulch, such as compost or pine needles.

Growing Tips. Water blueberry bushes regularly in dry summers, and keep the soil mulched with an acidic mulch or compost. If you fertilize your blueberries, use soybean meal or pesticide-free cotton-seed meal (both are acidic and will help keep soil pH low). In early spring, prune old or damaged wood and any crossing or rubbing branches. Rabbiteye blueberries don't need to be pruned as heavily as high-bush blueberries. Lowbush blueberries need heavy thinning once they're mature, or their harvest will decline.

Harvesting. Berries ripen in late summer to fall. You'll notice when they start to turn blue. It's a good idea to cover the bushes with bird netting at this point, unless you want to share your harvest with the birds. Wait about a week after the berries change color before picking, so the fruit can reach full sweetness. Ripe berries should drop off the plants into your hand. Pick daily to encourage the biggest harvest. Expect 5 to 6 pounds of fruit from a mature bush planted in a lasagna bed. I pick 2 to 3 pounds from each of my container-grown bushes.

PAT'S PICKS ~ BLUEBERRIES

'Blue Jay': Plant this blueberry and just 2 years later begin harvesting big, light-blue berries that resist cracking. Plants grow 3 to 4 feet high. Fruit ripens in July. Zones 4 through 9.

'Chippewa': This compact blueberry grows 3 to 4 feet tall, and mature plants produce 4 to 7 pounds of berries. Leaves turn bright red in fall. Zones 3 through 8.

'Dwarf Tophat': The smallest blueberry bush of all and great for patio planting in containers. Grows 2 feet tall and produces full-size berries that are round and firm, ideal for baking. Best of all, you only need one bush to produce fruit because no pollinator is needed. Hardy in Zones 4 through 10, it's the perfect berry for southern gardeners.

'Northblue': A cross of a lowbush and highbush variety, this midhigh variety grows only 20 to 24 inches tall. Very hardy; produces 2 to 5 pounds of dark blue berries in June. The big, dark green leaves turn crimson in fall, making this compact bush a perfect addition to a border or foundation planting. Zones 3 through 7.

'Northsky': Can survive temperatures as low as –40°F. A midhigh that grows only 18 inches tall, producing medium-size fruit. This variety is a good choice for container planting. Zones 2 through 7.

'O'Neal': Grows to 6 feet tall but can be kept contained. Big berries, another good choice for southern gardeners. Zones 6 through 10.

CITRUS

If you live in California, Florida, or balmy parts of Texas, Arizona, and the Gulf Coast, you may enjoy growing a small citrus tree right in your garden. Choose dwarf varieties of grapefruit, lemons, limes, or oranges, which range in size from 5 to 15 feet, depending on the type of fruit and the particular variety. Even gardeners who don't live in Zones 10 or 11 can grow citrus in containers and bring them indoors for the winter. Lemons are one of the easiest types to grow in a large pot.

Site and Soil. Citrus trees need full sun, although lemons and limes will tolerate partial shade in hot areas. They do best in moist but well-drained soil. Find a protected spot out of the wind, if possible. Limes are less hardy than other types of citrus, so only plant them if you can provide very warm, protected conditions.

Planting. Plant bareroot trees while the weather is cool but there is no danger of frost. You can plant trees in containers at any time of year, but it's better to avoid planting them in the heat of summer. Dig a wide, shallow planting hole, and check the level of the tree in the hole. The graft union should be 6 inches above the soil surface. Backfill with soil, and mulch the area around the trunk, leaving a 12-inch-diameter circle around the base of the trunk bare. (Or mulch the entire area around the tree with gravel, for fast drainage.)

To grow citrus in a container, use a 10- to 15-gallon pot, and provide a stake to anchor the tree. Try planting in a mix of 80 percent sand and 20 percent organic matter. You can harvest fruit from a single tree because citrus trees are self-pollinating. (Although you may need to pollinate them by hand.)

Growing Tips. Water young trees once a week during their first year of growth. If you're growing the trees outdoors in a garden bed, fertilize several times a year with bloodmeal, compost, or cottonseed meal. Don't feed the trees during late fall, or cold winter weather may damage the tender young growth that results.

Pruning citrus is easy—just cut out crossing or rubbing branches. Also make heading cuts on upright branches to keep the trees from becoming too tall. Wear gloves—most citrus is thorny.

Keep container citrus plants outdoors in full sun. Water them well, and occasionally water enough to

Set potted citrus trees on a wheeled caddy or platform so you can move them easily from outdoors to indoors with the seasons.

PAT'S PICKS ~ CITRUS

'Kaffir': This small lime variety is grown for its highly fragrant leaves, which are used in Thai cooking. (The peel is also used.) Leaves and fruits are both dark green. Good for containers, or for in-ground planting in Zones 10 and 11.

'Meyer Improved': Thought to be a cross between a lemon and orange, this small tree bears lemons with yellow-orange flesh and a sweeter flavor than standard lemons. Good for containers or in-ground growing. May be everblooming in mild climates.

'Minneola': A cross between a tangerine and a grapefruit, this small tree bears fruit with orange-red flesh and a tangerine flavor. Does well in containers.

'Nagami': A kumquat for planting in a container. Fruits are bright orange, and both the flesh and skin are edible. Good for fresh eating or making marmalade.

'Oro Blanco': A white-fleshed, low-acid grapefruit that will bear sweet fruit even in areas that don't get intense summer heat. Very fragrant flowers.

'Thornless Key Lime': If you love key lime pie, this is the lime to grow. Very cold sensitive, but quite productive in a container. Fruits are small and seedy, with excellent flavor.

flush the container, because citrus is sensitive to salt accumulation in the soil. In winter, indoor citrus needs as least half a day of sunlight. They like warm temperatures during the day, and they need high humidity. (You can boost humidity around the plant by misting the leaves several times a day.) Turn your thermostat down overnight because the plants prefer cool conditions (45° to 55°F). Fertilize container plants at least once a month.

Harvesting. Be sure to note when the varieties you've selected are supposed to ripen, because the outward appearance of the fruit doesn't give you reliable clues about ripeness. Ripe fruit can remain on the trees for up to 3 months; pick fruit as you need it.

CURRANTS, RED

Red currants are one of the greatest treasures in the garden. You can grow them as a standard bush or train them as a 4- to 5-foot-high cordon—a row of closely spaced plants trained as upright or angled single stems—to create a screen around the garden. The flavor of currants is incomparable.

If you want to plant currants, keep in mind that currants (particularly black currants) are thought to be hosts of white pine blister rust, a serious disease of white pine trees. Some states prohibit planting currants; check with your local extension agent if you are unsure whether currants are permitted in your area. Currants are hardy in Zones 3 through 7.

Site and Soil. Currants need rich, well-drained soil. Full sun is best, but they will tolerate light shade. Currants are very cold-hardy and do best where summers are not hot and dry for extended periods of time. Currants are self-fruitful.

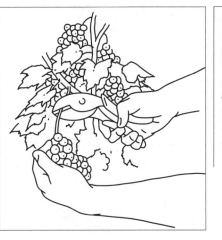

'Red Lake' currants are my personal favorite. When berries are dead ripe, I cut the whole stem, instead of harvesting one berry at a time.

Planting. Plant bareroot plants in late winter or early spring. Don't procrastinate, because the plants bloom early, and you might miss the bloom season. Open a shallow hole in the bed, and set the roots in the hole. Check the depth; the plants should be set slightly deeper than they were growing in the nursery. Adjust the depth of the hole if needed and push the soil back over the roots. Water thoroughly and mulch with aged compost to suppress weeds.

Growing Tips. Currants produce most of their fruit on 2- and 3-year-old branches, so you won't begin harvesting until the second year after planting. Shoots that are older than 4 years old produce little fruit. Once your plants are established, prune out branches that are more than 3 years old, and let the vigorous young shoots develop. Prune in late winter or early spring before the buds swell.

Birds like to eat currants, so thwart them by placing netting over fruits during the ripening season.

Harvesting. Currants ripen in the middle of summer. Taste-test the lowest berry on a cluster for ripeness, and harvest them near full ripeness for making jam. Wait until the berries are fully ripe to pick them for fresh eating. I clip off clusters with scissors or garden snips and then remove the individual berries from the stems once my bounty is safe in my kitchen.

PAT'S PICKS ~ RED CURRANTS

'Jonkeer Van Tets': Early producer of large, red fruits. Aphid and mildew resistant.

'Red Lake': This is an upright red currant bush with heavy yields and the most beautiful and tasty berries.

GOOSEBERRIES

A relative of red currants, gooseberries are an excellent dessert fruit that more people should be growing. (They're well loved in Europe.) Gooseberries are a fine fruit for the small garden when planted in a container or pruned to tree form. They are hardy in Zones 3 through 7.

Stick bamboo poles or lengths of plastic pipe into the ground around gooseberries and other fruit bushes and drape bird netting over the poles to thwart hungry birds.

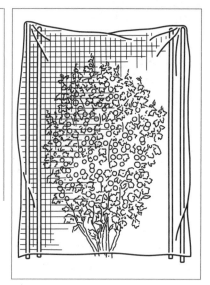

Site and Soil. Gooseberries grow best in full sun and partial shade. They need soil that drains well but stays damp and cool.

Planting. Plant bareroot plants in fall. Open a shallow hole in the bed, and set the plant in the hole. Check the depth; the plants should be set slightly deeper than they were growing in the nursery. Adjust the height if needed and cover the roots with soil. Water thoroughly and mulch well. Space plants 6 feet apart. Gooseberries are self-fruitful.

Growing Tips. In spring, mulch the plants with ½ inch of compost. Remove suckers around the bases. Gooseberries need moderate amounts of nitrogen but more potassium and magnesium. If your plants aren't thriving, test your soil to see if potassium is low. If it is, try applying greensand, an organic source of potassium, or a light sprinkling of wood ashes or kelp meal. You can also apply Sul-Po-Mag, which supplies potassium and magnesium. Follow the package directions for the amount to apply.

Prune gooseberries in winter to keep the bushes open so air can circulate. Cut off all but six new shoots, and remove any wood that is more than 3 years old. (Older wood doesn't produce much fruit.)

When harvesttime approaches, cover the bushes with bird netting to protect the fruit.

Harvesting. Fully ripe gooseberries are so sweet and tasty that, once you've tasted them,

PAT'S PICKS ~ GOOSEBERRIES

'Hinnomaki Red': Very productive with dark red fruit that has tangy skin and sweet flesh. Mildew resistant.

'Pixwell': Productive, upright variety with pretty purple foliage in fall. Light green berries are rosy pink when fully ripe. Mildew resistant.

'Poorman': Excellent for containers with upright growth and less-thorny stems than other varieties. The deliciously sweet fruits are reddish and pear-shaped.

you may decide never to have a garden without gooseberries again. Ripe fruit will hold on the plant for several weeks. For cooking, pick the fruit while it's slightly under-ripe. Each bush will produce from 2 to 10 pounds of fruit.

GRAPES

I grow grapes on an arch, intertwined with purple clematis. I prune some of the fresh vines for making wreaths. Some types of grapes are suited to dry climates, while others can cope with humidity. Hardiness varies by type, with some hardy as far north as Zone 4 and others able to tolerate heat up to Zone 10.

Site and Soil. Grapes need full sun and well-drained soil. Find a spot where breezes are frequent, to keep air circulating around the foliage—it will reduce the likelihood of disease problems.

Planting. Before you plant, build or install a sturdy support for your grapes. Grapes are very hardy if you plant types or varieties suited to your area, such as `Concord' in the North and muscadine grapes in the South. Plant in spring in cool climates and fall in warm climates. Open a shallow hole in the planting bed and set the plant in place. Check the depth; the graft union (crooked part of the trunk) should be 2 inches above the soil level. Adjust the height if needed, cover the roots with soil, water well, and mulch.

Grapes are self-fruitful, except for muscadines, which need a pollinator.

Growing Tips. Mulch in spring with a high-nitrogen mulch and water during the first year and in dry summers. After fruit sets, thin out the smallest fruits so remaining bunches are 12 inches apart. Continue mulching all summer with fresh grass clippings and nitrogen-rich compost.

Grapevines are vigorous and need training and pruning to produce a bountiful crop. (If you are growing grapes on an arbor and don't desire a lot of fruit, you can let them grow

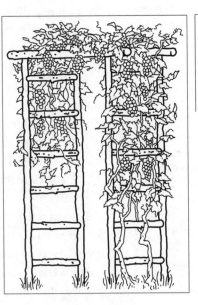

A strong wooden arch or pergola is a good choice for trellising grape vines.

PAT'S PICKS ~ GRAPES

'Concord': A disease-resistant American grape that's well suited to cool climates. Great for preserves, juice, and wine.

'Supreme': A disease-resistant muscadine grape with large, black fruit. You will need to plant a pollinator variety along with it.

with abandon.) There are many variations on training and pruning grapes. During the first few years, you will be establishing a strong trunk and developing the side branches (or arms). After the first few years, winter pruning will provide good air circulation and allow light into your vines.

Grapes are susceptible to a sackful of diseases. The best way to prevent problems is to choose grapes that are native to your area.

Harvesting. A mature vine can produce yields of 15 pounds or more for many years. Grapes don't continue ripening after you pick them, so wait until they're fully ripe to harvest. You can harvest whole clusters of 'Concord' grapes at once, but pick muscadines one by one because they ripen irregularly within a cluster.

AMAZING AUTUMN PIE

The Potager's Autumn Pie is one of our best-sellers, and it's reason enough to grow apples, pears, and plums. I'll share the recipe with you. For the crust, either use your own recipe for a double crust or buy a package of ready-made crust. Peel and slice 6 to 7 cups total of apples, pears, and plums. (I use about equal amounts of each.) In a large bowl, mix the sliced fruit, 2 tablespoons of lemon juice, 1 cup of sugar, 1 teaspoon of cinnamon, and 2 tablespoons of flour. Pile the fruit mix high in the bottom crust, dot the fruit with small pieces of butter, and lay on the top crust. Pinch the sides, cut vents in the top, and bake for 1 hour at 375°F.

PLUMS

Plums are a treat to grow and eat. They make the best preserves and add flavor and color to mixed-fruit pies (see my recipe at left). The small-space gardener has a couple of choices when choosing plums. You can choose a dwarf plum and grow it freestanding, or you can embark on espalier, training your plum tree against a wall.

With plums, you can match the tree to your climate because hardiness and bloom time vary quite widely. If winters are long and hard, choose varieties that flower later in the season. In warm climates, you can grow the early bloomers without fear of frost. The most difficult choice is picking a specific variety of a particular type of plum: American, European, Japanese, or Japanese-American hybrids. Plum trees will give you and yours a lot of pleasure for many years. Plant one as soon as possible!

Site and Soil. Plum trees need full sun, and different varieties will tolerate different types of soil. All types should do well in a well-drained lasagna bed.

Planting. In cool climates, plant trees in early spring, and in warm climates, plant in fall. Dig a hole in the bed and set the tree in place. Check the level of the graft union (the crooked area of the trunk); it should be above ground level. Adjust the depth of the hole if needed. Refill the hole with soil, water thoroughly, and mulch the area, leaving a 2- to 4-inch-wide space un-mulched all around the tree trunk.

To produce a full harvest, most plum varieties need cross-pollination, but most will bear a small crop even if you don't plant a second variety that blooms at the same time.

Growing Tips. Plum trees need about 1 inch of compost each year, topped off with a thin layer of mulch to suppress weeds and conserve moisture. A plum tree will naturally shed some of its young fruit in early summer. After that happens, check your tree and re-move additional fruits until the remaining fruits are spaced 4 to 6 inches apart.

European plums should be trained with scaffold branches, like apples. (See the pruning instructions for apple trees on page 202.) Japanese types are more spreading. Train them with an open center form with three or four main branches radiating outward from a main trunk. Plum trees do not need a lot of pruning after they are trained. Just prune out dis-eased or damaged wood. Prune out any black knot fungus (dark knobby growths) about 12 inches below the fungal growth, and destroy the dis-eased prunings.

Prune free-standing Japanese plum trees to an open center or vase-like form. This opens the trees to light and air, reducing the chances of disease problems.

Harvesting. A 10-year-old tree may produce as much as 50 pounds of fruit. Let plums become fully ripe be-fore you pick them. When they're soft and fully colored, they're ready to pick and eat.

PAT'S PICKS ~ PLUMS

'Damson': A European plum that's great for cold climates. The fruit is bluish purple with yel-lowish flesh and is excellent for home canning and preserves.

'Stanley': A European purple plum that's easy to grow, vigorous, and self-fertile (although it will yield more when pollinated with another variety). The sweet fruit is great for fresh eating and cooking.

'Weeping Santa Rosa': A self-fertile Japanese plum for small spaces. Makes great pies with its tart, red-skinned fruit and is also tasty for fresh eating.

RASPBERRIES, RED

Near my house in Westbrookville, there's an old raspberry patch where Mickey and I still pick large bags of berries for pies and cobblers for The Potager. The canes are nearly wild, but the berries are bigger and tastier every year. You probably don't have wild canes in your yard, so you'll have to buy raspberries for your garden. You can choose summer-fruiting or fall-bearing types; I grow both at The Potager. It's also smart to buy disease-resistant and certified virus-free plants because viral diseases can be a significant problem with raspberries. Raspberries grow well in Zones 3 through 9.

An old coffee table rescued from a garage sale is the perfect plant stand for my collection of potted berry bushes.

Site and Soil. Red raspberries have suckering roots that grow close to the surface and thrive in loose, rich, acid soil. The plants need constant moisture to put out a good crop of berries. They will be very happy in a lasagna bed where they get the nourishment they need and their roots will be unrestricted by heavy soil. Berries grow best in full sun, except in hot climates, where they prefer light shade.

Planting. Plant roots in early spring in cool climates and in fall in warm climates. Lasagna gardening is perfect for putting in an instant berry patch. Just pull back about 2 inches of layers and set the roots in place. Weight the roots down with a stone first, pull the soil back around the roots, and water. The roots simply will not grow if planted too deeply. Cut canes back close to ground level to reduce disease problems and to encourage root development. Keep moist after planting.

Growing Tips. Each spring, apply an inch or two of compost in your raspberry patch. Spread 1 or 2 sheets of wet newspaper over the compost and add a top mulch of bark chips or pine needles. Water during dry summers.

PAT'S SMALL SPACE STORIES

Beautiful, Bountiful Blackberries

I have wonderful memories of picking huge blackberries with my family when we lived on an old plantation in Albany, Georgia. Inspired by these memories, I still grow blackberries, even though they're not easy to fit in a small garden. The canes are large and generally take up lots of space. If you love blackberries as much as I do, though, follow my example and grow them along a fence that will support the canes. I have planted three plants 10 to 12 inches apart along a chain-link fence. (To grow your own blackberries, follow the planting instructions for raspberries on the opposite page.)

The vines don't need special support. I simply lay the canes along the chain-link and they remain in place. But to grow them against a smooth-surfaced wooden fence, I would string wire along the fence as shown on page 43.

To keep the berries in place, I periodically cut back growth that sprouts projecting away from the fence. A mulch of grass clippings at the base of the canes prevents weed problems.

I harvest my berries over a period of several weeks, pushing continued production by picking every day. My picking style is one for the bucket, one for me, one for the bucket, two for me. Even so, I still harvest enough to make a mean blackberry cobbler! You can expect up to 10 pounds of fruit from one plant.

After the harvest, I cut out the canes that produced fruit, leaving the new canes that will produce next year's crop.

Cut the old canes of summer-bearing varieties immediately after fruiting, leaving only two to four canes per square foot. Fall-bearing red raspberries can be cut to the ground at the end of winter. In my garden, I always cover my raspberries with bird netting, or they'll take my whole crop.

Harvesting. Expect about 12 pounds of fruit from a 10-foot row of summer-bearing canes.

STRAWBERRIES

What would summer be without the taste of red, ripe strawberries? I've been growing strawberries for most of my life and I still treasure every berry I pick, whether it's for eating fresh, making jam, or baking a pie. Strawberry plants are easy to grow and will thrive most anywhere. The plants spread rapidly, providing new plants for increased yields in successive years (although after 3 to 5 years, yields may decline). There are three types of strawberries: June-bearing, day-neutrals, and everbearing. I also grow alpine strawberries, which are a different species than standard strawberries.

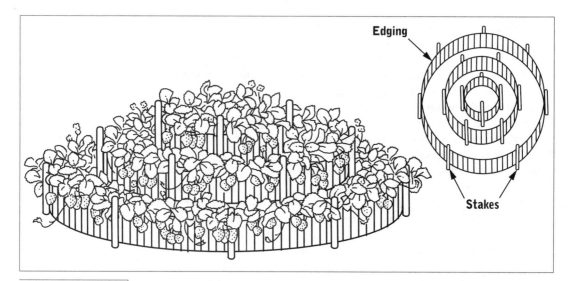

Plant up to 50 strawberry plants in a pyramid made of aluminum edging supported with stakes. Lasagna layering works perfectly for this system. I plant 25 June-bearing and 25 everbearing plants for an extended harvest.

June Bearers

If you want all your strawberries at once, this is the berry for you. June bearers deliver their harvest all at one time in spring, usually in June. You pick berries for about 2 weeks and then let the plants rest until next year. If you like to make lots of jam, then the concentrated harvest that June bearers provide is what you need.

Day-Neutrals

Day-neutral strawberries will provide fruit over the entire growing season. You can harvest fruit the first year you plant, but harvests will decrease after 2 years. Some gardeners grow them as annuals. Day-neutrals are more shallow-rooted and produce fewer runners than June-bearers. You'll need to water them during dry spells.

PAT'S PICKS ~ JUNE-BEARING STRAWBERRIES

'Dunlap': A super-hardy plant that produces even under harsh growing conditions. Tolerates drought, insects, and disease. Large, reliable yields of smooth, scarlet berries bursting with wild-berry flavor.

'Earliglow': The best early berry for canning and freezing. Extra fast to set and ripen fruit. Produces uniform, deep red fruit with outstanding sweet flavor. Resistant to red stele, root rot, and verticillium wilt.

'Sequoia': This variety will thrive in Southern heat and has a long bearing period. Produces very large berries that are dark red, juicy, and full of flavor.

Day-neutral strawberries are a natural for hanging baskets. I plant three or four plants in a 10- or 12-inch basket. You can harvest big, sweet fruits for several weeks and then enjoy the scalloped green foliage all summer. Best of all, you can root plants for next year's hanging pots if you use my double-decker pot technique shown at right.

Everbearers

Everbearing strawberries are not my favorite type of strawberry. Although they produce over a long period of time, production drops off after the first flush of berries. They're nice for a small bed for people who want a small ongoing harvest. (If you like a few strawberries on your breakfast cereal each morning, then everbearers would be right for you.)

Alpine Strawberries

Also called *fraise de bois*, these tidy plants bear plump little strawberries from early June until December. Plant them in window boxes, medium-size pots, and as a border in a garden bed. They don't send out runners, and the abundant foliage hides the fruit

Suspend a hanging basket filled with soil below a hanging basket of day-neutral strawberries. As the runners grow, pin them to the soil surface in the lower basket. They'll take root, and you'll have a head start on next year's crop.

PAT'S PICKS ~ DAY-NEUTRAL STRAWBERRIES

'Seascape': An early-ripening, large variety with great flavor. Long harvest season; does well in California and the Pacific Northwest. Disease resistant.
'Selva': A very good berry. Sugary sweet, wedge-shaped fruit is firm and delicious.

Plants are very hardy and prolific. Susceptible to red stele.
'Tristar': A very popular, cold-hardy variety with firm, sweet fruit. Bears its heaviest crop in spring, but fruits through the summer with a light crop in fall. Resistant to diseases.

PAT'S
PICKS ~ EVERBEARING STRAWBERRIES

'Eversweet': Perfect for hot, humid regions. Tolerates temperatures over 100°F without loss of fruit quality. Bred especially for southern gardeners. Very large, deep red berries are exceptionally sweet.

'Fort Laramie': An aromatic, sweet flavored variety. A good choice for colder climates, it is a vigorous plant that does produce runners. Use for fresh eating and preserves.

'Quinalt': Very large, sweet fruit. This everbearer is productive and disease resistant, and it is attractive in borders and containers.

during the season, cheating the birds of a tasty treat—but not you, if you look carefully. The foliage changes from dark green to red after the first frost.

Some visitors to The Potager seem to think alpines are too small to be worth bothering with, but you should see how quickly small children scout out these little gems. I love to see a child squatting by my alpine strawberry border, picking and eating the berries with delight.

You can grow this strawberry from seed and harvest the first year. Plants will freely self-seed or you can divide to propagate. As if those were not enough reasons to grow alpine strawberries, they also will tolerate growing in shade under trees or at the base of a shrub.

Site and Soil. Strawberries grow best in full sun, although alpine strawberries can take partial shade. Strawberries like good drainage and fertile soil, so they're very happy in a lasagna bed.

Planting. One of the joys of lasagna gardening is planting strawberries—it's so easy. I prepare a compost-rich bed and plant my virus-free plants by pulling the top layers apart and setting the roots in place, leaving the top of the crown exposed. The best time to plant is early spring. In mild-winter areas, you can plant in fall or late winter.

Strawberries will send out runners that produce new plants all along their stems and are perfect for hanging baskets, containers, and small beds. You can grow regular-size strawberries in most kinds of containers, from window boxes to pots. It's best to repot the plants each year to stimulate new growth and fruiting. When a container has finished making fruit, prop the container up onto a larger container. Set a couple of small pots alongside the mother plant pot and train runners to root into the small pots.

PAT'S PICKS ~ ALPINE STRAWBERRIES

'Alpine Yellow': I haven't tried this type of alpine, which has yellow fruit instead of red. But I think a mixed basket of red and yellow alpine strawberries would be quite pretty!

'Rugen': This is the variety sold most often. Berries are plump and red.

Cut off the rest of the runners and discard them.

Every 3 years or so, you'll need to discard the mother plants altogether, but by then, the baby plants you've rooted will be ready to produce a crop.

Growing Tips. Apply compost-rich mulch to feed the plants and a top mulch of straw to keep the fruit clean and the ground moist. After the crop is finished for the season, cut off the foliage. (You can use clippers or, if your patch is big enough to warrant it, your lawnmower.) Thin out the older plants and remove any weeds you find. Mulch the bed well.

Strawberries are susceptible to many diseases. Gray mold is the worst problem in my garden, especially during wet summers. To minimize diseases, water plants in the morning instead of the evening, and remove the first sign of mold or rot by removing the entire plant.

Birds can be a pesky nuisance in a strawberry patch. Protect the large berries from birds by covering the plants with a floating row cover or netting.

To overwinter strawberries in pots or hanging baskets, I just set them on the ground against a fence under a shade tree in fall. When the leaves drop, they cover up the baskets, and the snow provides additional insulation. (If you don't have a natural setup like this, put the plants in a protected spot and pile leaves loosely over the pots.) I pull out the pots in early- to mid-April and put them in a sunny spot to encourage new growth.

Every 3 years, move the youngest plants to a fresh bed or fresh soil (this crop rotation helps prevent disease problems), and discard the older plants. Rotating strawberries isn't hard for small-space growers because all that may be required is to replant the crowns in a fresh window box or hanging basket.

Harvesting. Expect about 2 cups of berries from each regular strawberry plant and a constant crop of small alpine berries. Wait until the berries are fully red and slip easily off the stems when you tug on them gently.

CHAPTER 7

ROCK GARDENS & TROUGH GARDENS

Rock gardening is intimate. You prepare small areas for planting and delicately tend the special plants that you've chosen specifically for their hardiness and unique appearance. These small plants, nestled in nooks and crannies among rocks, entice you to bend down and get close to your garden. Their blooms may be tiny and shy, too, or they may be almost unreal in their boldness. Give rock gardening a try, but beware—it can be addictive.

The Lure of Rock Gardening

From my first foray into the world of rock gardens and the special plants that inhabit them, I've been a champion of this very special form of gardening. Rock gardening is something that gets in your blood. There's something irresistible about rock-garden plants, which cling tenaciously to the tiny spaces between rocks and surprise us with their incredible flowers.

The inspiration for rock gardening is the beautiful communities of alpine plants that grow naturally among the rocky outcroppings high on mountain slopes. Some gardeners work intensively to re-create these conditions on their property, building artificial slopes and lugging in gravel and rocks by the ton. This kind of rock gardening isn't for me, though, and I'll bet it's not for you, either.

Rock gardens nowadays offer the impression of an alpine planting, but they don't require building an artificial mountainside and they aren't limited to plants native to areas above the tree line. You can make a simple rock garden by taking advantage of rocks that are already in your yard or by acquiring a few special rocks. Your garden may include some of the same annuals, perennials, bulbs, and herbs that you grow in your other gardens, or it may contain species that are related. For example, one of my favorite perennials to plant in a rock-garden setting is 'Homestead Purple' verbena. I fell in love with this plant when I saw it growing at the top of a sloping bank amid azaleas in Henry County, Georgia. I knew I had to have it, and I added it to my garden that same year. As the name indicates, it has wonderful purple flowers that look perfect spilling over rocks or stone steps. It grows just 6 to 10 inches tall, and it's mildew resistant to boot.

The only true rule of rock gardening is that the garden should look natural, as if nature spilled out the rocks exactly where they sit. If you're new to rock gardening, take time to view natural formations of rocks in your area so you have a mental picture to follow when building your own rock garden.

TAKE A LESSON FROM MOTHER NATURE

In the Hudson Valley and lower Catskills where I live, a drive down any country road or a walk in the woods will bring you to just the right terrain to study rock gardens. The same applies to mountains in Tennessee, Vermont, or the back roads of Maine. Naturally, gardeners in the Rocky Mountains are surrounded by natural rock gardens. It might be a little harder to find examples in the flat areas of the Midwest, but ask nature-loving friends for guidance or get in touch with the North American Rock Garden Society by visiting their Web site at www.nargs.org or by writing to NARGS, PO Box 67, Millwood, NY, 10546. I'm sure there are lovely examples of rocky gardens in almost every part of North America.

Rock Gardening the Lasagna Way

As with any garden project, there are a few essentials to keep in mind for successful rock gardening: soil, climate, and location.

One of the main requirements of alpine and rock-garden plants is fast drainage. These little plants don't like to have their roots sitting in wet conditions at all. They're adapted to gravelly conditions where rainwater quickly percolates through the upper layers of soil and away from plant roots. Following conventional garden thinking, would-be rock gardeners with slow-draining clay soil have dug out that heavy soil with pickaxes and brute strength, replacing it with a mix of light soil, sand, and gravel.

Recently I watched a television show where a very old woman was installing a new plant in her hilly rock garden. I wanted to call her and tell her not to work so hard! Her gardens were 35 years old and she was still using a pickaxe and shovel to make a deep depression to which she hauled buckets of compost to enrich the soil.

I don't do pickaxes, so I decided to create rock gardens lasagna-style. It seemed to me that covering the soil with layers of wet newspaper and organic material would soften the soil underneath, and earthworms attracted to the lasagna layers would create drainage tunnels in the soil below. It works!

Fast-draining soil is the primary requirement for a rock garden, but also be sure to check the light and hardiness requirements of the plants you choose. You'll find that most rock-garden plants do well in full sun, and some will tolerate partial shade. As long as you give the plants the conditions they need, you'll find that rock-garden plants are fairly undemanding and trouble-free.

Gardening among Existing Rocks

You may already have a site in your yard that's crying out to be a rock garden. Perhaps you have a garden bordered by a rock retaining wall or some fieldstone steps up to your door.

In sites like these, you may not need to prepare the soil at all, lasagna-style or otherwise. Poke around in the wall to see whether there are any pockets where soil has collected. If there are, you can simply tuck some low-growing plants into the pockets. After planting, you can mulch around the plants—leaf mold (thoroughly composted leaves) is a good choice, but you can use whatever you have on hand. One of my favorite mulches—triple-ground, dark brown bark mulch—also looks nice

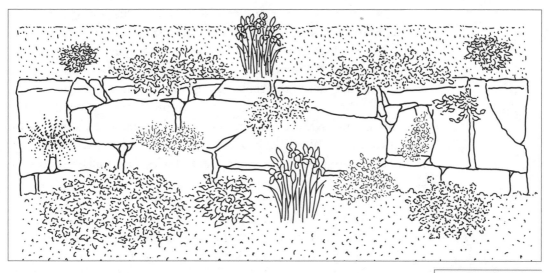

around rock-garden plants. The most important tip for establishing rock-garden plants in planting pockets among stone is to water daily for the first week. After that, the plants should do fairly well on their own, especially if you've mulched them to conserve moisture.

Planting on the Mountainside

I've planted several small, rocky sites at my home in Westbrookville. The property is part of an old farm that was literally dug out of the side of the mountain. The mountainside is one rock after another, with little pockets of soil in and around the rocks. It has the potential to be the most amazing rock garden imaginable.

The farmer used stone to build walls marking the boundaries of the property and also to build terraced garden beds around the house, a small courtyard, and stone steps leading up to the main house. Each time I climbed the steps and walked through the courtyard, I felt a need to add color and texture to the mossy greens and grays of the rocks.

I started with a few plants harvested from the abundance of the gardens at The Potager. I lifted small tufts of blue fescue (*Festuca glauca* 'Elijah Blue') that had seeded in the paths and tucked them into sunny spots among the courtyard flagstone.

Next I lifted a 'Red Fox' veronica that had planted itself outside the fence at The Potager. Only 12 to 15 inches tall in full bloom, I knew this veronica would be perfect in a partially sunny spot at the outer edge of the courtyard.

A stone wall at the front or rear of a garden bed is the perfect spot for rock-garden plants that spread, such as creeping baby's-breath.

221

As I continued to clear and thin gardens at The Potager, I found other plants to tuck among the rocks at home: sedums, sedums, sedums! I could have planted a community of gardens with all the sedums I harvested. One of my favorites is 'Dragon's Blood' (*Sedum spurium*), with its red to bronze foliage and red bloom. With a height of just 4 inches and a penchant for traveling, I knew it would fill in beautifully through the random nooks among the stone steps. I also took a snippet of 'Vera Jameson' sedum from the tiny stone wall next to the café, along with some hens-and-chicks, and tucked them into crevices in the steps, as well.

I could see remnants of creeping phlox (*Phlox subulata*) already in evidence along the steps, but they were in need of new blood. Using divisions that I harvested from the wood planters in the side garden at The Potager, I reintroduced creeping phlox to the sunnier spots in the steps.

PAT'S SMALL SPACE **STORIES**

Recycle the Rubble

If you end up with leftover stone or even broken-up concrete from a remodeling or landscaping project, put it to use. Make a rubble wall and plant it as a rock garden. A rubble wall is a boxlike structure, and it can be any height and length that works for you. In the past, I've built extensive rubble walls at my inn and farm, but I've had to downsize my rock-building projects. I've created one 5-foot-long wall at the bottom of some stone steps along the walkway at The Potager. It's about 18 inches high.

The principle in building a rubble wall is to use the largest, flattest stones to make the outside of the "box" and then fill up the inside with the rough, smaller leftovers. I work layer by layer on the outside wall, throwing the rubble into the center as I go. I offset the joints between rocks in each layer of the outer walls to increase their stability. When I've finished building the wall, I dump topsoil onto the rubble and spray it with a hose to force it down among the spaces in the rubble. (I also keep "feeding" the wall from time to time by emptying the soil mix from spent containers onto the rubble.)

For my wall at The Potager, I brought some attractive flat stones from my home in Westbrookville (where I have enough stone to last a lifetime) to fashion the outside walls, and I filled the inside with cracked stones and pieces of brick that I'd collected during a general cleanup of The Potager property. I inserted pieces of lamium into the pockets of soil among the rocks, and in just one summer the wall was covered with its spreading stems and pretty pink flowers. The following year, I continued the theme by planting a container with the same lamium and setting it on the steps. There's a small shade garden nearby planted in shades of pink. I was inspired to add lamium there, too, as a groundcover among the shrubs and perennials. The lamium unifies the whole scene, and if you didn't know better, you'd think I had it all planned from the start!

The small, terraced gardens alongside the steps were in need of attention, too. The existing soil was poor and barely supported the daffodils planted there by the past owner, so I started with the soil. While the daffodils were all in bloom, I carefully covered the soil with one or two sheets of wet newspaper, tucking it around the clumps of bulbs. Then I added layers of organic matter lasagna-style.

I'd noticed old plantings of pulmonarias in the stone terraces, so I brought in *Pulmonaria longifolia* 'Bertram Anderson', with blue-green foliage and pink to blue blooms. Next I added *Iberis* 'Alexander's White' and coral bells (*Heuchera* spp.) with petite marbled burgundy leaves and creamy pink blooms.

The conditions in my planting area are perfect for hardy cranesbills (*Geranium* spp.), and I had just one to divide, *G. sanguineum* var. *striatum*. It grows to 8 inches tall and gently spreads its salmon-colored blossoms over stones to reseed in other spots. I've promised myself to add other varieties to keep it company.

Next, I was ready to begin on creeping thymes, but that's another story. See what I mean about rock gardening being addictive? I have trouble stopping, and really, why should I?

Creating a Rock Garden on a Slope

A slope is also a natural choice for a rock garden. If the slope is naturally rocky, you can work with the existing stones. If not, you can add stones to the garden as you build up the lasagna layers.

To begin with, clear the site of any brush. If the site had woody plants growing on it (shrubs or tree seedlings), cover the site with cardboard. If the only growth is green plants or grass, use layers of wet newspaper. Then layer on organic materials: garden wastes, compost, peat moss, whatever you have on hand.

If you need to add rocks to your site, set them in place as you work. Your goal is to have the rocks partially buried, so they'll look like a natural part of the landscape. This is where lasagna-style rock gardening has it all over traditional rock-garden building. No need to dig holes for the rocks! You just set them on top of the newspaper and layer up around them. I like to cover up about one-quarter to one-third of the mass of a rock. (By the way, if you'd prefer to build the bed first and then play with the arrangement of rocks, that's fine, too. It's easy to scoop aside the loose materials of the layers to set the rocks in place. Just be sure not to disturb the base layer of newspaper.)

Planting large rocks in the layers of a lasagna garden on a slope helps anchor the soil and plants.

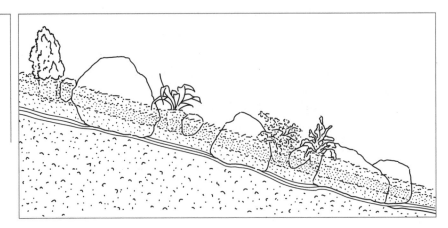

Once the bed is deep enough to plant in, slip the plants into place. To ensure that the plants won't be washed down the slope before their roots have time to grab hold and establish themselves, I also arrange smaller stones around the plants to anchor them in place. I remove these rocks later or I leave them in place, as seems right. Sometimes the plants grow up around these smaller stones and they look like a natural part of the garden, too.

In traditional rock gardens, you'll see a surface mulch of gravel, but I don't bother with this because it's expensive and heavy to haul. Instead, I mulch with compost or shredded leaves. In an established rock garden, plants usually cover the soil surface completely, and the rocks don't need to be mulched!

Faux Hills to Climb

Once the passion for rock gardening takes hold in your heart, you may need to manufacture more rocky sites around your property to plant. Creating a stone accent in the small garden is as simple as hauling in a few boulders and arranging them to form a jumbled faux hill. It gives the impression of going from one height to another when you are actually on level ground.

In the past, I carried a board in the back of my car so that if I spotted a particularly desirable rock along a road cut, I could pull over and roll the rock up the board and into my trunk or onto the floorboards. At home, I would drive across lawn or field as needed so I could roll the stone out of my car near my next rock-garden site. Call me crazy!

There are plenty of ways to acquire rocks for a faux hill garden. Perhaps you have friends with an old rock wall on their property, or you know a contractor who digs out stone during excavations. Quarries and garden centers sell rock, or there's my roadside raid method.

If this is all too much for you, contact a local sand and gravel company and have them dump a load of "fill material" right where you want the garden to be. Tell

them you want fill that includes some small boulders. When the stones tumble out of the dump truck, voilà, you have a faux hill arranged in a random design much as it would be if the rocks had tumbled down a mountainside during a rockslide. After all, Mother Nature does not have a stone designer do her arranging.

After the rocks are in place, you'll need to dump soil among the rocks for planting. Scrounging soil is an option that works for me. I find piles of it along the roadsides in the spring, carried there by snowplows that scraped away topsoil as they plowed the roads. I've also begged soil from the local road crew when they were out clearing drainage ditches. It's not the best quality soil, but for a rock garden, it works just fine. I "spike" this fill soil with small amounts of compost in the spots where I tuck in plants, to make sure they'll have a source of nutrients. Or, to prevent problems with weeds (this type of soil inevitably contains weed seeds and the roots of perennial weeds), I cover planting pockets with newspaper and top the paper with peat or compost and grass clippings. I let it sit and decompose for a few months, and then I plant.

Here's a great idea: If you're importing a pile of stone for a rock garden, add a small pool beside it and turn the rocks into a miniature waterfall. You'll have the double pleasure of admiring your rock-garden plants while listening to the soft splash of flowing water.

Choosing Plants for Rock Gardens

The list of plants suitable for rock gardens is long and varied, so how do you choose what to grow? I start by thinking about three categories of rock-garden plants: tuft-forming plants, mat-forming plants, and spreading plants.

Tuft-forming plants. Columbines, candytuft, and primroses are three examples of this category. The plants grow as small clumps or tufts with upright stems or basal rosettes of foliage topped by upright flowerstalks. They bring your rock garden up above ground level and add a variety of textures.

(continued on page 228)

EASY ROCK-GARDEN PLANTS

My listing of rock-garden plants is eclectic because that's the way I plant my rock gardens. This list includes annuals, perennials, bulbs, and even a shrub or two. Start with some of these plants, and experiment on your own. Many of the plants I've described in other chapters will also work well in rock gardens, including agapanthus, sweet alyssum, dwarf asters, bleeding hearts, candytuft, crocuses, Roman chamomile, daffodils, geraniums, lavender, lemon balm, creeping phlox, pinks, primroses, snowdrops, spurges, thymes, veronica, violets, and woolly yarrow.

All of the plants listed below are less than 12 inches tall unless otherwise stated, and they all need well-drained soil. These plants do best in full sun; I've noted those plants that will also grow in partial shade.

PLANT NAME	DESCRIPTION	GROWING TIPS
Ajugas, bugleweeds (*Ajuga* spp.)	Spikes of blue or white flowers in late spring. Some cultivars have lovely variegated leaves. Zones 3–9.	Plant in sun or shade. This ground-cover will spread to clamber over rocks or cover a slope in a short time.
Dwarf columbine (*Aquilegia* Biedermeier Group)	Beautiful flowers with long spurs in many colors including blue, lilac, pink, purple, and white. Blue-green lobed leaves form a soft mound of foliage. To 10 inches tall. Zones 3–9.	Likes partially shady wooded settings and will self-seed in and around rocks. For small rock gardens, the Biedermeier columbines are a better choice than larger hybrid columbines.
Basket-of-gold (*Aurinia saxatilis*)	Cheerful yellow flowers bloom in late spring over rosettes of gray-green leaves. Zones 3–7.	Needs sun for prolific bloom. Plant three plants on 4-inch centers to embrace a large rock.
English daisy (*Bellis perennis*)	From early spring to late summer, rounded green leaves are covered with 1-inch daisylike flowers. Forms low-growing mounds that branch out. Zones 4–8.	Easy to grow in sun or shade. Prefers cool, moist conditions. Deadhead the flowers to prevent them from self-sowing.
Carpathian bellflower (*Campanula carpatica*)	Cup-shaped purple-blue or white flowers in spring over clumps of rounded or heart-shaped leaves. Grows 6 to 9 inches tall. Zones 3–8.	Full sun to partial shade. Clip faded blooms to stimulate summer-long bloom. For white flowers, choose 'Alba'; for blue flowers, try 'Blue Clips'.
Snow-in-summer (*Cerastium tomentosum*)	Soft, gray-green foliage is evergreen and topped by cascading white flowers in summer. Zones 2–8.	Give snow-in-summer a haircut after blooming and it will bloom again. Plant toward the back of the garden and watch it tumble forward.
Glory-of-the-snow (*Chionodoxa luciliae*)	Hardy bulbs with star-shaped blue flowers in early spring. Zones 3–9.	These bulbs will thrive and increase over the years without assistance. To create a carpet of blue, plant lots of the marble-size bulbs as close as 1 inch apart. I plant them with 'Tete-a-Tete' minidaffodils as a spring groundcover.

PLANT NAME	DESCRIPTION	GROWING TIPS
Barrenworts (*Epimedium* spp.)	Unusual, semi-evergreen foliage that becomes bronzy in cold weather. Flowers in early spring, but grown more for foliage than flowers. Spreads very slowly. Zones 4–9.	Full sun or partial shade; tolerates dry shade. Set small containers of bright-colored annuals among the foliage for an eye-catching effect. Try *E. alpinum* 'Rubrum', with large, red-tinged leaves and crimson flowers, as a backdrop for small spring bulbs.
Winter aconite (*Eranthis hyemalis*)	Early spring-blooming bulbs with rounded clusters of narrow leaves below bright yellow flowers. Zones 4–9.	Plant these with snowdrops, and they will break through the snow crust to catch your eye as winter wanes.
Cornish heath (*Erica vagans*)	A spreading shrub with sweeping stems of narrow leaves and spikes of bell-shaped pinkish purple flowers in fall. Zones 5–9.	'Valerie Proudley' and 'George Under-wood' have lovely pink blooms and grow well in rock gardens (and in containers, too). Both thrive in acid soil.
Creeping baby's-breath (*Gypsophila repens*)	A low-growing form of this popular plant with clouds of small, creamy white flowers that look beautiful tumbling over rocks. Zones 4–8.	I grow 'Pink Baby', a pink- flowered variety, in a small, sunny space between the sidewalk and the street, and it has survived both dogs and skateboards.
Lamium (*Lamium maculatum*)	Attractive oval leaves on creeping stems and clusters of white, pink, or rose-pink flowers in spring and summer. Zones 3–8.	Plant in partial shade. The creeping stems will root; clip them back or pull out un-wanted stems to keep the plants under con-trol. Variegated cultivars with lots of sil-vering to the leaves don't spread as rapidly.
Rose campion (*Lychnis coronaria*)	Low rosettes of silvery woolly leaves with tall flower spikes bearing star-shaped magenta flowers. Flowerstalks can be 2 to 2½ feet tall. Zones 4–8.	Looks best when planted in drifts where the intense flowers will draw everyone's attention.
Common beardtongue (*Penstemon barbatus*)	Lance-shaped leaves and spikes of deep rose, fuchsia, pink, and rose-violet tubular flowers. Dwarf varieties are 12 to 18 inches tall. Zones 3–8.	Sow seed in fall; the plants may bloom the following summer. This plant may attract hummingbirds to your rock garden.
Hens and chicks (*Sempervivum* spp.)	Cactuslike plants with many perfect rosettes of fleshy leaves. Some types are very hardy and all have great character. Hardiness varies with species and variety.	Some rock gardens consist of only sempervivums. Easy to divide or start from cuttings. Main rosettes die after flowering but may reseed, and new rosettes form along lateral stems.
Lamb's-ears (*Stachys byzantina*)	A hardy perennial with layers of woolly leaves that give the plant a silvery appearance. Flowerstalks are silvery, too, with small purple flowers in late spring. Zones 4–8.	May rot in very rainy summer heat. Cut rotted parts away, and the foliage will resprout when conditions turn cooler. Cut flowerstalks early to prevent self-seeding.
Purple mullein (*Verbascum phoeniceum*)	Rosettes of fuzzy leaves with very tall (up to 4 feet) spikes of bright magenta flowers in late spring. Zones 5–7.	Because this plant has such tall flower-stalks, plant it in the middle or back-ground of a rock garden.

Mat-forming plants. Snow-in-summer is one of my favorite mat-forming plants. These plants have prostrate or low-growing stems that form dense cushions of foliage and flowers. Ajuga is another excellent mat-forming plant. These plants look great filling spaces between rocks and at the feet of tuft-formers.

Spreading plants. When you want plants to spill down a slope or weave in and out among steps, choose a plant with spreading stems, such as creeping phlox or corydalis, two of my favorites. These plants send out running stems that root at various points along their length (phlox) or spread prolifically by self-sowing (corydalis).

I try to include some plants from each category in my gardens. Each category includes perennials, annuals, and herbs that fill the bill. (I enjoy herbs in rock gardens planted along a path so that whenever you brush by them or step on a bit of the foliage, they release their aroma.)

Dwarf Trees and Shrubs

I use dwarf trees and shrubs as the backbone of my small rock garden. There is something about a dwarf evergreen that is as charming as a small child. Best of all, you don't have to send the plant to college! Seriously, these plants are relatively maintenance-free and they add year-round interest to a rock garden.

When I began to garden with dwarf plants and shrubs, I chose cotoneasters (pronounced coh-TOE-knee-ass-turs) as part of my first collection. I began with rockspray cotoneaster (*Cotoneaster horizontalis*) because it was the hardiest member of the genus I could find. At that time, I was living on my mountaintop farm, which could have been considered either Zone 3 or 4. Rockspray cotoneaster is reliably hardy only to Zone 5. I planted it in the very first pile of stones I heaped up to form a rock garden. I was delighted with the deep pink spring buds, the little white flowers in early summer, and the deep red berries that lasted all winter.

Next I tried *Cotoneaster adpressus* 'Little Gem', a dwarf variety. This prostrate cotoneaster has a wonderful ability to take root in soil on a steep bank and hold it in place. Ten-year-old plants measure only 6 inches high and 12 to 15 inches across. Although it doesn't produce showy flowers or berries like those of rockspray cotoneaster, 'Little Gem' is wonderful in a small garden.

Two other dwarf evergreens that are good starter plants are dwarf Alberta spruce (*Picea glauca* var. *albertiana* 'Conica') and Hinoki false cypress (*Chamaecyparis obtusa*). Alberta spruce is easy to find at nurseries. It grows slowly, but over time it may outgrow your space. If so, I suggest that you transplant it to a bigger space (or give it away) and replace it with something smaller because it won't respond well to strong pruning.

Hinoki cypress is not as familiar in garden centers and is a bit more expensive, but it's easy to grow. 'Kosteri' has elegantly twisted dark green foliage on globular plants. Distinctive, lacy stems and branches of 'Nana Gracilis' are less globe-shaped and are covered with cup-shaped sprays of foliage. These very dwarf shrubs will not outgrow the small rock garden. They grow slowly and reach heights of just 3 to 4 feet in 15 years.

Want more choices? *Cryptomeria japonica* 'Elegans Compacta' has soft, feathery foliage that grows in tiers at first but after about 10 years will form a mound-shaped plant just 3 feet high. *Picea abies* 'Little Gem', globular in shape, is a dwarf of a dwarf that reaches just 1 foot at maturity.

I'm fascinated by the trailing form of weeping Norway spruce (*Picea abies* 'Reflexa'). This prostrate tree can be trained up a short pole and then allowed to "weep" into a rock garden. The new growth is a pretty pale green that matures to dark green. A dwarf hemlock, *Tsuga canadensis* 'Minuta' is one of the smallest varieties at just 3 inches tall, while `Bennet' is a flat-topped spreader at 18 inches and 'Cole's Prostrate' lies flat on the ground at 12 inches.

Trough Gardens:
The Ultimate Small Gardens

For gardeners who live in apartments, container gardening on a balcony, terrace, or fire escape is the only outlet for indulging their passion for plants. Lucky for them, there's a way to create a rock garden in a special type of container—a facsimile of a stone trough. Trough gardens can be planted with miniature and dwarf evergreens, flowering shrubs, and groundcovers. They can also include perennials that mimic their larger counterparts. (And of course, gardeners with in-ground space can still enjoy trough gardening, too.)

Whether you buy or construct your own trough, be prepared to fall in love with this wonderful type of gardening. Particularly rewarding to those who need elevated gardens, troughs can be placed at whatever height is most convenient for planting and maintenance. Troughs offer the ideal environment not only for dwarf and alpine plants, but also for many herbs and creeping perennials.

The trough that you'll plant your garden in is modeled after stone livestock troughs that were used to feed and water livestock on farms in England and Europe. These troughs were hand-hewn from local stone, many times right on the spot where the stone was found. Stones large enough to water the herd were much too heavy to be moved, so the farmer would chip away at a stone in the field.

When the troughs were no longer used for livestock, they were filled with gritty soil mixtures and planted with small plants. These original troughs had to have holes chipped into their bottoms to provide good drainage.

The troughs became quite popular as planters, but the supply of real stone troughs was limited, so people began creating substitutes. At first these were made with heavy materials, but lucky for us, some inventive gardeners dreamed up hypertufa. This is a lightweight mixture of cement, sand, and peat moss that makes a very authentic-looking trough planter. You can buy hypertufa containers at garden centers, or you can make your own container, following the directions on page 232.

TUFA AND HYPERTUFA

Tufa rock is a soft, porous, calcium-containing rock that is formed when water containing carbon dioxide seeps through limestone formations. As the water cools and evaporates, it leaves irregular calcium deposits around debris and decaying matter. When the debris and other organic matter has finished rotting, just the lime deposits are left, and that's tufa. Soft when it's dug from the ground, tufa hardens in the air. Tufa is an interesting material for planters, but it's not readily available. Hypertufa is the manufactured substitute for this unique natural rock.

Planting a Trough Garden

Growing plants in a trough is not very different from other kinds of gardening. You match the soil mix to the plants you want to grow, taking into consideration your zone and microclimate.

I make my soil mix for a trough first and then add it to the trough, rather than making lasagna layers in the trough. I use leaf mold, compost, and peat moss in about equal parts, and then I add about an equal amount of coarse builder's sand.

Start with a layer of small to medium pebbles in the bottom of the trough, and fill the trough to the top with your soil mix. Set in plants and surround them with a mulch of grit. You can purchase grit from a home and garden store. Ask for chicken or turkey grit.

Choosing plants for your trough is the fun part. Think small, small, small! Dwarf trees and shrubs set the stage for all the other plants. Select a perfect little dwarf hemlock or pine as the focus plant. For draping interest, try a dwarf juniper. For blooming interest, try one of the diminutive rhododendrons.

Place some rocks in and around your trough for plants like sedum, thymes, and creeping phlox to grow around and over. My favorite tool for planting and maintaining troughs is a narrow trowel. Purchased just for this purpose, my stainless steel trowel is perfect, but I have also adapted several household and kitchen tools.

I have been experimenting with alpines in containers for years. I'm finally good at pruning, and I've become inventive about raising the troughs up on cinder-block platforms so they can be viewed at close range. I just stack cinder blocks two or three blocks high, to create a base of the same dimensions as the trough. Then I coat the blocks with hypertufa mix to disguise them. They look like a natural extension of the trough! If I ever have to move again, I may have to hire a moving van just to carry my trough gardens. It would be worth it, though, because they're the most valuable works of art I own.

Because I enjoy trough gardens so much, I set aside enough money to buy special plants every year. I've learned to water my trough gardens when they need it and feed them before the plants show stress.

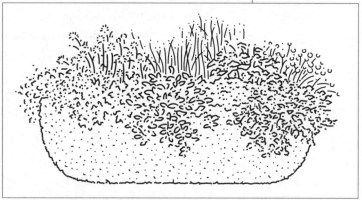

Making a Hypertufa Trough

Making a trough out of hypertufa is a fun project, but there's no disguising that some parts of the process are a lot like work! (Remember, I'm the *lazy* gardener.) And if your experience is like mine, you may find that you spend more time collecting the materials you need than you do making the trough itself.

The basic steps of making the trough are making the hypertufa mix, spreading it over a form, and allowing it to cure.

I recommend using a plastic dishpan as the form for your first trough, because it's a good size and shape, and it's easy to acquire. Washtubs and cookie tins work well, too. If you adopt trough gardening as a hobby, you can also make your own forms out of wood or polystyrene insulation board held together with duct tape. You can also experiment with free-form troughs, made by shaping a pile of coarse builder's sand as the form. (Personally, I don't want to work that hard. I think that using old buckets, bowls, and pans as forms is much easier.)

Materials and Supplies

Plastic sheeting	1 bag Type II portland cement
Old dishpan or other form	2 cubic feet of peat moss, sifted
Scissors	1 bag of perlite
Duct tape	Wheelbarrow
Rubber gloves	Hoe or small-bladed shovel
Safety goggles	Water
Dust mask	Wooden dowels
2-pound coffee can	Wire brush or chisel

1. Spread out the plastic sheeting on the floor of your basement, garage, or other indoor area that you don't mind getting dusty.

2. Prepare your mold by covering it with plastic. You can put the plastic inside the mold or turn the mold upside down and put the plastic on the outside. Use scissors to cut away excess plastic if needed. Secure the plastic in place with duct tape.

3. Put on the rubber gloves to protect your hands and the safety goggles and dusk mask to protect yourself from dust. Using the coffee can as a measuring scoop, measure 3 parts cement, 4 parts peat, and 5 parts perlite into the wheelbarrow.

4. Use the hoe or small-bladed shovel to mix the ingredients together.

5. Begin adding water and blending it into the mixture. Add small amounts at a time, mixing it in as you go. Once the mixture is easy to stir, stop adding water.

6. Spread the mixture over the form. The coating should be at least 1½ inches thick. After you've finished coating the mold, push several short dowels through the hypertufa coating on the bottom of the container. (You'll remove them later, creating drainage holes in the container.)

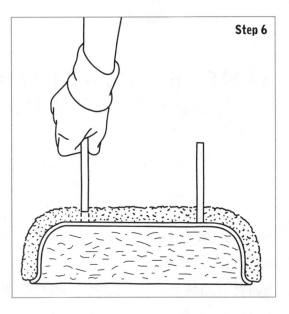

Step 6

7. Cover the trough with plastic, and leave the whole thing sitting for about 24 hours.

8. The next day, remove the plastic so you can texturize your trough. Use a wire brush or old chisel to scrape the surface of the container until it has a texture that appeals to you.

9. Re-cover the container and let it sit for about 2 weeks. Every few days, twist the dowels so they won't bond too firmly to the container.

10. When it's time to "unpot" your trough, remove the dowels, take the container off the form, and set the trough outdoors in a shady spot away from your gardens. Let it sit for 4 to 6 weeks so that rain can soak through the trough, which will leach excess lime out of the cement.

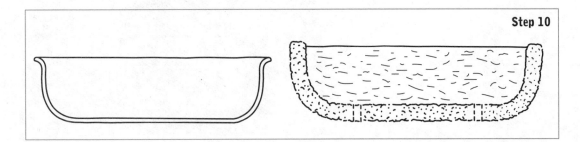

Step 10

CHAPTER 8

SIMPLE SOLUTIONS TO SMALL-GARDEN PROBLEMS

One benefit of gardening on a small scale is that you won't have to cope with any large-scale problems. Plus, when you garden lasagna-style, you'll find that weeds, insects, and diseases usually aren't a problem at all. Small-space gardening can offer some unique challenges, though, and occasionally you'll spot signs of pests or diseases on plants. I've developed a grab bag of solutions to garden problems, and I'll share my best ideas with you here.

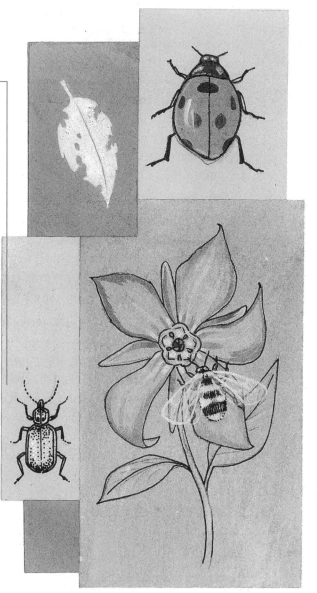

A Lasagna Garden Is a Healthy Garden

My lasagna gardening method has become famous because of its promise of "no digging, no tilling, no weeding." But there's another wonderful benefit of lasagna gardening: It reduces pest and disease problems.

Even before I started lasagna gardening, I did my best to avoid pesticides, and now I just don't need to spray. As I've learned more about organic gardening, I understand why. Many scientific studies show that healthy, vigorous plants aren't as susceptible to insect attack or diseases as stressed plants are. And the layers of wholesome organic ingredients in a lasagna garden provide the fundamental soil conditions plants need to be healthy.

Over the years, I have watched as many gardeners living in my community made the change from labor-intensive and chemical-supported gardening to lasagna gardening. As they experienced growing success from the fast-and-easy layering method, they gave up using chemicals, too. Each and every one came to know the value of keeping the earthworm population alive and well, and of feeding the soil rather than killing it.

A Little Knowledge Makes a Great Garden

Gardeners sometimes set themselves up for gardening problems because they haven't learned gardening fundamentals. One of the best ways to ensure the success of your garden is to arm yourself with knowledge. Whether you're a new or an experienced gardener, read through the following section. Are you observing these basic tenets of good gardening? If you're not, even building the best lasagna bed in the world won't bring you success.

Understand Your Local Weather

Every gardener should know what hardiness zone they garden in, but that's just one important climate factor that affects gardens. (If you don't know which zone you live in, you can figure it out by checking the USDA Plant Hardiness Zone Map on page 288.) What's the weather like in your area during a typical growing season? If you have very humid summers, you may need to pay more attention to providing good airflow in your garden to prevent disease problems. If you garden in an area with cool summer nights, you may need to choose cold-tolerant tomato varieties, or you may never harvest many tomatoes. (Tomato fruit-set is poor when nights are cold.)

Local geography may also affect your gardening. The Potager is a great example. According to the USDA Hardiness Zone map, The Potager is right on the border of Zones 4 and 5. However, because the village of Wurtsboro is snuggled in a protected valley, the zone is actually much closer to a full Zone 5, possibly even close to Zone 6 conditions. We call this special type of climate area a microclimate.

Microclimates occur on much smaller scales, too. There may be different microclimates right within your yard. For instance, growing conditions on the south side of your house can be several degrees warmer than the north side, which is exposed to wind and shade. Small-space gardens often end up being protected from the elements by fences, walls, or adjoining buildings. Plus, because they are small, you can devote more time to the plants you choose to grow. This makes small gardens great places to experiment with plants that might not normally be hardy enough or well adapted to the climate in your area.

HOW MUCH RAIN?

You can buy a simple rain gauge for just a few dollars at most garden centers or hardware stores. Or you can make your own from a straight-sided jelly glass. Use a permanent marker to draw a scale on the glass in ½-inch increments. Set your rain gauge in the garden, away from any overhanging trees or bushes and out of the path of walls or fences that might block the rain.

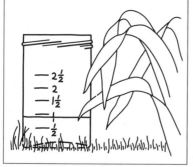

Keep Track of the Rain

Gardeners have a love-hate relationship with rain. Of course, we love it when it rains just after we've planted a garden, but sometimes we curse rain on Saturdays when we'd planned to garden all day. Whether rain falls at the right time or the wrong time, it's a good idea to keep track of how much is falling. Install a rain gauge in your garden and check it after each rainfall. As a general rule of thumb, 1 inch of rainfall per week is enough to keep your garden growing.

Monitor the moisture level of the soil in your beds, too. Just push aside the surface mulch and stick your finger into the soil. If the soil is dry more than an inch below the surface, your plants need watering.

My favorite way to water is to install soaker hoses. It's a low-effort way to water, and it delivers water precisely where it's needed: to the soil and the roots of your plants. In a small garden, it's easy to lay out a soaker hose and leave it in place all season. Cover the hose with mulch so it doesn't show. When you need to water, just attach your regular garden hose to the end of the soaker hose, and turn it on at low pressure so the soaker hose drips steadily. (Adding a breaker between

the hose and soaker hose is helpful for regulating the flow of water.)
If you know you'll need to water on a regular basis in summer, you
can put the hose on a timer, too.

Read the Local Plant Life

Observing the plants that are already growing in your local area can
tell you a lot about what will grow well in your garden. Even observing wild plants helps because they're a clue that you can grow do-
mesticated plants from the same family. For example, in my area, a
type of spirea grows wild in any unplowed field or ditch. Seeing that
spirea could grow well untended in my area, I knew that cultivated
types would do well in my garden, too.

Make Smart Plant Choices

Small-scale gardeners also need to be extra-picky about selecting the
right varieties of plants. One big consideration is mature size. Let's
use the spirea that I mentioned above as an example. If you just drop
in at a garden center and ask for spirea, you'd probably be told that
the most popular type of spirea is bridalwreath. It deserves to be popular because it's a gorgeous shrub with cascading branches covered
with white blossoms in late spring. It's also unmistakably large. If

INSPECT BEFORE YOU BUY

Save yourself time, money, and frustration
by educating yourself before you shop and
by inspecting plants thoroughly before you
buy them. Too often we're lured by beautiful blossoms and we make snap buying
decisions. To avoid problems, follow these
instructions when you shop:

1. **Look for whiteflies:** Brush your hand
over the foliage and watch to see if white,
specklike insects fly up.

2. **Inspect the condition of the foliage.**
Leggy stems and yellow, wilted, or curled
leaves are signs that the plant has suffered
heat, cold, light, or water stress.

3. **Check the undersides of leaves for
webbing** (spider mites) or raised bumps
(scale).

4. **Tip the plant out of the pot to inspect
the roots.** Healthy roots are plump and
white; dead or diseased roots can be limp
and dark.

5. **Lift a six-pack out of the flat to check
for slugs lurking underneath.**

you bought it and tried to control it in a small space, you'd do the plant a great injustice. However, there are some small types of spirea that are perfectly wonderful in a small garden, such as *Spiraea japonica* 'Anthony Waterer', which is easy to keep pruned to manageable size. I also like 'Goldflame', 'Little Princess', and 'Magic Carpet'. You just need to know what to ask for when you shop! If you haven't homed in on a specific small-space cultivar, check with a knowledgeable nursery owner or salesperson for good cultivar choices for small gardens.

Disease-resistance is another important quality to check for when buying seeds or plants. You can save yourself a lot of grief, get a jump on the season, and avoid problems by using plants that have been bred to resist disease. Catalog descriptions will include information about disease resistance. Research first, and take the information with you when you shop. Choosing disease-resistant plants is as easy as keeping a little notebook of info that fits in your pocket.

Solving Pest and Disease Problems

Keep an old pair of metal tweezers in your garden tool caddy. They come in handy when hand-picking plant pests, especially slimy slugs!

Growing plants in lasagna beds and making smart plant choices will solve 90 percent of potential insect and disease problems before they ever get started. For the remaining 10 percent, my advice is to seek out solutions that are easy on you and easy on the environment.

Early detection is easy. The earlier you discover a pest problem, the easier it is to control it. When you have a small garden, it's also easier to find time to observe the condition of individual plants. Suppose you spot a few shoot tips on your peas covered with aphids. Snip off the badly infested areas and dunk them in soapy water to kill the aphids. Spray the pea plants with a strong stream of water to wash off any remaining aphids, and chances are your problem is history.

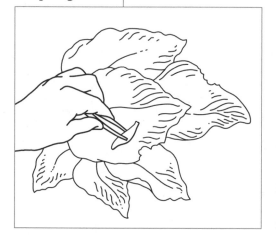

Your garden is naturally diverse. With small spaces, it's unlikely you'll have any large plantings of a single type of crop. Your gardens will be a diverse mix of plants, and diversity is one of the best natural methods for minimizing problems.

Replanting is an option. Making a fresh start when problems develop can be a great choice in a small-space garden. For example, if you've planted a rose bush and it develops a horrendous black spot problem, it's not too heartbreaking or costly to dig it out and replant (and maybe the next time you'll be able to choose a variety that's resistant to blackspot).

Hand-picking can get the job done. Hand-picking is easy, fast, and it's certainly inexpensive. If you're squeamish about touching insects, use tweezers or chopsticks to pick the pests off the plants. Drop the offending insects into a can of soapy water to kill them.

Keep Up with Plant Care

We small-space gardeners tend to plant our beds and containers very intensively in our quest to fit in as many of our best-loved favorites as we can. Lasagna beds can support intensive growth, so fertility isn't usually a problem. However, our lush, crowded plantings can be an invitation to plant diseases. Many bacteria and fungi that cause plant rots, spots, and blights enjoy moist, dark conditions just like the atmosphere in and under the foliage of a dense garden. The secrets to minimizing disease problems are wise watering, frequent trimming, and regular dividing.

The Right Way to Water

Picture this: You spend the day at work and, once home, more for yourself than the plants, you decide to slip outside and do some watering. It's a mindless job, and it's a great stress relief to stand there for 15 to 20 minutes, watching the arcs of water droplets and feeling the coolness in the air from the spray—but it's murder for your plants. Water drenches the foliage and lingers there through the evening and into the night. It's the perfect conditions for the bacteria and fungal spores that spread in water droplets. Watering in the evening is never a good idea.

Instead, develop the morning watering habit: Get out there between 5 and 10 A.M. And no spraying from above! Shape small wells or depressions around the bases of your plants, and direct a slow stream of water into the wells. A watering wand is a great tool for watering both garden beds and containers, and of course, an old-fashioned watering can will do the job, too.

SPRING CLEANING

I like to leave my gardens "messy" for the winter because the dried plant stalks and seedheads look pretty covered with snow, and more important, they provide excellent shelter and food for birds and beneficial insects. When spring comes, though, I spring-clean my garden just as I do my house. As soon as the garden is dry enough to work in, I remove all spent vegetation: leaves, stalks, stems, and old fruits and vegetables. As I work, I check for damaged or broken limbs on trees and shrubs, and I prune them out. I pull mulch back from the crowns of perennials and cut spent foliage back from ornamental grasses. This opens the way for new growth and also removes materials that may harbor insect pests and disease spores.

FUN AND FREE TOOLS

I believe in paying for good quality when I buy tools at the garden center, but I also revel in finding improvised tools and garden supplies for free. Search your kitchen junk drawer—I bet you'll find items that will be perfect tools for small gardens.

A long-handled spatula, one that has seen better days at the barbecue grill, serves as a mulch pusher. Bend the spatula blade down and use it to push mulch around and under plants.

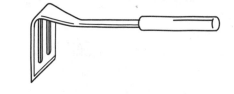

En garde! Cut the roots of a pesky weed with an old butcher knife. Wrap the handle with layers of duct tape to make it comfortable to hold. Plunge the blade into the soil in the middle of the plant and twist.

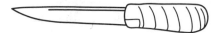

A meat fork is perfect for aerating and loosening compacted soil. Whether the soil is surrounding plants grown in containers or in the ground, it helps plant performance to open up channels for air and water to penetrate the root zone.

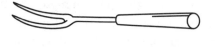

I'm a fan of soaker hoses—those rough-textured black hoses that leak water slowly all along their length. A 25-foot length of soaker hose usually snakes nicely through a small garden bed, providing adequate coverage for all the plants. Cover the hose lightly with mulch to disguise it. When you need to water, attach the end of the drip hose to your regular hose, turn the water on at a low pressure, and let it soak. An hour to two is usually sufficient to thoroughly wet the soil.

Drip irrigation systems are also very water- and time-efficient, but I'm so technically challenged that I avoid using them. If you enjoy tinkering with do-it-yourself projects, try one of the simple kits available at garden centers or from mail-order catalogs.

A Clip in Time

Take your garden clippers or shears along with you every time you stroll through your garden. If you see areas of growth that look very dense, clip out a few stems to open things up. Anything you clip may look good as part of a flower arrangement, even if it's not a blooming flower stem. This discipline is natural for me because I'm constantly harvesting material from The Potager gardens to decorate the shop and café, or for arrangements to sell. But you can develop the same good habits, and you'll have fresh plant materials to accent every room in your house.

Three Cheers for Beneficials

One of my favorite tactics for fighting insect pests is to call on their natural enemies. Yes, pests have predators, both seen and unseen. Some songbirds are terrific insect eaters. I hope that birds are already visiting your yard, but if they aren't, entice them. Food, water, and shelter are sure-fire ways to enlist their help in your war against harmful insects. Put out birdfeeders, a birdbath, and perhaps a birdhouse or two. In return for your hospitality, birds will consume enormous quantities of harmful insects.

Some of the best predators of pest insects are other insects. We call these pest-eaters "beneficial insects." Lady beetles are the best-known beneficial. Both adult lady beetles and their larvae eat copious quantities of aphids. Ground beetles, tiny lacewings, and wasps are some of your other insect allies.

What you plant in your garden and how you plant it influences how attractive your garden is to beneficial insects. Beneficials like areas with permanent cover where they can hide. Many beneficial insects are very tiny, and they seek sheltered spots protected from dust and wind. Plants that form clumps that persist throughout the year, such as ornamental grasses and some perennials, are generally good for beneficials. These plants provide shelter from heat and dust in the summer, and they're excellent overwintering sites for ground beetles and lady beetles (as long as you leave them standing through the winter).

Beneficials eat pollen and nectar as well as insects, so a garden planted with nectar flowers can also attract their attention. Due to their small size, these insects prefer to feed at flowers with very small blossoms.

Research studies have identified particular plants that attract beneficial insects, and I make it standard practice to include some of these plants in my garden. Planting to attract beneficials is a fascinating topic, and the more you look for information on beneficial insects in magazines, books, and on the Internet, the more you'll learn. Not all of the plants that attract beneficials are suitable for small gardens, but I recommend several for small gardens and containers.

MOTHER NATURE'S NIGHT CREW

Wouldn't it be great if assistants patrolled your garden at night, tracking down plant pests while you slept? It can happen, and you can encourage it. Mother Nature supplies the crew if you supply the housing: a bat house! Don't get squeamish. Bats aren't going to suck your blood or build a nest in your hair. They are insect eaters and will devour thousands of mosquitoes and other insect pests in one night's feeding. One bat house will house up to 300 bats. That number of bats can have a major impact on the pest population. Some mail-order catalogs and wild-bird supply stores sell ready-made bat houses and simple bat-house kits that you can assemble yourself.

Hardy marguerite (*Anthemis tinctoria* 'Kelwayi'): In a garden or a large container, this drought-tolerant perennial is a beautiful, ferny plant, and its wide yellow flowers are highly attractive to lady beetles, lacewings, flower flies, tachinid flies, and tiny beneficial wasps.

Borage (*Borago officinalis*): I love this annual herb for its bright blue flowers that are both beautiful and edible. The flowers are also exceptionally attractive to good bugs. Borage's flaw—at least in the small garden—is that it self-sows prolifically, but I think it's easy enough to pull out any seedlings that spring up in places where they're not wanted. (I also use the flowers for my own purposes when I entertain: I freeze borage flowers in an ice ring and float it in a punch bowl with a red wine punch. It always attracts lots of compliments.)

Bachelor's buttons (*Centaurea cyanus*): Fluffy pink or purple flowers provide early nectar for flower flies, lacewings, lady beetles, and beneficial wasps. It's easy to grow from seed sown in fall or spring.

Sweet alyssum (*Lobularia maritima*): The tiny white, pale pink, or pale purple flowers that cover this low-growing annual throughout summer attract aphid-eating flower flies. This is a wonderful edging plant that will reseed itself.

Mountain mint (*Pycnanthemum virginianum* and *P. muticum*): All mints are excellent plants for attracting beneficials, and their dense foliage also provides shelter for spiders. In a small garden, always

From shrubs like pussy willow to perennials and groundcovers, there are a surprising variety of plants that attract beneficial insects to a garden.

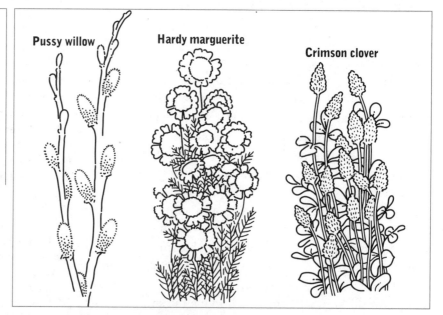

Pussy willow   Hardy marguerite   Crimson clover

plant mint inside a root barrier or in a container so it doesn't take over the garden.

Pussy willow (*Salix discolor*): This shrub is easy to grow, either in the garden or in a pot. Pussy willows produce pollen in very early spring, providing an important food source for beneficials just as they're emerging from winter dormancy.

Sedums (*Sedum* spp.): These perennials have flat-topped clusters of tiny flowers that make great "landing platforms" where beneficials can alight and feed.

Crimson clover (*Trifolium incarnatum*): Crimson clover and other clovers are used as a green manure crop for improving soil. With the lasagna gardening method of soil-building, planting green manures isn't necessary, but I grow small patches of crimson clover because it's such a pretty plant and because it attracts many types of beneficials. When I'm ready to get rid of the clover, I don't dig it in, I just cover it with some sheets of wet newspaper and mulch and let the earthworms do the work!

Corn (*Zea mays*): A corn patch may not be what comes to mind when you think about attracting beneficials to a small garden, but why not? Corn tassels produce large amounts of pollen that lure good bugs to your garden. Even if you don't have enough space to grow corn for food production, try growing a few stalks in a large pot as a striking focal point for a grouping of containers.

What to Do When Problems Hit

Sooner or later, you *will* find a pest or disease problem in your garden. It's no cause for panic, though. The first step is always to make a diagnosis. Identify the pest so you know what control measures will be effective. It's a good idea to buy a pest identification guide (you'll find some listed in "Pat's Picks (Recommended Reading)" on page 274). Or catch a few of the bugs, imprison them in a jar, and take them to your local Cooperative Extension office for identification. Once you know what the culprit is, you can do some research and decide on the best control method.

With diseases, identifying the specific problem can be tricky. Making a general diagnosis is helpful, at least to determine whether it's a fungus (which you can prevent in the future with a homemade spray) or a virus (which there's generally no cure for, and the best course of action is to pull out badly infected plants).

Some Simple Suggestions

When it comes to solving a pest problem, I try simple control methods first. As I mentioned before, with relatively large, slow-moving pests like slugs, Japanese beetles, and Colorado potato beetles, you can often win the battle just by hand-picking. Here are some other simple controls that work well for me:

Water sprays. For infestations of aphids or spider mites, use a watering wand to direct a strong stream of water on the infested plants. The water washes the delicate insects off the plants, killing most of them in the process. Be sure you direct the water to wash both the tops and undersides of leaves. You can repeat this tactic as needed.

Row covers. Floating row cover is a synthetic fabric that lets air and water through but keeps pests out. You must use row covers preventively, though; once the pests are on your plants, it won't be effective. If you know from past experience that a certain crop will be troubled by insects, or if your neighbors have warned you to expect problems with a certain pest, cover the crop with a very lightweight row cover (row covers come in different weights) at planting and seal the edges against entry by weighting them down with boards or soil. Row covers are terrific for controlling pests in the vegetable garden. (Of course, you won't want to use them for pest problems in a flower garden.)

Barriers and traps. Barriers and traps are helpful for specific pests. (That's where diagnosis plays a role.) You can foil cutworms by putting a barrier of heavy paper or cardboard around plant stems. You can trap slugs in shallow containers of beer. Gardeners have come up with many ingenious ideas for keeping pests away from crops. A little reading and research about this topic is worthwhile.

Homemade spray. For whiteflies and fungus, I find a homemade oil and baking soda spray to be quite effective. In a 1-gallon container, I combine 1 tablespoon of baking soda, 1 tablespoon of vegetable oil, and a few drops of dishwashing liquid. Fill the container to the top with water. When you want to spray, shake or mix the solution well and pour it into a pump spray bottle. At the first sign of any fungus problem,

WHAT ABOUT WEEDS?

Many gardeners with large gardens name weeds as their number-one problem, but I predict that you'll almost never have weed problems in your small-space lasagna gardens. Weeds find it easiest to invade bare soil and unplanted garden beds. When you have lots of big garden beds to plant, weeds often plant themselves before you have time to fill the space. But it's easy to plant a small-space garden quickly and completely. In a short time, your small gardens will be bursting with desirable plants, crowding out any weeds. Each layer of top mulch applied to the soil's surface will also keep weeds out. If a few weeds do poke through, pulling them out is a snap, especially from the rich, loose soil of a lasagna bed.

spray the entire plant, including the undersides of the leaves. This spray is effective on black spot on roses, and it's a good idea to spray even before you notice problems. I've also found it helpful in reducing problems with gray mold on raspberries and other cane fruits.

Outfoxing Aggravating Animal Pests

Animal pests are the number-one problem for some gardeners and only a minor irritation for others. If you garden on an apartment balcony, your only potential animal marauders are birds. But if you have a small garden in a suburb or rural area, you may have to contend with deer, skunks, squirrels, rabbits, woodchucks, and more.

Don't let fear of animal pests keep you from the joy of gardening. One advantage of gardening on a small scale is that it's easier to set up barriers that keep pests away from your plants. As with insect pests, knowing your enemies is your first line of defense.

Some animal pests are bold, eating your plants in broad daylight. With other pests, you may need to piece together the identity of the culprit by adding up clues: animal tracks, the type of damage, and the experiences of other local gardeners. Here are some of my tried-and-true techniques for foiling animal pests.

Throw Them off the Scent

Animal pests use their sense of smell to find food, and sometimes you can repel them by putting out strong-smelling deterrents. Strong-smelling soap seems to deter animals, including deer. You can make a "soap ornament" like the one shown below to hang from tree limbs,

I saved my new dwarf apple trees from deer damage by decorating them with soap ornaments. To make them, use an ice pick to poke a hole through the wrapped bar of pungent-smelling soap (*below left*). Feed twine or wire through the hole for hanging the ornament (*below right*).

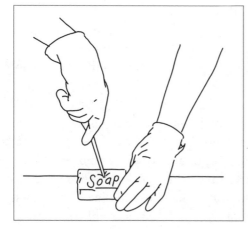

berry bushes, on the lips of containers, or along a fence. Some gardeners have success leaving smelly old shoes in the garden. Rabbits and other animals seem to dislike the smell of blood, so sprinkling dry bloodmeal on and around plants can be an effective tactic.

Apply the Heat

A natural ingredient in hot peppers called capsaicin is a potent pest repellent (it works on some insect pests, too). You can mix up a spray solution that will deter many animal pests. Combine 2 tablespoons of hot sauce (the hottest you can buy), 1 teaspoon of chili powder or cayenne pepper, a few drops of dishwashing liquid, and 1 pint of water in a pump spray bottle. Spray the mixture directly on the leaves of the plants you want to protect. Also spray it all along the edges of your garden; it may be enough of a deterrent to keep animals from exploring your garden. Try shooting the spray into planting holes when you plant bulbs in fall; it may deter squirrels from digging up the bulbs. Also, sprinkle a little of the mixture around the bases of young fruit trees to deter bark-gnawing mice.

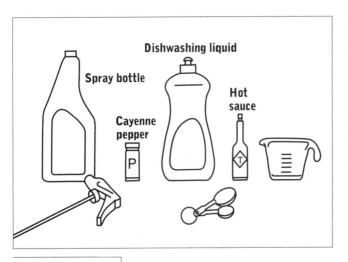

These simple ingredients are all you need to concoct an effective pest-repelling spray.

Try a Dose of Castor Oil

When tell-tale tunnels appear in your lawn or garden beds, it means you have visiting moles. The moles don't actually eat your plants; they feed on grubs and other soil-dwelling insects. But their tunnels certainly can be unsightly.

If you have a white grub problem in your lawn, fighting the grub problem may reduce the mole problem, too. You can apply parasitic nematodes to attack the grubs (see "Resources for Lasagna Gardeners" on page 271 for nematode suppliers). However, moles also eat earthworms, so you may need to take other measures to send them packing more quickly. One technique I like to use to discourage them is flooding their homes with a nasty-smelling castor-oil concoction.

A favorite recipe of mine is a combination of 1 cup of water, 4 tablespoons of dishwashing liquid, and 3 or 4 tablespoons of castor oil. Whisk these together, and store the mixture in a glass jar with a lid.

Arm yourself with a sharp spade or other sharp tool, and go in search of mole tunnels. When you find one, add 2 tablespoons of the castor oil mixture to 1 gallon of water. Use the tool to open up the tunnel, pour in about 1 cup of the castor oil mixture, and step on the tunnel to close it. The moles will flee when they encounter the yucky smell.

If treating individual tunnels doesn't seem to get rid of the moles in your lawn, try treating the whole lawn, instead. Mix 1 ounce of castor oil (⅛ cup) into a gallon of water along with a few drops of soap (this helps mix the oil into the water). Use a sprayer to apply the solution to your lawn. This recipe should cover about 300 square feet. You can also use the diluted castor oil mixture as a deterrent spray for squirrels and chipmunks. Just spray it directly on the garden areas you want to protect.

Block the Way

For small vegetable gardens, a simple 2- or 3-foot-high chicken wire fence will keep out rabbits and possibly woodchucks. The key is to put up the fence before you plant the garden. If the animals don't know what they're missing, they won't be motivated to try and trespass beyond the barrier. But if they've gotten a taste of yummy young lettuce or peas before you put up the fence, they may be more persistent about getting over the fence or digging underneath.

Another barrier that we discussed using against insect pests (see page 244) also works for some animal pest problems: floating row cover. Drape this over rows of vegetable seedlings and weight it down in a few spots with rocks to keep animals away.

If deer are a problem in your area, you'll need something taller than a chicken wire fence. Gardeners devise all types of barriers to deer: double fences, electric fences, tall barriers of special plastic netting.

In my experience, the way to deal with deer is to intercept their usual pattern of travel and "reroute" them around the garden. When I've figured out where the deer path is, I set up metal fence stakes at 6- to 8-foot intervals across their usual path. I hook plastic netting over the top hooks of the metal stakes and let it hang down. I also tie long strips of survey tape to the top of the netting. The tape flutters in the breeze, alerting the deer to the presence of the fence. The deer may push against the netting, but when it resists, they walk along the fence until it ends rather than trying to force their way through. You'll need to leave the fence in place quite a long time, but eventually you'll change their habits.

Baffle the Birds

Birds are a gardener's ally, but sometimes they're also a competitor for the harvest—especially when the harvest is berries and some tender vegetable plants. I love birds, and in the winter I keep my feeders filled every day. I stop feeding in late spring, and I usually have few problems with birds in the garden. The exceptions are tender lettuce and strawberries. I've found that covering the plants lightly with floating row cover keeps the birds away. I've also used shiny reflective tape tied between stakes at the ends of rows of plants as a deterrent. An old-fashioned pinwheel on a stick is a fun garden ornament, and its noise and motion may also deter birds. Friends tell me that CDs suspended from strings have the same effect as the reflective tape because they move and flash in the breeze. So if you receive CDs in the mail with offers promising you free Internet access or other promotions, don't throw them away—use them in your garden, instead.

Technical Difficulties in Small Gardens

Some small-garden problems have nothing to do with insects, diseases, or animal pests. They're unique to vertical, small-space, and container gardening, and you may find that coping with these technical problems may take more of your time and energy than pest problems will. I call this section, "Help! What do I do when...?"

Q. Not only is my garden small, but I have next to no space for storing my gardening supplies. How do I keep my gardening "stuff" organized and under control?

A. Discount stores sell a wide variety of plastic storage containers at low cost. Many of these are intended for storing household items in closets or under the bed, but they work well for gardening supplies, too. I first saw them used this way on a rooftop garden. The boxes were discreetly stored under the stairs that led from one level of the roof to another. I was so impressed that I put this system to work at home right away, storing boxes in an area under the deck outside the door of my second-floor apartment. I keep tools in one "sweater box," potting soil in another, mulch in a third, and composted cow manure in a fourth, all stacked one on top of the other. I've even turned a plastic sweater box into a composting box. I drilled holes in the bottom and set the box on strips of wood. It's tucked behind the other storage boxes out of sight, and I throw garden wastes into the box whenever I'm trimming plants or pulling out spent annuals.

If you have extremely limited space, such as in a balcony garden, keep your tools and supplies in a container that's sturdy enough to fill in as a table or a bench, and cover it with an attractive throw when company comes to visit.

Here's another storage tip: At The Potager, I keep my gardening tools contained in an old golf bag. It's compact enough to wheel along even the narrowest pathway, and it holds a full load of tools.

Q. What can I do when one aggressive plant takes over a small bed?

A. Do what I do: Accept defeat gracefully, cover the entire bed with a thick pad of wet newspaper, and start over. The paper will smother the rogue plant. Cover the paper with compost or any organic material and layers of grass clippings and chipped leaves. As soon as you have 3 to 6 inches of material on top of the paper, plant a new garden. Sound like a lasagna garden? You guessed it!

Q. What can I do if the trellis that I thought was plenty strong turns out to be too weak or rickety to properly support plants? How can I prevent it from being blown over or pulled down by the weight of the plants?

A. Call in reinforcements! Don't be afraid to get in around the trellis and prop it up with 2 × 4s or metal fence posts. Set them in line with the trellis frame and lash them together. Rebar is also excellent for reinforcing a vertical structure. These steel bars come in 12-foot lengths, and you can buy them at the lumberyard (ask them to cut the rebar to the lengths you need). I keep 18-inch sections handy so I can install vertical supports with extra protection against toppling. When I decide where my trellis or other vertical accent will be placed, I install sections of rebar next to each leg. I pound each 18-inch piece about halfway into the ground and attach it to the leg of the trellis with stout wire. You can paint rebar and wire the same color as your trellis and you will never even notice it's there.

Q. What can I do if a vine outgrows its supports?

A. One thing you can do is cut the vine back hard, remove the support, and replace it with a larger support. Or, if you don't want to cut the vine back that much, you can reinforce it with a temporary support. I've found that I can use a wide board as a support, or a metal fence post cushioned with a rag tied around the top so it won't damage the vine's bark. Prop up the vine, install the new support, and then take the temporary support away.

Q. My container plants suffer from heat stress whenever the temperatures rise above about 80°F. How can I help them?

A. The obvious answer is to move the containers into some shade, but sometimes that's just not practical because of a lack of shade or because the pots are too heavy. In that case, bring the shade to the pot! Prop an old umbrella over the plants; it can provide temporary relief for several small containers. Commercial growers cover their greenhouses with shade cloth in the summer to reduce the intensity of the sun. You can mimic this by creating supports from bamboo poles set into gardening pots with quick-setting cement and draping canvas shade cloth over the poles. Or buy an inexpensive bamboo roll-up shade, attach one end to your roof or siding, and prop up the other end with 6-foot bamboo poles. Setting containers in saucers filled with stones and filling the saucers with water daily may help a bit, too.

If you get tired of fussing with these temporary solutions, investigate the cost of installing an arbor or lath-covered sunshade to create a permanent partially shaded area for container plantings. (You'll enjoy it as a way to escape heat stress, too!)

Q. My potted plants always seem to be dry, even though I do my best to keep up with watering. What can I do?

A. Self-watering pots might be just what you need. These are designed so that you fill a reservoir at the base of the pot and the plant roots wick up water as it's needed. You'll find them for sale at garden centers, home centers, and mail-order suppliers. If they're too pricey for you, try creating your own

Just like vacationers on the beach, container plants appreciate the simple shade of an umbrella when the sun beats down bright and hot.

watering reservoir for large potted plants using a plastic soda bottle. (This technique is shown on page 149.)

One other technique I've used to combat the problem of containers that dry out too quickly is to mix a water-retaining polymer into my potting soil. Water-retaining polymers absorb large quantities of water and release it over time. I think they're quite effective, but I must tell you that according to the new federal organic standards, these polymers aren't allowable because they're made from a synthetic material. Starch-based water-retaining granules serve the same purpose, though, and they're fine for organic gardeners to use because they're a natural product. The catch is that starch-based granules are very hard to find; in fact, I can't track down a single source where I can buy them. This is a case where the power of consumers could have an impact. If you grow lots of plants in containers and want an organic product to help you garden more successfully, you should be asking your garden center and mail-order suppliers to sell starch-based water-retaining granules!

Wind can contribute to the drying of container plants, so keep an eye on your plants for a few days. If you notice that they're frequently windblown, try to set up a windbreak to protect them. A small section of decorative fencing can be very effective for this.

Finally, I have two decidedly low-tech suggestions for keeping container soils moist. The first is to increase the amount of compost you use in your containers. Compost can retain a large quantity of water. You may want to make the bottom layer of your containers straight compost to create a "sink" of moisture that will sustain plants. The second suggestion is to cover the surface of the container with a sheet of newspaper. This blocks evaporation from the soil surface quite effectively. Top the newspaper with a decorative mulch, for appearances' sake.

Q. What do I do about the opposite problem: waterlogged containers?

A. I have to reply with a question of my own: Did you check the containers for drainage holes? The most common cause of waterlogging is that excess moisture can't escape from the bottom of the pot. Check for drainage holes. If the container has them, make sure they're not blocked. You may want to set the container on small blocks of wood or pieces of brick or concrete so extra water can drain freely. Don't set outdoor containers directly in saucers or cachepots, though; they can become flooded when it rains.

Also, think about the mix you're using. If you used too much heavy material and not enough light material (like perlite), that could be causing the problem. If you suspect that this is your problem, the best answer is to repot in a lighter mix.

Q. What should I do with all of my container plants at the end of the growing season?

A. That depends on the plant and the container. Annuals and vegetable plants get composted; hardy perennials stay outside, as do evergreens. Plastic or composition pots can withstand the winter with plants in them, but terra-cotta pots will crack. Old cement pots filled with old soil and old plants seem to be able to get through any kind of weather. (New cement pots seem to be more fragile and can't be trusted to make it through the slightest freeze without disintegrating.)

Some plants can spend the summer outside and make the transition inside for the winter, while others wither and die. Many times the difference is as simple as acclimating the plant to being inside. I always like to bring a few herbs inside, so from the start I grow them in containers that I "plant" in the garden. Toward the end of the growing season, I dig up the pots and bring them close to the house. I keep them out of direct sun and make sure they have enough water. Next I bring them onto the deck, under the overhang. Before the heat goes on in the house, I move the plants inside and place them on a tray of pebbles out of direct sun. Add water to the pebbles to create humidity and keep the plants away from drafts.

CHAPTER 9

ROMANCING THE SMALL GARDEN

No matter where you live or what size your garden is, your garden can have a romantic attitude. Don't worry about what zone you're in or whether your garden is sunny or shady. Romance in the garden is about creating an atmosphere and about including unique accents that have special meaning to you—something sentimental, something nostalgic, and a touch of something silly.

The Art of Garden Romance

Romance is not just for young lovers. Anyone can be a romantic. All the women in my family have been romantics who surrounded themselves with small, sentimental icons and nostalgic keepsakes. My great-grandmother wore a mourning pin, and I still remember how touched we were when we found a lock of hair from her old flame, whose young life was ended during the war, tucked in the back of the pin.

My life is full of romantic memories and images, and my gardens are no exception. What makes a garden romantic? Perhaps it's a pair of old Adirondack chairs, with well-worn dark green paint, sitting side-by-side in a tiny alcove waiting for you and a friend to share the view. It could be a small wrought-iron table and ice cream parlor chair placed where a lone gardener can watch the sunset each evening. It might even be a fanciful arrangement that includes a piece of recycled art that evokes fond memories. After all, romance is in the mind of the beholder.

My grandmother planted flowers for the romance of the bloom. Fragrant roses grew along the fence and annuals bordered her vegetable patch. All the flowers found their way into the house, where they brightened tables and perfumed the air.

At our old house, the porch was shaded from the midday sun by honeysuckle vines growing on a wooden trellis. When you sat on the swing you felt hidden from view, and you could imagine that you were invisible. As a child, this is where I went to read, and I was convinced that no one could ever find me there.

Having a small garden is no excuse for ignoring the possibilities for romance. In fact, there's something about a small garden that lends itself perfectly well to romantic touches.

I've always thought that having a mini-lawn of low-growing thyme would be romantic. To me, it evokes a dream of an estate in the English countryside. Once I switched to gardening on a small scale, I had the time and place to plant my thyme lawn. It's the perfect finishing touch for the edge of a patio or a space between planting beds and a path.

When you walk along a path bordered by a thyme lawn, your feet will brush the thyme foliage and release its fresh scent.

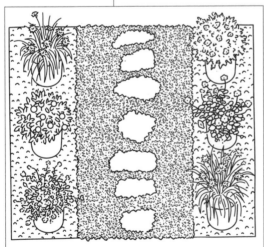

Another romantic fixture in my garden is the green picket fence bordered by narrow beds filled with cosmos and cleome. It doesn't matter that these plants are too big for my small spaces, I jam them in and they fill the beds, spilling over the path. To me, they're among the most romantic flowers, and I can't imagine gardening without them. You can ask anyone who has visited my gardens, and they are sure to remember my mixture of cleome and cosmos behind the green picket fence.

Create Garden Rooms

One unfailing strategy for creating more atmosphere and interest in your outdoor space is to create "garden rooms." Now, a garden room doesn't need sills, rafters, or beams. It doesn't even require four walls. It's more about impression than structure.

A garden room is an outdoor area that gives you the sense of being separated from the rest of your surroundings. Perhaps it's a garden bench in the middle of a flowerbed, or a table and chairs on a patio that's screened from view by a lattice trellis. Creating garden rooms allows us to set different moods and provides us with areas to be active in, areas to be social in, and a place to retreat to and be alone. Urban gardeners, you can do this, too! Even a fire escape can be an outdoor room if you add window boxes to the railings and keep a folding chair handy for times when you want to sit outside.

The curled iron base of my grandmother's treadle sewing machine is the centerpiece of one of my garden rooms near the entrance to The Potager café. The sewing machine base supports a slab of marble for a tabletop. I added a collection of four wooden slat chairs surrounding the table, inviting visitors to sit a while. An arbor covered with lushly growing 'Concord' grapes marks the entrance to the room. A large bench beside the arbor adds to the sense of atmosphere, as do plantings of edible flowers, gooseberries, herbs, and rhubarb. A pot of lettuce, nasturtiums, and pansies is the centerpiece for the table.

One of my favorite garden rooms is an outdoor "dining room" under an arbor complete with a painted chandelier hung with silk ivy. What could be more romantic than this private outdoor dining area?

255

One impediment to creating a sense of romance in this room is that it's right next to The Potager driveway. To separate the room a bit from the blacktop, this summer I will install some sections of post and rail fence between them.

Arches and Arbors

In Chapter 2, I talked about using plant supports such as trellises and arbors to increase your gardening space by growing plants vertically (see page 42). I also love arbors, arches, and pergolas because they exude romance, and they're great tools for creating an entrance or roof for a garden room. A rustic arch or an arbor made of white lattice gives a garden a country or cottage atmosphere. A classic pergola lends regal elegance to a garden room.

If you are planning an arbor that people will walk through, be sure it's taller than head height (even for very tall visitors, not just yourself). Also make sure it's wide enough for two people to walk under it at the same time—now *that's* romantic!

On the other hand, don't limit yourself to arbors as entrances. Some charming arbors are only for style or for supporting plants, not for people to pass underneath. One of the loveliest arches I've seen was in an Ontario garden I visited on a garden conference tour. The gardener had woven flexible, twiggy saplings to form a narrow, curving arch in the midst of a perennial bed. At the time I visited, it wasn't even supporting a vine. But the twigs made a lovely pattern against the sky, and the arch framed a view out across the water to the city of Toronto. I stood admiring the scene for a long time.

Sometimes a romantic arch or arbor evolves by accident. When we bought the old church that we converted into The Potager, we struggled to figure out what to do with the contents of the church, including some curved copper tubing that had been used to support a low curtain surrounding the altar. It was winter, and after Mickey had dismantled the copper tubing, she tossed it outside onto a snowbank.

It lay there all winter, and it nagged at me each time I passed it. It was too valuable to throw away, but what to do with it? One day I mentioned to Mickey that it would work well as an arbor, although it wouldn't be tall enough to walk under.

When spring came, we turned our attention to the outdoor fix-up, and that tubing was still sitting there. Mickey dragged the tubing to the middle of the front garden and attached it to the wood post that held our sign. Indeed, it wasn't tall enough to walk beneath, but it looked quite pretty. I decided there was no rule that an arbor has to be tall enough to walk under, and I tied climbing rose to one side and planted honeysuckle on the other. I placed two large terra-cotta pots on either side of the arch. Just before Memorial Day, I filled the pots with flowering annuals, and the results were spectacular.

I also have a collection of cedar fences, gates, arbors, and planters that I was lucky enough to acquire at a nursery trade show for a fraction of what they're worth. One of my favorite pieces is a moon gate and pergola in the middle of the fence that surrounds the side gardens. The gate doesn't open, but it's intriguing to look through the circular "moon" opening, and the pergola is a great support structure for climbing vines. (My customers love to include the pergola in the background when they take photos of the main building at The Potager.)

Cast-off shutters and doors find new life in your garden as charming supports for climbing vines.

Screens and Fences

Screens and fences are a practical reality of living—in many cases, we use a fence or hedge to indicate where our property ends and our neighbor's begins. Used as screens, they hide views that may be distracting or unattractive. If we have a pet, we may need a fence to keep the animal from roaming. Screens and fences are also great assets in creating a garden room, so why not use these practical realities as a romantic opportunity?

Solutions to Street Noise

There's nothing romantic about hearing honking horns and traffic noise when you sit outside in your garden. When street sounds intrude on your peace and quiet, your best bet is to install a solid wood fence—a picket fence or lattice won't block noise as well. Thick evergreen hedges can also block sound well, but they'll take time to mature and fill in.

Solid wood is pretty but plain, so the natural solution is to grow plants on the fence. They will help to block more sound, which will

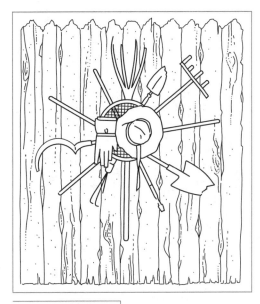

Unsold leftovers from one of my gift shops provided materials for a rustic wall hanging. No one had wanted to buy the tools individually, but once I created this sculpture, everyone wanted it!

make being outside more pleasant, and they'll certainly improve the view. Try a fragrant vine, or one with flowers that attract hummingbirds, and you'll delight your senses even further.

Occasionally, it's not practical to grow a vine up a fence, but that's no reason to settle for a view of naked wood. Just as you'd decorate the walls of your home with artwork, you can mount decorative items on a fence. Display a rugged piece of sculpture, or create a work of art of your own, like the tool sculpture shown at left. Or try mounting a mirror to give the impression that your garden is larger than it seems. I've hung a few old mirrors with interesting frames (barn sale finds) on the walls of the shed at The Potager. They reflect the narrow path that leads to the shed, creating the impression that the path disappears mysteriously beyond the shed's walls.

Screening Unpleasant Sights

When you only need to block an unwanted view, but not noise, you have more options. One of the easiest screens to work with is premade lattice. Even a tool-challenged person like me can do a pretty decent job of camouflage using lattice.

I used lattice to spruce up the view of the greenhouse at The Potager. It's a utilitarian hoop-style house, basically a glorified, plastic-wrapped coldframe that had no romance to it at all. I mounted green lattice panels on both sides of the entrance door and added wooden planters at the bases. I planted them with herbs and honeysuckle to climb the lattice. Now the greenhouse blends beautifully into the scenery.

You probably don't have a greenhouse, but you can use the same technique to block the view of a heat pump or your garbage cans, or to dress up the entrance to a storage shed.

Marking the Boundary

If you're putting up a fence to mark a boundary, you can still be creative about how you do it. The back of The Potager property is off-limits to customers, and I used my cedar post-and-rail fence as the boundary. I punctuated the fence with arbors to support vines, and I planted narrow gardens all along it, even in the openings of the arbors. The arbors are a great focal point and create more of a sense of a garden room, while the gardens at their feet make it clear that no trespassing through the arbors is allowed!

I also love rustic fences like the one I saw between the sidewalk and the front yard of a home in San Antonio, Texas. The posts were rough logs, with saplings woven between in lattice and arching patterns; the fence itself was lashed together with stout twine. It certainly didn't block noise or conceal any views, but it created a wonderful romantic atmosphere for the whole property.

Garden on the Balcony

It's easy to imagine adding romantic touches to country gardens, or even to small urban courtyard gardens. But what if you're an apartment-dweller in an anonymous apartment complex? No problem—even if you only have a balcony to garden on, you can still create a romantic atmosphere.

Balconies are usually small, hemmed in by railings, and surrounded by buildings. However, if you are lucky enough to have one, a balcony

Lavish your balcony with plants for an inviting outdoor retreat you'll love. Include perennials, shrubs, and vines to create the feeling of a woodland or even a jungle.

is the perfect place for a romantic garden. After all, what's more romantic than feeling like you're in a secluded hideaway in the midst of hundreds of people? You can add privacy to a balcony by setting up trellises at each end to hide your balcony from your neighbors. The trellises will also act as windbreaks, making it more comfortable to sit outside. Use the trellises for climbing plants, and you'll double the charm of your balcony garden.

By necessity, your balcony garden will be a container garden. To create the impression of being in a natural environment, try arranging some of the containers on a plant stand, to bring foliage and flowers closer to eye-level. Also, take full advantage of your balcony railings by hanging window boxes from them. Leave enough room for a pair of chairs and a tiny table so you can sit in your balcony garden. On a practical note, choose materials that won't add excessive weight to the balcony. Buy lightweight plastic pots or fiberglass pots.

To add privacy, set up a lattice screen or suspend bamboo or canvas blinds at either end of the balcony. (You can lower these when you're outside, to separate your space from your neighbor's balcony.) If your balcony has a ceiling, screw hooks into the roof and string twine from the balcony railing to the hooks for training vines as a living screen. (You can plant annual vines like morning glories or black-eyed Susan vine in a large pot and position it by the railing.)

PAT'S SMALL SPACE STORIES

My Lake Helen Balcony Garden

I'll never forget my first balcony garden. It was off the master bedroom of a wonderful old colonial house in Lake Helen, Florida. There was enough room for a small table, two chairs, and a few potted plants. It was shady, but I could grow vines that clung to the railing and up the support posts, as well as pots of hosta and columbine. It was the most romantic place I have ever lived. Old oaks grew close by, and Spanish moss hanging from the branches swayed in the wind. In the moist heat of summer, begonias and impatiens flourished in pots in the shade.

Alone on my balcony, I felt I had an island of calm in my busy life. I could escape my children, ignore my full calendar, and put off my deadlines curled up in a comfortable chair, nestled amid a jungle of plants with my favorite book. In the evening, my husband and I could sit with a drink and relax after herding the children through baths and off to bed.

Recently, I visited Palm Coast and Lake Helen. My old house was now Chauser's Bed and Breakfast. Mr. Chauser gave me a house tour, including my old room with the balcony. It was even smaller than I had remembered, but there were remnants of a container garden still growing there. One of the pots looked familiar, but it had been 30 years since I'd gardened there. It couldn't be, could it?

Growing conditions on a balcony can be less than ideal: You may have scorching afternoon sun or daylong shade cast by surrounding buildings. Plants for sunny balconies include dahlias, zonal geraniums, marigolds, nasturtiums, petunias, salvias, verbena, annual vinca, and zinnias. Vines that can take hot, dry conditions include black-eyed Susan vine, canary creeper, moonflowers, morning glory, purple bells, and old-fashioned climbing roses.

If your balcony's stuck in shade, try planting begonias, caladiums, coleus, impatiens, and pansies. Perennials to try include hostas, lamium, and lily-of-the-valley. Cardinal climber and English ivy are vines that will grow well in containers in partial shade.

No Balcony Too Small

Although balconies are usually small, the balcony of a hotel room I'd booked in Daytona Beach, Florida, won the prize. I had an oceanside room, and the balcony was intended only as a safety precaution when guests opened the sliding glass doors to catch the ocean breeze. It measured 12 feet long by 14 inches wide and was equipped with the customary iron balcony rail.

I thought to myself, could I garden here? Absolutely! It would be the perfect site for the special vertical container garden systems that I've seen at Epcot Center and garden shows. These systems use styrofoam or other types of pots that stack one atop the other or are suspended from a single rod. Some of these systems are hydroponic, meaning that a soil substitute is used in the pots and the plants are fed with an organic liquid fertilizer solution. This would be helpful on a balcony—no mussing with messy soil mix. I've seen vertical systems that are so compact that one would fit at each end of that narrow Daytona Beach balcony. Systems like these are great for raising herbs, lettuce, strawberries, and even patio tomatoes. Of course, I don't ever intend to make my home in a hotel in Daytona Beach, but if I did, I could still have a garden!

Wind chimes are a delightful accent for a balcony. Try making your own from 4-inch clay pots strung with fishing wire. Tiny craft-type pots from a craft store serve as the clangers inside the larger pots.

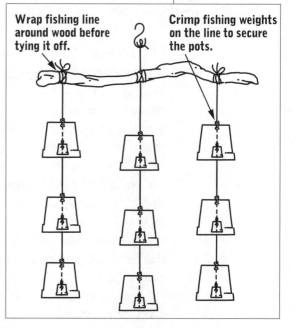

Wrap fishing line around wood before tying it off.

Crimp fishing weights on the line to secure the pots.

My Garden above the Ground

When my daughter Mickey and I moved to our adjoining house and apartment in Westbrookville, it was an experiment in mother-daughter relationships. With only a bit of lawn and a fieldstone patio separating our residences, we had to be careful at first not to infringe on each other's privacy. After the first year, we knew things would be fine. We were two independent people who could successfully share both a business and a laundry room. We even turned the fieldstone patio into a beautiful small garden room we could share.

My apartment is on the second story above a garage. There's a balcony/deck outside my front door, with 13 steps to traverse before reaching ground level. I couldn't wait that long to get to the garden below, so I decided to bring the garden up the steps and onto the deck. The deck is only 12 feet long and 3 feet deep, but lucky for me, it's quite sturdy. I started by creating an on-the-deck entry garden consisting of two bright green arborvitaes in outsize pots, one on each side of the door. (The arborvitaes do double duty during the Christmas season, when I decorate them with small white lights.) Then I added smaller matching pots with lush hostas, and for bright color, some pots of flowering annuals. To the side is a small, marble-topped table and chair where I practice serious sitting.

The garden continues down the steps with herbs and summer flowers that I've planted in a collection of old watering cans and enamel pitchers. On the landing of the stairs, I've set up an old tea cart as a stand for still more plants!

Of course, my life is full of plants and gardens because of The Potager, and there's that perfectly lovely garden in the courtyard between my house and Mickey's. But for those times when I want absolute solitude in the garden, I know I can retreat to my garden above the ground.

Patio and Terrace Gardens

Patio and terrace gardens are only limited by the size and scope of your imagination. A patio doesn't necessarily have to be attached to the house or even close to the house. It can be in any part of the yard, at the end of a path or under a sheltering tree. It is a paved area that allows you to enhance the rest of the garden rather than intrude on it. You may use it for outdoor entertaining or as a place to escape to for quiet time.

If you already have a patio, then you have a garden room ready for finishing touches. Container plantings are a must on a patio, and you may want to choose containers that match the material or color of your patio surface. As with a balcony, setting up a trellis or even a lattice screen at one side of a patio can lend it the atmosphere of a secluded retreat.

If you're designing your patio from scratch, choose a paving material that blends with the rest of the garden and design a shape that is pleasing to the eye. The most popular shape for a patio is a square or rectangle, but why not try designing a circular patio, or one that's a series of overlapping circles?

Materials for patios range from cement to natural stone and bricks to prefabricated pavers. I prefer using what I can find nearby for free rather than materials that have to be delivered and paid for. Some of my favorite patio-making materials have been natural stone collected from fields on my property and used bricks donated by a friend. If you don't live in the country like I do, you may find it harder to scrounge patio materials. In that case, bite the bullet and buy your materials, or have a professional install your patio. It will be one of the best investments you make.

Plants in the Patio

One of my favorite techniques for softening the look of a patio and adding an appealing atmosphere is to chip out some material at the edges, or even to remove a section of bricks or pavers to create areas for growing plants. (That's another reason I like to lay my patios with found materials.) Low-growing annuals such as sweet alyssum, pansies, and portulaca look beautiful spilling over the edges of patio stones, and so do perennials such as creeping phlox and low-growing sedums. A square of golden marjoram, creeping speedwell, and thyme works well, too. You can even grow vegetables, as shown in the illustration on page 109.

Patio on Demand

Have you ever planned a garden party and wished that you could expand your patio on short notice to accommodate your guest list in style? Necessity is the mother of invention, and when I was faced with a seating crisis at The Potager, I invented my instant patio technique.

My emergency wasn't due to a party, it was due to a garden tour from the Brooklyn Botanic Garden. On the morning of the tour, I got a confirmation call telling me the precise number of visitors to expect. I hung up the phone and screamed when I realized I would be short on seating for lunch, let alone having enough space to set out the punch bowl.

Grasping at straws, I thought of the large cardboard boxes that had protected mattresses I'd had delivered recently. I stripped the tape

Need an inviting spot for entertaining guests? Create an instant patio by covering part of your lawn with cardboard topped with a generous layer of bark chips. Add a table and chairs and some potted plants, and you're ready for a party!

and staples off the boxes and laid them down on the grass, overlapping all the edges. I enlisted my friend Charlie to spread bark chips over the cardboard. This done, we put out a patio table with umbrella and chairs. Near the edges of the "patio" I pushed the chips aside and placed small herb plants in pots so they would look as if they were planted there.

At one corner, we set up a second table with chairs to accommodate the final two expected guests. We finished the job in less than an hour, and I was putting the punch bowl on the table as the tour group arrived.

I hope you'll never face such a tight deadline when you entertain, but next time you're planning a garden party and want to add more people to your guest list, you'll know what to do.

Set a Garden Personality

My gardens have attitude. They reflect my personality, and I'm definitely a believer in the power and importance of emotions. I romance my gardens with special touches that mean something to me.

I've toted two chipped stone statues of boys carrying Grecian urns from garden to garden because they give me a sense of continuity with the past. The statues were a gift to me in the early part of my stint as an innkeeper. When I bought the inn, the gardens around it were quite bare. I planted and planted, but they still needed more. Many of my new neighbors brought me plants and other special items to display in the garden. The statues were a gift from two of my faithful customers, Peter and Florence Pizzarro. Peter and Florence were selling their property and retiring to smaller quarters. The statues had long graced their gardens and they wanted to give them a good new home. With me, they've had several! Once I set the statues down in a garden, I feel at home.

I keep a collection of wrought iron fern stands on my deck planted with Boston ferns, spider plants, and Christmas cactuses—all because they launch wonderful flights of imagination about what it would be like to live in Victorian times. (Yes, I'm a hopeless romantic!) In winter, they stand stark and empty, but I feel like they're my special sculpture collections. The tender plants they support in the summer spend the winter indoors in Mickey's sunroom. When I walk through the courtyard, I can look up at the sunroom and see all that greenery snuggled together, and I look forward to their return to my deck when summer comes.

An old piece of furniture that looked like junk indoors can be perfectly at home in the garden. Many guests at The Potager have asked where I got the old coffee table that holds my berry collection, and they always laugh at my story of retrieving it from the cast-off pile years ago to use "temporarily." The table has now been there so long that it looks as if it is rooted to the ground.

Dress your scarecrow in some of your favorite old clothes—you know, the ones you don't wear anymore but can't bear to part with. You'll smile every time you see your "alter ego" in the garden.

Even my scarecrow has special meaning, as she peeks seductively around the side of the shed at The Potager. She wears my old ruffled apron and a long-sleeve blouse I couldn't bear to throw away. I had worn that blouse for some of my most memorable and romantic times. Now, when I look at it in the garden, when the breeze lifts the apron skirt and the sleeves on my blouse flutter, I remember myself dancing. The hat my scarecrow wears, the one with the faded ribbon around the brim, has done more than keep the sun off my face. It's become part of my identity, and now that I have a new straw hat, I've passed the old one down to my alter ego.

Trash or Treasure?

How many home and garden magazines or television shows have you seen that portray scenes that contain all the right "stuff" for decorating romantic gardens? Each time I see an appealing photo or image on the screen, I take inventory of my storage spaces in my mind. I know I have some of that great stuff tucked away—if I can just find it.

If you have a bit of the pack rat in you, you may have a cache of stuff waiting to decorate your garden. My garage has never had a car inside it because a car would displace my precious stuff. The best thing is that I haven't seen some of my stuff in 4 years, so when I come across it again on a "stuff-sorting" day, it will all be new again!

Some of the items from my "stuff" collection are ornaments in my garden now, and they also help reflect my personality in the garden. I've collected iron gates, sections of fencing, and fancy embellishments to buildings that are now a part of history. The tiny garden between the two houses in Westbrookville hasn't the need or the room for a fence, but it does accommodate an old wrought-iron gate. I inserted two 4 × 4 posts to hang the old-fashioned iron gate on to create a romantic entry to our small garden and patio. It was also the perfect spot to install an arbor on which to grow an old-fashioned climbing rose. Our little garden took on a new dimension with the addition of these treasures.

Another of my treasures was a lone section of iron fencing made up of fanciful leaves and oversize acorns. In another life, it was probably

I've uncovered some of my favorite containers and gardening equipment, such as old metal wash tubs and a genuine Radio Flyer wagon, at tag sales and auctions.

part of a porch railing. It was painted white when I bought it, and it now has a bit of rust. It leans against the lower wall of my daughter's house, looking beautiful. Ivy has begun to cover parts of it.

I enjoy looking for farm implements and architectural or decorative pieces from old buildings that I could put to use in new ways in my garden or home. I have always loved old ornate frames, and I'm delighted when I find a good buy. I remove the glass and picture or photo in the frame. I paint the frame with a whitewash and sand a little paint off here and there to "re-age" them. In my house, I might stand a frame on my mantle, or hang it on the wall as-is. In the garden, I might prop a frame against a post. I also like the effect of hanging the frame over a mirror mounted on a shed wall or fence. (I don't worry about matching the size of the frame and mirror. Chances are the plants in the garden or climbing the shed wall will hide the edges of the mirror, anyway.)

ACQUIRING YOUR OWN STUFF

Recycling is one of the things I do best. I have long been at home and at work in old buildings that had served other purposes for previous owners. An old boarding house became my country inn. For a while, I lived in a building that had been a general store. My current business, **The Potager**, used to be a Methodist church.

Just as I've learned to recognize buildings that are gems waiting to be reclaimed, I've honed my skills at finding recycled treasures of all kinds. Here are my tips for acquiring treasures with style, and without spending a fortune.

Where to look. Tag sales, garage sales, yard sales, flea markets, and antique sales. Estate and auction sales are usually advertised in the newspaper days ahead of time.

What to bring. Cash, a tape measure, a flashlight, snacks, and a beverage.

What to wear. Old clothes, comfortable shoes, no jewelry, and a hip pack or backpack (a purse will get in your way, and it's easier to lose).

Price. Memorize these questions: "Is this your best price?" "Will you take $5 (or $2, or $20—whatever you hope will snag the sale) for this?" "Is that your final answer?" However, if a price tag is marked "Firm," don't haggle. If you try to negotiate, you'll just make someone angry.

When you're on a shopping expedition and find a piece you think you can't live without, inspect it thoroughly before you buy. Flea markets and auctions aren't like department store shopping, where you can always return something a day later. Use your flashlight to look under the drawers or into dark corners and under the bottom. If the piece is damaged, will it break apart when you transport it? Are you the type who will fix something that's broken? Take measurements, too, especially if you have a specific spot in mind for your treasure. If it's too big, let it go. The perfect piece is sure to be somewhere down the road at another sale.

Share Your Garden with Friends

A final theme that keeps my gardening spirits and creativity fresh is sharing my garden with others. Now that *Lasagna Gardening* has made me something of a gardening celebrity, I have the privilege of sharing my gardens with hundreds of people who send me letters and e-mails, thousands of visitors to The Potager, and tens of thousands of people who've read my book.

I never could have believed I'd have such a vast network of gardening ties, and it gives me a charge to think about it. But my deepest satisfaction and joy in gardening is the smaller group of close personal friends that I've connected with through gardening. Once you get bitten by the gardening bug, I hope you'll discover the joys of gardening friends like mine.

The Temple Arbor

I have a very special arbor at The Potager, made by my friend Lou Temple. It's actually the second arbor Lou built for me. The first was for my first white garden, a magnificent color-theme garden that was one of the highlights of the property at our inn. (I wrote about the evolution of this garden in my first book about lasagna gardening.) Leaving that garden was one of the hardest parts of giving up the inn.

When friends contribute to your garden, like my friend Lou Temple did by building this lovely arbor for The Potager, you'll feel close to them every time you work among your plants.

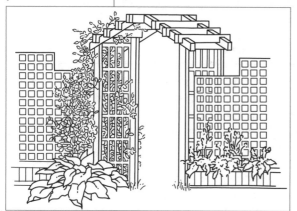

You can imagine how touched I was when, at age 91, Lou showed up at The Potager with another one of his beautiful arches. He dug the holes for the arbor posts himself, climbed the ladder to check the top piece, and made sure the whole arbor was plumb. He never got to see the blossoms of the pink 'Henry Kelsey' rose that I planted to climb the arbor. If I ever have to move again, the arbor, and my memories of Lou Temple, go with me.

My Gardening Joy

One of my best friends is truly a Joy—that's her name! A mutual friend who thought that Joy and I had some things in common encouraged Joy to look me up. One day she came knocking on my door. We discovered that we both had been married to servicemen, we both had grown children, and we were both struggling on our own with the upkeep of our houses.

In addition to tending my house and property, I had a growing business and needed help dividing perennials and potting them for sale. Joy volunteered to help, and soon we were standing side-by-side, potting up plants. We shared our trials and triumphs of life as single women, and we taught each other new skills. Joy quickly caught on to lasagna gardening and was soon layering her own gardens at home.

Joy brought me off the mountain and into a social life again, and I led her down the path to easy gardening. What did that have to do with romance in the garden? Everything!

When Joy received an invitation to attend her late husband's West Point Reunion, she sought my advice, and I talked her into going. Despite a case of nerves, she went, and while she was there, she met her future husband. He was also part of her husband's graduating class and had been widowed 3 years before. When she brought him to meet me, I could tell as they walked toward me that they were perfect together. But without our garden chats, it might never have happened.

Making Garden Friendships

How do gardening friendships like these spring to life? Sometimes it's serendipity. You never know where you'll encounter someone who shares your passion for plants. There are ways to increase the odds, though. Take a gardening class at a local college or nursery. Join a gardening club or the Master Gardener program at your local Cooperative Extension office. I've had dozens of clubs and Master Gardener groups visit The Potager, and it's easy to see that many wonderful friendships exist in those groups.

Lasagna gardening is ideal for sparking friendships because the simple act of making a lasagna garden is an attention-getter. People will stop to ask why on earth you're covering your lawn with newspaper. At first, they may make fun of you—take their ribbing with good grace, and invite them back the following day to see the results and share a cup of tea. Once they see how well lasagna gardening works, they'll want you to tell them your secrets!

Friendship can also happen by chance or with the tiniest nudge. Sometimes all it takes is showing up at someone's door with a plant you've potted up after dividing a perennial from your own garden, or some extra seeds you'd like to share. Try it yourself and see what takes root.

EPILOGUE

It's been 5 years since I sold Shandelee Herb Farm and turned my attention to developing my business and small-scale gardens at The Potager. What was once a Methodist church is now a veritable potage of goods and services: a gift and antiques shop, a café, a catering service, a greenhouse, and a garden center. On a summer weekend, hundreds of visitors may browse through the shop and gardens.

As The Potager grew and thrived, my first book, *Lasagna Gardening*, also saw huge success. A billboard along Route 209, the main tourist route in the southern Catskills, proclaims The Potager as "The Home of the Lasagna Gardener." Enthusiastic gardeners who've read the book and adopted my methods stop in regularly at The Potager to thank me for revolutionizing their gardens and to see what I'm up to now.

I know that there's an audience of potential gardeners nationwide who just need a bit of encouragement to get out in the garden. I strive to reach as many of these people as I can in person, through lectures and demonstrations. I've visited locales as far flung as San Diego, Boston, Atlanta, and even Disney World. I was so proud when I was chosen to appear at Epcot Center as one of America's Six Great Gardeners of 2000.

Through e-mail, I've also opened a dialogue with men and women from all over the world who either want to stay in the garden or get into the garden for the first time. I'm excited that this new book will introduce me to a brand-new audience of would-be gardeners: those with little or no gardening space or those with limited time to garden.

Encouraged by the outpouring of mail from readers of *Lasagna Gardening*, I hope to embark on yet another book project, *Lasagna Gardening with Friends*. This book would take me across the country, visiting the gardens of folks who have made their gardens with the lasagna method, and I'd share all their best new ideas with all of you. I also have dreams of a *Lasagna Gardening* newsletter, both in paper and electronic form. If you're a lasagna gardener who'd like to help me with either of these efforts, I'd love to hear from you at patlasagna@aol.com.

Life is good and getting better every day.

Your friend in the garden,

Patricia Lanza

Patricia Lanza

The following list of mail-order suppliers just scratches the surface of the garden shopping world that's available via mail-order catalogs and Web sites. If you have Internet access, you have an almost unlimited range of choices of garden plants and products at your fingertips. I've listed sources here that I've come to know and trust, but there are many other fine companies as well. Some of the companies I've listed under "Seeds and Plants" also offer a range of gardening equipment and supplies. For a state-by-state listing of soil test labs, you can also visit www.organicgardening.com.

Don't overlook local tag sales, garage sales, and farm auctions as sources of garden treasures, especially unusual plant supports and ornaments. See my guidelines for tag sale shopping on page 267 for ideas.

Seeds and Plants

Bear Creek Nursery
PO Box 411
Northport, WA 99157
Phone: (509) 732-6219
Fax: (509) 732-4417

Bluestone Perennials
7211 Middle Ridge Road
Madison, OH 44057
Phone: (440) 428-7535
  or (800) 852-5243
Fax: (440) 428-7535
Web site:
  www.bluestoneperennials.com

Bountiful Gardens
18001 Shafer Ranch Road
Willits, CA 95490-9626
Phone: (707) 459-6410
Fax: (707) 459-1925
Web site:
  www.bountifulgardens.org

Brent and Becky's Bulbs
7463 Heath Trail
Gloucester, VA 23061
Phone: (877) 661-2852
Fax: (804) 693-9436
Web site: www.brentand
  beckysbulbs.com

W. Atlee Burpee & Co.
300 Park Avenue
Warminster, PA 18991-0001
Phone: (800) 888-1447
Fax: (215) 674-4170
Web site: www.burpee.com

The Cook's Garden
PO Box 535
Londonderry, VT 05148
Phone: (800) 457-9703
Fax: (800) 457-9705
Web site: www.cooksgarden.com

Goodwin Creek Gardens
PO Box 83
Williams, OR 97544
Phone: (541) 846-7357
Web site: www.goodwincreek
   gardens.com

Harris Seeds
PO Box 24966
Rochester, NY 14624-0966
Phone: (800) 514-4441
Fax: (877) 892-9197
Web site: www.harrisseeds.com

Indiana Berry and Plant Co.
5218 West 500 South
Huntingburg, IN 47542
Phone: (812) 683-3055
Fax: (812) 683-2004
Web site: www.inberry.com

Ison's Nursery & Vineyards
PO Box 190
Brooks, GA 30205
Phone: (770) 599-6970
Fax: (770) 599-1727
Web site: www.isons.com

Johnny's Selected Seeds
Foss Hill Road
Albion, ME 04910-9731
Phone: (207) 437-4301
Fax: (207) 437-2165
Web site: www.johnnyseeds.com

Pinetree Garden Seeds
Box 300
New Gloucester, ME 04260
Phone: (207) 926-3400
Fax: (888) 527-3337
Web site: www.superseeds.com

Raintree Nursery
391 Butts Road
Morton, WA 98356
Phone: (360) 496-6400
Fax: (888) 770-8358
Web site: www.raintreenursery.com

Renee's Garden
Phone: (888) 880-7228
Fax: (831) 335-7227
Web site: www.reneesgarden.com

Richters Herb Catalogue
357 Highway 47
Goodwood, Ontario
L0C 1A0 Canada
Phone: (905) 640-6677
Fax: (905) 640-6641
Web site: www.richters.com

Sandy Mush Herb Nursery
316 Surrett Cove Road
Leicester, NC 28748
Phone: (828) 683-2014

Seeds of Change
PO Box 15700
Santa Fe, NM 87506-5700
Phone: (800) 957-3337
Web site: www.seedsofchange.com

Territorial Seed Company
PO Box 158
Cottage Grove, OR 97424-0061
Phone: (541) 942-9547
Fax: (541) 942-9881
Web site: www.territorial-seed.com

Thompson & Morgan Inc.
PO Box 1308
Jackson, NJ 08527-0308
Phone: (732) 363-2225
Fax: (732) 363-9356
Web site: www.thompson-morgan.com

Van Bourgondien Bros.
PO Box 1000
Babylon, NY 11702-09004
Phone: (800) 622-9997

Well-Sweep Herb Farm
205 Mt. Bethel Road
Port Murray, NJ 07865
Phone: (908) 852-5390
Fax: (908) 852-1649

Gardening Equipment and Supplies

Bricko Farms
824 Sandbar Ferry Road
Augusta, GA 30901-1946
(706) 722-0661

Gardener's Supply Co.
128 Intervale Road
Burlington, VT 05401-2850
Phone: (800) 427-3363
Fax: (800) 551-6712
Web site: www.gardeners.com

Gardens Alive!
5100 Schenley Place
Lawrenceburg, IN 47025
Phone: (812) 537-8651
Fax: (812) 537-5108
Web site: www.gardensalive.com

Harmony Farm Supply and Nursery
3244 Gravenstein Highway N
Sebastopol, CA 95472
Phone: (707) 823-9125
Fax: (707) 823-1734
Web site: www.harmonyfarm.com

Peaceful Valley Farm Supply
PO Box 2209
Grass Valley, CA 95945
Phone: (530) 272-4769
Fax: (530) 272-4794
Web site: www.groworganic.com

Plow and Hearth
PO Box 5000
Madison, VA 22727-1500
Phone: (800) 627-1712
Fax: (800) 843-2509
Web site: www.plowhearth.com

The Potager
PO Box 729
116 Sullivan Street
Wurtsburo, NY 12790
Phone: (845) 888-4086
Fax: (845) 888-4386

Soil Testing Laboratories

For a state-by-state and province-by-province listing of soil test lads, visit: www.organicgardening.com/library/soil_test_labs.html

Timberleaf Soil Testing
39648 Old Spring Road
Marrieta, CA 92563
Phone: (909) 677-7510

Wallace Labs
365 Corel Circle
El Segundo, CA 90245
Phone: (310) 615-0116
Fax: (310) 640-6863
www.wallace-labs.com

PAT'S PICKS
(RECOMMENDED READING)

Books

Allen, Oliver E. *Gardening with the New Small Plants*. Boston, MA: Houghton Mifflin, 1987.

Armitage, Allan M. *Armitage's Garden Perennials*. Portland, OR: Timber Press, 2000.

Brickell, Christopher, and David Joyce. *The American Horticultural Society Pruning and Training*. New York: DK Publishing Inc., 1996.

Cebenko, Jill Jesiolowski, and Deborah L. Martin, editors. *Insect, Disease & Weed I.D. Guide*. Emmaus, PA: Rodale Inc., 2001.

Cole, Rebecca. *Potted Garden*. New York: Clarkson Potter, 1997.

Fell, Derek. *Bulb Gardening with Derek Fell*. New York: Friedman/Fairfax Publishers, 1997.

Gilkeson, Linda, Pam Peirce, and Miranda Smith. *Rodale's Pest and Disease Problem Solver*. Emmaus, PA: Rodale, 1996.

Greenwood, Pippa. *The New Gardener*. New York: Dorling Kindersley Publishing, 1998.

Grounds, Roger. *Small Garden*. New York: Canopy Books, 1994.

Hillier, Malcolm. *Container Gardening Through the Year*. New York: Dorling Kindersley, 1995.

Hodgson, Larry. *Annuals for Every Purpose*. Emmaus, PA: Rodale, 2002.

———. *Perennials for Every Purpose*. Emmaus, PA: Rodale. 2000.

Lanza, Patricia. *Lasagna Gardening*. Emmaus, PA: Rodale, 1998.

Lloyd, Christopher, and Richard Bird. *The Cottage Garden*. New York: Dorling Kindersley Publishing, 1999.

Pavord, Anna. *The Border Book*. New York: Dorling Kindersley Publishing, 2000.

Search, Gay. *Gardening without a Garden*. New York: Dorling Kindersley Publishing, 2000.

Yang, Linda. *The City and Town Gardener*. New York: Random House, 1995.

Magazines and Newsletters

Country Living Gardener, 224 W. 57th Street, New York, NY 10019.

Hortideas, 750 Black Lick Road, Gravel Switch, KY 40328.

OG, Rodale, 33 E. Minor Street, Emmaus, PA 18098; www.organicgardening.com.

ACKNOWLEDGMENTS

I have had many wonderful friends, but gardening friends are the best. Without them, I could never have made it through the ups and downs of my life. I'd like to thank them all, but I'll have to content myself with acknowledging the following special people.

Ron Tissot was the first friend to ever work in my gardens. Though not a gardener, he taught me about pickup trucks, power tools, and perseverance. Ron also laid out beautiful fieldstone paths that gave my gardens great character.

As soon as I would dream up a new idea, I would call Doris and Ed Wehner. Ed helped me convert the little building that had stood over the well into a tool shed. Ed built a pergola to shade potted plants waiting to be sold. When I bought 22 sections of old picket fence at auction and needed it installed, I called Ed. When I wanted the fence painted, I called Doris. Ed built the garden supply building, greenhouse, decking around the back of the house and gift shop, and store shelves. Doris helped me pot hundreds of plants and host busloads of guests. I could do anything when Doris and Ed were by my side.

Joy Rhyne's wisdom in all things helped smooth the bumpy road to my new life: Learning to live alone after a lifetime of marriage or coping with a powerful mower, a filled septic tank, a leaky roof, an overflowing oil tank, a power failure, 400 poppies to pot, 50 seniors on a bus an hour early, and whether to accept a date. Even when she didn't know the answer, she stood by me as we learned together.

When I met Doug Bury I was up to my eyeballs with tough times: starting a new business, selling the farm, moving to a new town, and trying to meet deadlines for a book. I was so busy I couldn't get beans planted or mow the grass. Doug found time to help me with both planting and mowing. He also took care of hungry woodchucks, relocating them far from my vegetables, and many times he provided my dinner. As if that were not enough, Doug gave me all the space I needed to plant gardens on his property. I divided my most loved plants and took divisions to his gardens in Roscoe, New York. His lawn soon became a series of lasagna gardens, planted instantly with the divisions. He helped me with many, many gardening projects, large and small.

Many other wonderful friends have saved the day at one time or another. Charlie Huber would stop by to help me prune evergreens. Vera Huber would bring me a special lunch and stay to make sure I ate it. Ed Lowe kept my vehicles running and saw to the proper restoration of my collection of wrought-iron furniture. The Barbanties came with their bulldozer to move truckloads of soil to fill in a sloping yard. Alan and Mary Fried led me by the hand down the path to easy mountain gardening. Cathy Barash introduced me to the Garden Writers Association of America. And when the writing made me crazy and I felt like giving up, Walter Chandoha sent huge bouquets of yellow flowers with notes telling me I could do it.

In the long run, it was my publisher who made it all happen and deserves my most heartfelt thanks. The folks at Rodale are a family and have given me support and encouragement, as families do. From my first encounter with editor Deb Martin and throughout the production of *Lasagna Gardening*, I have felt that I was a part of the Rodale family. With this second book, I have had the pleasure of working with Fern Marshall Bradley: editor, therapist, and friend. As the professional editor she is, she made my work the best it could be. As the wise woman she is, she understood me and kept me focused and at my desk. During the process, we became friends.

When life seems full of gray days, friends bring sunshine. My very best friends were, and still are, my seven children, their spouses, and my grandchildren. They have bolstered my spirit, boosted my ego, and balanced my checkbook. They have traveled far to help put my tearoom together, build my stairs, prune the roses, and serve my guests. I could not ask for better.

USDA PLANT HARDINESS ZONE MAP

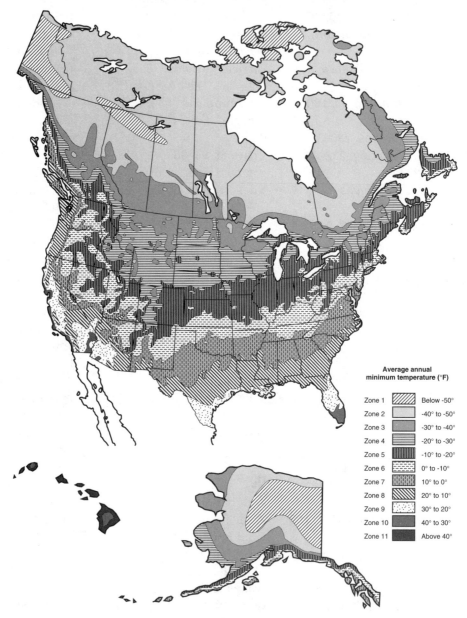

Average annual
minimum temperature (°F)

Zone 1		Below -50°
Zone 2		-40° to -50°
Zone 3		-30° to -40°
Zone 4		-20° to -30°
Zone 5		-10° to -20°
Zone 6		0° to -10°
Zone 7		10° to 0°
Zone 8		20° to 10°
Zone 9		30° to 20°
Zone 10		40° to 30°
Zone 11		Above 40°

This map was revised in 1990 and is recognized as the best indicator of minimum temperatures available. Look at the map to find your area, then match its pattern to the key. When you've found your pattern, the key will tell you what hardiness zone you live in. Remember that the map is a general guide; your particular conditions may vary.